D1034035

TEXTUAL MASCULINITY AND THE EXCHANGE OF WOMEN IN RENAISSANCE VENICE

Contents

Acknowledgments

It is a great pleasure to thank the many people and institutions that have helped bring this book to fruition. My earliest interlocutors at the University of Chicago first introduced me to the puzzles and delights of early modern Italian culture and have been crucial to the evolution and growth of this project. Elissa Weaver read every single word of its earliest incarnation and offered meticulous and insightful comments on every single page. Martha Feldman taught me the value of scholarly exchange, challenged me to think about cultural history in new ways, and helped me tighten both my prose and my arguments. Paolo Cherchi, Armando Maggi, and Rebecca West dazzled me with their erudition and continue to touch me with their kindness. They all know, I hope, how much they have enriched my work and life through their own vibrant example.

The groundwork in Italy was done with the aid of the Fulbright Foundation. I later completed essential archival and library research in Venice with the generous support of the Gladys Krieble Delmas Foundation and the Leslie Center for the Humanities at Dartmouth College. The Office of the Dean of the Faculty at Dartmouth College provided indispensable financial support for the preparation of the manuscript. In Venice, I benefited especially from the scholarly expertise of Francesco Bruni and Daria Perocco. Rosella Mamoli Zorzi and Marino Zorzi made me feel at home in Campo Santa Maria Formosa and offered help with some of the trickier dialect passages. Special thanks are due to the staffs of the Biblioteca Nazionale Marciana, the Archivio di Stato di Venezia, and the Biblioteca del Museo Correr for their invaluable help in locating the documents, manuscripts, and rare books that shed light on the literary fraternities I examine here. At the Marciana, Stefano

Trovato and Orfea Granzotto were particularly instrumental in making my research more fruitful. A band of merry and knowledgeable fellow Venetianists offered guidance in navigating the city's research institutions and many happy hours over spritz and *polpette*: Alexandra Bamji, Jane Stevens Cranshaw, Julia DeLancey, Esther Brummer Gable, Sharon Gregory, Chriscinda Henry, Sally Hickson, Nan McElroy, Alison Sherman, Anna Swartwood, and Jill Weinrich. Rosa Salzberg and Krystina Stermole, especially, know how much I appreciate their friendship and their intellectual companionship, which has so enriched my understanding of Venice past and present.

I am deeply grateful to my colleagues in the Department of French & Italian at Dartmouth, who have generously offered support, guidance, and critical insight at every turn: Faith Beasley, Nancy Canepa, Lynn Higgins, David LaGuardia, Keala Jewell, Larry Kritzman, Graziella Parati, John Rassias, Andrea Tarnowski, Roxana Verona, Keith Walker, and Kathy Wine. Many of my students have helped shape this project through their fresh and often fearless readings of many of the primary and secondary sources that made their way into this book. I thank especially the members of my 2014 seminar on sex and gender in the Italian Renaissance, whose enthusiasm and intelligence energized my revisions. Naaborko Sackeyfio-Lenoch, my partner in writing and crime, has been a steady source of companionship as we both brought our books to press. Moira Killoran provided kind and indispensable advice on navigating the writing process.

I am particularly indebted to the administrators and scholars at the Leslie Center for the Humanities at Dartmouth, who organized and participated in a review of an early draft of this book. My Dartmouth colleagues David LaGuardia, Adrian Randolph, Andrea Tarnowski, and Michelle Warren read every word, offered copious and valuable suggestions, and spent many gruelling (if convivial) hours helping me clarify my plans for revision. The outside reviewers, Guido Ruggiero and Jane Tylus, cheerfully travelled long distances to contribute their expertise and provide encouraging and incisive feedback. Their insights have deepened my understanding of the literary, social, and sexual economy of Renaissance Italy immeasurably and have made this a better book.

There are several others who have contributed in important ways, and whose roles I must acknowledge specifically. First among them is Tita Rosenthal, whose path-breaking work on Veronica Franco and her world has so enlivened the ideas here. I have benefited immensely from her generosity of time, spirit, and intellect since the time I was a graduate student. I am indebted, also, to Diana Robin for her unflagging support and for our countless lively conversations that have broadened and deepened my approach to early modern women's interactions with their literary world. Karen-edis Barzman took me under her wing on my first day in the archive in Venice, showed me the ropes, and then helped me think through my ideas about the dynamics of collective literary discourse. Elizabeth Cohen read the introduction, offered invaluable comments, and has helped me develop my ideas about the power dynamics of early modern prostitution. Julia Hairston offered an extraordinarily helpful critique of chapter 5, as well as her unparalleled knowledge of the literary career of Tullia d'Aragona.

At the University of Toronto Press, I profited from the formidable skills of the editorial team, especially Leah Connor and Matthew Kudelka. The anonymous readers for the press provided thorough and thoughtful comments; their invaluable suggestions have helped shape the final product. Senior Humanities Editor Suzanne Rancourt shepherded me and my book through the publication process with efficiency and grace, even in the face of the sudden and sad loss of Ron Schoeffel. He will be remembered for his kindness to first authors like myself and for the depth of his contribution to Italian Studies. Many thanks go to the wonderful and infinitely patient Beth McAuley for her care and expertise in the preparation of the manuscript, and to Barbara Kamienski for her intelligent and meticulous help with the index.

Finally, I want to thank my family and friends for their loving support over the years. I am grateful to Carmen Nocentelli for introducing me to the joys of all things Italian and for her wise and witty council; to Parke Treadway for her steady encouragement and sense of humour; to my father for his enthusiasm and his volunteer proofreading services; and to my mother, whose intellectual curiosity, grit, and zest astound and inspire me every day. I dedicate this book to her, with admiration and gratitude.

TEXTUAL MASCULINITY AND THE EXCHANGE OF WOMEN IN RENAISSANCE VENICE

Writing the Whore in Renaissance Venice

Ma perch'io sento il presente all'odore,
un'operetta in quel cambio galante
vi mando ora in stil ladro e traditore
intitolata: la *Puttana errante*,
dal Veniero composta mio creato,
che m'è in dir mal quatro giornate inante.

Because I can smell the gift coming,
I am sending you, in courteous exchange,
a little work in dishonest and perfidious style,
entitled *The Whore Errant*,
composed by Venier, my creation,
who is four days ahead of me when it comes to speaking ill [of others].
Pietro Aretino, "Capitolo al Duca di Mantova," 1530[1]

In 1530, Pietro Aretino wrote from Venice to Federico II Gonzaga, the newly named duke of Mantua. Although Aretino cloaked his request in witty satire, he made no bones about the purpose of his missive. It had been over a month since Aretino had heard from Gonzaga, and he was beginning to worry that his long-time benefactor had abandoned him: "Has the hour come when I must die of cold and thirst, to atone for my sins? What shall I say? What shall I do?"[2] The solution to the dilemma, Aretino writes, came to him in a dream. If all went according to Aretino's plan, the duke would soon provide his faithful servant with "a suitcase bursting with silver, along with that other item I asked for a short time ago."[3] In other words, Aretino needed cash, and he hoped the duke would provide it.

To sweeten the deal, Aretino sent Gonzaga a gift, carefully chosen to appeal to his patron's tastes. The gift was a poem entitled *La puttana errante* (The Whore Errant), penned by a man Aretino called his "creation," a young Venetian patrician named Lorenzo Venier. As its title suggests, *La puttana errante* capitalized on the popularity of chivalric epics such as Ariosto's *Orlando furioso*, first printed in 1516 and a best-seller throughout the century and beyond. But instead of Ariosto's male knight errant, Venier's poem features a woman who sets out from her native Venice on an epic quest across the Italian peninsula to "farsi puttana errante" (make herself a whore errant).[4] Her sexual odyssey culminates in Rome, where she is paraded through the streets in mock triumph with a "corona di cazzi" (crown of cocks) on her head.[5]

Aretino's strategies for obtaining patronage included traditional techniques such as presenting and dedicating his works to his intended patrons.[6] But he was a shrewd observer of both individual and public taste, and his literary offerings were usually chosen to appeal to both. What better gift for a man like Federico Gonzaga – a man who appreciated both novelty and explicit sexuality – than a new poem, still in manuscript, recounting the exploits of a fictional whore? By the time Aretino presented Gonzaga with *La puttana errante*, he had been cultivating the duke's favour for some time. The two men had met in February 1523, when Aretino arrived at the Gonzaga court in Mantua with a letter of recommendation from the Cardinal Giulio de' Medici in hand.[7] A few weeks later, Gonzaga begged the cardinal to allow Aretino to remain in Mantua, adding that he could not bear to part with "the elegance of the compositions, the diverse discourses, and the sweetness that abounds in [Aretino]."[8] Aretino returned to de' Medici's service in April, but Gonzaga would continue to solicit his latest writings during his absences from the court throughout the 1520s. "I beg you to allow us to enjoy some of your compositions," Gonzaga wrote in 1524 to Aretino, "especially when you create something that might delight us."[9]

When Aretino returned to Mantua in 1526, he joined Giulio Romano, the Roman artist and architect whom Gonzaga had engaged to remodel and decorate his new summer palace, the Palazzo del Te.[10] A few years earlier, Giulio and Aretino had both been major players in what would turn out to be one of the biggest editorial scandals of the century. It all began in Rome in the early 1520s, when Giulio made a series of sixteen drawings of couples engaged in as many sexual positions.[11] In 1524, the printmaker Marcantonio Raimondi created a set of engravings based on Giulio's drawings, collectively known as *I modi* (The Positions). Shortly thereafter, as Giorgio Vasari would recount, the images turned up "in the least likely places one could imagine" and Raimondi was imprisoned, presumably for his role in circulating such unseemly material.[12] Giulio Romano, by then safely ensconced at Federico Gonzaga's court in Mantua, was seemingly untouched by the scandal.

In a letter to his friend Battista Zatti, published well over a decade after the uproar in Rome, Aretino claimed to have been personally responsible for convincing the Pope to release Raimondi.[13] In the same letter, Aretino dramatizes the tale of the genesis of the *sonetti lussuriosi*, sixteen sexually explicit sonnets he wrote to accompany Raimondi's engravings: "After I obtained Marcantonio's freedom from Pope Clement ... the desire came to me to see the figures ... and I was touched by the same spirit that moved Giulio Romano to draw them."[14] When exactly Aretino began to work on the sonnets is unclear, as is the date they first appeared in print.[15] But it seems likely that Aretino drafted and circulated the sonnets while he was still living in Rome, where they were probably part of the reason the papal datary Gian Matteo Giberti ordered Aretino's assassination in July 1525. Aretino survived the attempt on his life and wisely left Rome for good. For a year or so, he was in the service of the famous *condottiere* Giovanni de' Medici (delle Bande Nere). When Giovanni died in Mantua, Aretino remained there, joining Giulio Romano at the Gonzaga court. In any case, the sonnets must have been complete by 1527, when Aretino sent a gift he described as "il libro de i sonetti e de le figure lussuriose" (the book of sonnets and lascivious figures) to the Paduan *condottiere* Cesare Fregoso.[16] Written in dialogue form, Aretino's sonnets give voice to the couples represented in Raimondi's engravings, who take turns commenting on the sexual acts in which they are engaged.

Like the drawings that inspired Aretino's sonnets, many of the frescoes Giulio designed for the Palazzo del Te feature nude bodies both male and female. The main banquet hall is adorned with episodes from the story of Cupid and Psyche, a tale that can be traced back to the *Metamorphoses* of the Roman writer Apuleius. On one wall, Cupid reclines with a languid Psyche, her buttocks and breasts turned invitingly towards the viewer. The daughter born from their union, Voluptas (Pleasure), peeks out from between her mother's legs. Intertwined with the story of Cupid and Psyche are representations of other famous mythological lovers. Nearby, a voluptuous Venus is shown bathing with a heroic Mars. In the next scene, Venus restrains Mars, who brandishes his sword as he pursues Adonis. In one of the lunettes, Jupiter in the form of a serpent ravishes Olympias, who raises one arm over her head in alarm even as she parts her legs obligingly. As Bette Talvacchia has argued, the explicit sexuality of these frescoes was moderated by the mythological frame in which it was presented.[17] The drawings that became *I modi*, on the other hand, were scandalous precisely because they lacked such a frame.

At least one art historian has argued that Aretino was involved in the narrative program for the Palazzo del Te frescoes, perhaps as adviser to Giulio Romano.[18] Direct evidence for this is sketchy at best, but what is clear is that Aretino and Giulio had a mutual interest in erotic imagery and its uses. Even after Aretino left Mantua, he continued to curry Gonzaga's favour, in part through attempting to provide the duke with works of art and literature in accordance with his taste.[19] In 1527, a few months after settling into his new home on the Grand Canal in Venice, Aretino wrote to assure the duke that the sculptor Jacopo Sansovino was in the process of creating for him "a [statue of] Venus so realistic and so full of life that she will fill the thoughts of anyone who looks at her with lust."[20] Gonzaga would reply that Aretino's description of the statue made him even more eager to receive it.[21]

Given the abundance of eroticized images of the female body with which the duke surrounded himself, Aretino's decision to present his patron with *La puttana errante* was a strategic choice. In the end, it also appears to have been a fruitful one. About a month after Gonzaga received the poem, he wrote to thank Aretino for his "divine compositions" and to assure him that compensation was on its way in the form of "alcune cosette" (a few little things).[22] In this exchange between writer and patron, the fictional body of the *puttana errante* was clearly valuable currency.

Textual Masculinity

This book explores how men in sixteenth-century Venice consolidated their bonds with one another through the creation, circulation, and consumption of literary fictions of women. Aretino's gift to Gonzaga is a ready example of this paradigm; that same gift also marked the beginning of his collaboration with the vast network of writers in sixteenth-century Venice that is my particular focus here. By the time Lorenzo Venier died in 1550, his brother Domenico had become one of the most influential literary patrons in the city, and the family palace in Santa Maria Formosa had become a gathering place for a heterogeneous group of writers who included both Venetian aristocrats and foreign-born intellectuals of the middling sort.[23]

Not the least of these was Aretino, whose direct connections to Domenico can be traced back to at least 1537, when he extolled the patrician's developing literary talent in a letter: "the flowers of your youth will ripen in their autumn into the sweetest fruits that have ever been tasted."[24] Aretino's letters to Domenico are found in all six volumes of his letterbooks – a distinction shared only with another patrician poet named Federico Badoer, Domenico's childhood friend and a literary man himself. Aretino wrote to both patricians in 1538 to exhort them to come and visit him more often.[25] By the mid-1540s, Aretino was well-integrated into the group of poets who gathered at Domenico's house, with whom he shared stylistic and thematic affinities.[26] When Aretino died in 1556, it was Domenico who wrote the epigraph engraved on Aretino's tomb in the church of San Luca – a tomb he would share with two other writers who were also members of Domenico's circle, Girolamo Ruscelli and Lodovico Dolce.[27]

The Venier salon's literary network was vast, extending well beyond the Venetian Republic to include many of the most illustrious writers of the day – Bernardo Tasso and his famous son Torquato, the influential Florentine academician Benedetto Varchi, and the poet and playwright Annibale Caro, who was based in Rome. Domenico Venier and his cohort were renowned among their contemporaries for the elegant verse they published in the highly successful *Rime di diversi* series of lyric poetry anthologies inaugurated by the Ferrarese printer Gabriele Giolito in 1545.[28] Venier's own poetry first appeared in print in the third volume of the series, published in 1550, alongside verse by Aretino, Girolamo Parabosco, and many other writers connected to the salon – their first appearance in print as a group. For the public arena of print, the group composed high-toned sonnets, often in dialogue with one another, on conventional themes such as patriotism, the deaths of literary greats, and the beauty of women. Their love poems featured fictional female beloveds, who, like Petrarch's Laura before them, were evoked through fragmentary, disembodied images: strands of golden hair, ruby-red lips, eyes like stars, and snow-white hands.[29] These images of stylized female beauty and purity, published throughout the sixteenth century and well beyond, were instrumental in solidifying the salon's renown as a centre of poetic excellence well beyond the confines of Venice.

Another aspect of the salon's literary activity was just as instrumental in consolidating relationships among its members, although it was not for the wider public to see. Even as they lamented the unattainability of chaste ladies in print, Venier and his cohort wrote and exchanged among themselves poems in Venetian dialect featuring hyperbolically promiscuous whores. In doing so, they were participating in a flourishing culture of manuscript exchange of dialect poetry. That culture has received scant critical attention, especially from scholars writing in English. Yet without considering dialect production, our understanding of early modern attitudes regarding gender, sex, and love is incomplete. In the dialect poems, too, women are represented in fragments. But while the ladies of the love sonnets are characterized by the surface perfection of their chaste bodies, the whores of the dialect poems are composed of defiled body parts available to all: a gaping vagina, sagging breasts, and skin marred by the pustules of disease. On the surface, these two strands of writing about women appear to be diametrically opposed, but that was so only on a stylistic level. Whether high or low, public or private, the texts penned by the Venier circle are preoccupied with preserving ideals of feminine beauty and comportment, aligning beauty with resistance and unattainability. At the same time, they reinforce normative modes of masculine behaviour and access to power, which is acquired through the cultivation of connections not with women but with other men.

Until the 1990s, what little secondary scholarship there was on sixteenth-century Venetian dialect poetry was silent regarding Domenico Venier's contribution to this phenomenon, perhaps because Venier's moralizing eighteenth-century biographer Pierantonio Serassi had cast his subject as a paragon of virtue.[30] Yet a codex in the British Library, rediscovered by Martha Feldman and discussed briefly in her *City Culture and the Madrigal* (1995), proves that Venier was in fact an avid composer of dialect poems. The codex preserves a lengthy poetic dialogue in dialect between Venier and another patrician named Benetto Corner, composed in the 1540s.[31] Taking the form of an erotic diary, the exchange chronicles the relationship between the two poets and Elena Artusi, a woman with whom they both claim to have had a sexual relationship.

In the opening sonnet, Venier highlights the triangular relationship between the three protagonists, boasting that while he has "za chiavà" (already screwed) Artusi in the past, his friend Corner "adesso la chiava" (is screwing her now).[32] As the fictive chronology unfolds, we are told that it was Venier who initiated the exchange, after a flare-up of gout (which would plague him for the rest of his life) left him bedridden and his affair with Artusi came to an end. When he learned that Corner had begun a relationship with his ex-lover, Venier proposed that they make her the centrepiece of a new, collaborative poetic project. Each time Corner saw Artusi, he was to write Venier a poem recounting the details of their encounter, "ponto per ponto" (point by point), as well as describing "giusto co la fò" (exactly what she did).[33] Whatever Artusi may have been in her lived life, in the dialect manuscript she is figured as a "puttana di natura" (whore by nature) whose defining characteristic is her promiscuity. At the same time, through the trope of the commodified female body, the dialect exchange foregrounds the relationship between the two men.

What are we to make of this literary threesome? One way to begin to untangle the sexual politics at work in these texts is to note that they often involve some form of triangulation between two (or more) men and one woman. My readings here will focus on that triangulation, taking as a point of departure the basic paradigm of male traffic in women as articulated by Claude Lévi-Strauss, Gayle Rubin, and Eve Kosofsky Sedgwick.[34] In revisiting this paradigm, I do not mean to translate it into a metaphor for gender roles and relations with the attendant casting of women as passive recipients of male desire and men as their privileged oppressors. That is one plotline in what is a very complex story, since early modern Venetian culture was patriarchal but not monolithic. Neither was masculinity itself. To be sure, the exchanges of fictional women that follow are concerned both with ideals of masculinity and with the control of women and their sexuality. At the same time, the texts I focus on here do not always represent these things as unproblematic. So I begin with the triangular paradigm of traffic in women not to smooth over these rough edges but to provide a starting point for thinking about how the exchange of fictional women reflected, affirmed, and sometimes resisted normative ideals of behaviour for both sexes.

In *Between Men*, Sedgwick used Rubin's anthropological critique of male traffic in women as an enforcer of patriarchal heterosexuality to analyse the power dynamics of the erotic triangle in English literature.[35] Sedgwick would later summarize her project as an exploration of "the oppressive effects on women and men of a cultural system in which male–male desire became widely intelligible primarily by being routed through triangular relations involving a woman."[36] Crucial to

Sedgwick's argument was her notion of male homosocial desire, which she defined as the entire continuum of men's relations with other men, including but not limited to relationships of genital homosexual desire. This attention to sexuality was an important revision to René Girard's foundational but symmetrical vision of the erotic triangle in the European novel.[37] While Girard had highlighted the intensity of the bond between the two (usually male) rivals for the affections of the (usually female) beloved, he did not make explicit the possibility that the male–male bond might involve sexual desire.

Sedgwick, on the other hand, is ultimately most interested in the erotic triangle as an expression of the forbidden desire of men for one another. It is not that she reduces men's relationships to sexual desire alone, or that she is insensitive to the constraints of patriarchal heterosexuality as they apply to women as well as men. But there is a sense in which, for Sedgwick, the erotic triangle is as much a register of homophobia and homosexual panic as it is a metaphor for male traffic in women. I point this out not to diminish her important argument regarding the ways in which homophobia and misogyny can be interconnected, but instead to emphasize a change of focus in my own readings, which consider male–male desire as one element in a complex spectrum of homosocial relationships. For the men I study here, literary fictions of women served to consolidate relationships up and down the social spectrum, and of many different types. In the world of the text, the poets are sometimes (yes) lovers, but they are also friends, literary partners, patron and courtier, or teacher and student. It also seems important to add what Sedgwick called "the quicksilver of sex itself" back into relationships of heterosexual desire.[38] After all, if men's desire for one another was constrained by patriarchal systems, so too was men's desire for women.

The power dynamic in the erotic triangle is even more asymmetrical (to continue Sedgwick's geometrical analysis) when the female mediator between men appears in the guise of whore, as she does in so many of the texts produced by Venier, Aretino, and their network. Of course, the exchange between men of texts on whores can be traced back to antiquity, and thus the subject offers a rich array of intertextual significance to both writers and readers.[39] Then, as in Renaissance Italy, male poets deployed the trope of the whore (and the "whorish" behaviour of the beloved) as a means of performing and negotiating relationships with one another. To cite just one example, the poems of the Latin poet Catullus, many of which are addressed directly to his friends, are scattered with invectives against women. In one poem he demeans Ameana, "this crazy girl, so thoroughly fucked over ... the worthless whore"; in another, he accuses a "wretched slut" of stealing his writing tablets.[40] A woman he calls Lesbia (who in life was probably his married lover) is alternately idolized for her powers of seduction and denounced for her whorish tendencies: in a poem addressed to his two friends Furius and Aurelius, Catullus accuses Lesbia of sleeping with three hundred other men.[41]

These intertwined themes of male friendship and misogynist invective continued into the sixteenth century, when literary representations of prostitutes took on a new vigour and valence as anxieties about the circulation and accumulation of capital continued to build.[42] As Walter Benjamin observed in *The Arcades Project*, "the whore is, fundamentally, the incarnation of a nature suffused with commodity appearance."[43] In the work of sixteenth-century Venetian writers, too, the whore trope illuminates the mechanics of a social system that commodifies women's bodies. She is at the fulcrum of sex, power, and money. Yet the whore is much more than a simple exchange object. As a literary trope, her symbolic resonance is complex and malleable, a quality that Aretino and other writers of this period capitalized on in their representations of her in their works. Even as she is evoked for tangible gain, the whore becomes the incarnation of the corrupt other, something to be vilified and debased. In that sense, she is a foil against which to construct a positive, powerful masculine identity.

The figure of the whore was particularly resonant in Venice, the lagoon republic known for its relatively unrestricted atmosphere of intellectual and literary exchange, its status as the centre of print culture, and its abundance of sensual pleasures. In 1509, the Venetian diarist Marin Sanudo recorded that there were almost twelve thousand prostitutes in Venice among its forty-eight thousand women and children.[44] While Sanudo's figures are probably exaggerated, he was not the only one to comment on the relatively high numbers of prostitutes in Venice. Venice was of course not unique in being a site of prostitution in the sixteenth century, yet it does seem to have been a particularly hospitable environment for the sale of sex – or at least that is how it was represented. Lorenzo Venier, for example, lamented around 1531 that there were "tre legion o quattro di puttane" (three or four legions of whores) in his city, adding that they were the "ruina de' patrizi e de' plebei" (the downfall of both patricians and plebes).[45] About fifty years later, one of the characters in Giordano Bruno's comedy *Il candelaio* (The

Candle-Bearer, 1582) noted wryly that all three major urban centres of Renaissance Italy – Naples, Rome, and Venice – were overrun with "puttane, o corteggiane come vogliam dire" (whores, or courtesans, or whatever we want to call them). But in Venice, he continued, "because of the magnanimity and the liberality of the illustrious Republic, whores are exempt from every hardship; and they are less bound by laws than any of the rest [of the inhabitants], even though there are so many of them."[46]

Bruno's interlocutor uses *puttana* and *cortigiana* as synonyms, bringing into focus the inherent ambiguity in the terminology used for prostitutes of all types, an issue to which we will return in detail. For now, I want to emphasize that those two words, along with the more neutral *meretrice* (a rough equivalent to the English "prostitute"), were used interchangeably in both legal documents and literary texts to refer to women who exchanged sex for gifts or money. This slipperiness underscores the profound ambivalence with which prostitutes were viewed by the men who patronized them and by society as a whole.

Puttana, Meretrice, Cortigiana: What's in a Name?

In 1523, Marin Sanudo reported that while walking through the banking district near the Rialto Bridge he saw "molte lettere grande [*sic*] di carbon in vituperio di banchieri e di alcuni altri" (many large letters in black carbon insulting bankers and a few others) scrawled underneath the portico.[47] Most of the insults were directed at various Venetian bankers whose offices were in the area. But among these was a slur targeting a woman named Cornelia Grifo: "Cornelia Grifo, ch'è in tal reputation, sapiate è una puttana trista, per aver fato fioli un million" (Let it be known that Cornelia Grifo, who has a certain reputation, is a wretched whore who has done it with a million men).[48] Nearby was another phrase suggesting that the slur against Cornelia was probably motivated by her relationship with a wealthy Venetian patrician: "Cornelia sarà la to ruina, Piero da Molin!" (Cornelia will be your downfall, Piero da Molin!)"[49] Still another proclaimed that the banker Polo Zigogna had been consorting with a certain "Eugenia putana" (Eugenia the whore).[50]

Less than a week after Sanudo recorded seeing the graffiti, during an examination by the Signori di Notte, a young nobleman named Domenego Mocenigo confessed to having written some of them.[51] Mocenigo's slurs, written in rough imitation of rhyming couplets, had a comic, literary tone. Even so, his disparagement of two fellow patricians was no laughing matter. As punishment, Mocenigo got the silent treatment: an announcement was posted in the Ducal Palace forbidding other nobles to speak to him.[52] As such a punishment suggests, the problem was not only what the epithet "whore" did to the reputations of Cornelia and Eugenia but also what it implied about men who associated with such women.

About three years later, Cornelia raised hackles again when she married a Venetian patrician, an event that was newsworthy enough to be recorded in detail by Sanudo: "Today one heard openly about the wedding between ser Andrea Michiel … and a certain Cornelia Grifo, a most beautiful and sumptuous widowed prostitute. She is rich and has been publicly kept by ser Ziprian Malipiero, and for a while she belonged to ser Piero da Molin … and to others, who have given her a dowry of [amount left blank] ducats. The wedding was held at the monastery of San Zuan on Torcello and has cast great shame on the Venetian patriciate."[53] Although Sanudo emphasizes the shameful nature of the misalliance between a nobleman and a prostitute, he devotes most of his entry to a description of Cornelia herself, highlighting her beauty, her wealth, and her connections to powerful men.

As Stanley Chojnacki has suggested, Cornelia's marriage was probably the driving force behind a new law, enacted just ten days after the scandalous nuptials, that required all noble marriages to be registered with the *avogadori di comun* (state attorneys).[54] The registration procedure required that two relatives of each spouse swear to both the legitimacy of the marriage and the status of the bride (confirmed by the status of her father). Any offspring resulting from an unregistered marriage would no longer be eligible for membership in the patrician class, nor would they be registered as noble in the *Libri d'Oro*, the so-called golden books.[55] These new requirements, while aimed at preventing illegitimate sons from claiming noble status, also made it much more difficult for a woman who lacked status or respectability to marry a nobleman.

According to the Council of Ten in a law passed the same year as Cornelia's wedding, the pollution of noble blood threatened the very "honor, peace, and conservation" of the Venetian Republic.[56] Seen in this light, the sexuality of women like Cornelia Grifo was unsettling because it posed a threat to carefully drawn social and class boundaries. Small wonder, then, that our noble graffiti artist Domenico Mocenigo warned Piero da Molin that Cornelia would bring about his downfall.

And small wonder that his insults interpellated Cornelia as a *puttana trista*, calling her into subjectivity not as a sought-after courtesan but as a disempowered whore.[57]

Cornelia would appear in the guise of *puttana* once again in *La tariffa delle puttane di Venegia* (The price list of the whores of Venice), a satiric dialogue printed about 1535.[58] The author of this text is unknown, but flattering references to Aretino and his circle within the text suggest that it was likely written and published under Aretino's auspices.[59] The dialogue takes place between a Venetian *gentiluomo* (nobleman) and a *forestiere* (a visiting foreigner), who asks the Venetian to describe for him the courtesans of Venice, their prices, and their *ruffiane* (procuresses). The *gentiluomo* obliges, but not without admonishing the *forestiere* to remember that whores are "come statue ... dentro hanno il fango, e son di fuora ornate" (like statues, they have mud inside, but are decorated on the outside).[60] By the end of the poem, having exposed the dirt hidden by their artificially beautified exteriors, the nobleman has succeeded in convincing his guest to swear off courtesans forever.[61] This stance, which frames *La tariffa* as moralistic and pedagogical in its intent to teach men to preserve themselves from the dangers posed by prostitutes, is a common one in such texts, perhaps in part as a way to legitimize unseemly content and deflect possible censorship.[62] At the same time, the conversion of the visiting gentleman, like the rest of the text, is ambiguous, since the conversation between the two men emphasizes the pleasures as well as the dangers of consorting with courtesans: "O che dolce morir, morir soave, / Morir felice, a chi le muore in braccio!" (Oh, what sweet death, to die sweetly, to die happily, awaits those who die in their arms!).[63]

The list of courtesans begins with "la Lombarda, che d'oro e terreni / Ricca si fè con la virtù del tondo" ([Giulia] Lombardo, who has managed to become rich in both gold and land through the virtues of her round [ass]).[64] Cornelia Grifo, second in line, is introduced as a "buon pasto e robba ghiotta, se pur ghiotto mangiar fa ghiotta carne" (good meal and tasty stuff, although greedy eating makes for tasty meat).[65] She is also taken to task for putting on airs and overcharging her clients:

Costei vi chiederà, per essere dotta,
in far l'altera et un puttanesmo honesto
quaranta e più, solo a chiavarla in potta.
Ma questo egli è pur prezzo dishonesto
e forse miglior robbe nei bordelli
ha per due soldi alcun che porta il cesto.

She will ask you for forty *scudi* or more just to screw her in the cunt, because she proudly claims to be erudite and to engage in honest whoring. But this is truly a dishonest price, and even a porter can probably find better merchandise for a few bucks in the brothels.[66]

Such condemnation of courtesans for their pretensions to erudition, elegance, and social status is commonplace in sixteenth-century discourse.[67] On the one hand, their beauty, erudition, and wealth made them suitable and desirable companions for aristocratic men; on the other, these very attributes could be unsettling, in part because of the social mobility they enabled.

As for Cornelia Grifo, while the outcome of her marriage is unclear, even as late as the 1540s she was still wealthy enough to engage the artist Lorenzo Lotto to paint her portrait.[68] It appears that she later decided to retract the commission. Even so, such a request suggests that she had achieved and held on to relatively high social and economic status. This status is reflected in Lotto's account books, where he refers to Cornelia as "Magnifica Madonna" (Magnificent Lady), a respectful honorific that was often bestowed on noblewomen. To complicate matters even further, Cornelia was addressed as "Cortigianissime Cornelie Grifo venete" (the most courtesanly Cornelia Grifo of Venice) in a satiric dedication preceding a collection of invectives targeting a Venetian prostitute named Jacomina.[69] This last example is evidence of how early modern writers sometimes transformed the term *cortigiana* into a satiric barb, poking fun at its connotations of courtliness and social elevation and at the social ambition of the women who identified themselves as *cortigiane*.

These shifting representations of Cornelia Grifo – she is at once *puttana trista, meretrice somtuosa, cortigiana*, and *Magnifica Madonna* – point towards a deceptively simple question that is at the heart of my inquiry here: What did it mean to call a woman a whore in sixteenth-century Venice? We might begin by recalling, with James Grantham Turner, that early modern discourse on prostitution often "exploits the ambiguous relationship between two elements that would eventually combine: pornē (signifying the prostitute openly revealed and reviled) and graphē (the expressive mark or engraved sign, verbal as well as visual."[70] In his work on libertine culture in early modern England, Turner uses this etymology as the basis for what he calls "pornographia" – the prostitute revealed through literal or figurative signs that mark her as whore. For Turner, this process can be thought of as "an act of *designation* or *marking*, at once accusation, distinction, signage, and signature. At its crudest it means uttering and affixing the single word *whore*."[71] Like the graffiti on the Rialto Bridge, which inscribed the word *puttana* on the reputations of Cornelia and Eugenia, the texts I examine here wield the epithet whore as the ultimate weapon of defamation.

Even as they mark the women they target as whores, these texts have much to tell us about the men who exchanged them. The problem with Cornelia had as much to do with the very human dangers she posed as an inspirer of desire – a dangerous force, indeed – as it did with her alleged pretensions to erudition and class. It was that power that made her a threat to her noble lovers, who risked financial ruin and loss of status as a consequence of their involvement with her. In that sense, we can read the literary transformation of Cornelia from a beautiful, erudite, wealthy courtesan into an overpriced piece of "tasty meat" as an expression of anxieties about the disruptive power of sexual desire – and, yes, perhaps even love.[72] Taken collectively, texts like *La tariffa*, with their obsessive rehearsing of the trope of the courtesan exposed as whore, mediate concerns about the fragility of masculine identity and authority, especially in the complex realm of human desire and sexuality. What more effective way to put a courtesan back in her place between men after she has threatened to escape triangular transaction than to figure her as a piece of flesh to be bought and sold?

Words for women who participated in the sex trade were many and varied, but in the early modern Venetian context there were three that dominated both legal documents and literary texts: *puttana, meretrice,* and *cortigiana*.[73] All three are found in a decree issued in 1524 by the Provveditori alla Sanità, an institution of the Venetian government that oversaw public health and that in the fifteenth century was empowered to control the movements of prostitutes.[74] Here, perhaps for the first time in Venetian legislation, courtesans are mentioned as a distinct category of prostitute: "le cortesane e altra sorte de putane over meretrice" (courtesans and other kinds of whores or prostitutes).[75] The distinction, however, is semantic rather than legal. Courtesans are simply one kind of whore and therefore they are bound by the same rules as the rest. At least in terms of legal discourse, if not in common parlance, a courtesan was a prostitute; therefore, she was also a whore.

Or was she? As we saw with Cornelia Grifo, the same woman could be interpellated in multiple ways regardless of her economic, social, or moral status. As Elizabeth Cohen has argued, the choice of words often depended "less on the status of the woman described, than on the circumstances and personal pretensions of the speaker."[76] In other words, a man might use the epithet *puttana* when intending to insult a woman, but he might refer to her as a *cortigiana* when wanting to raise his own status. The source of this ambiguity in terminology, as Cohen has pointed out, lies precisely in the equivalent ambivalence with which women who exchanged sex for material compensation were viewed by the very men who patronized them, as well as by the society in which they lived and worked.[77]

The term *cortigiana* probably originated in the late fifteenth century, in Rome, where it was used to denote the prostitutes who were patronized by the elite, highly educated men employed at the papal court. In 1498, Johannes Burchard, the master of ceremonies to Pope Alexander VI Borgia, described in his diary a certain Cursetta as a "cortegiana, hoc est meretrix honesta" (courtesan, that is, honest prostitute).[78] Three years later, Burchard used the same definition – "meretrices honeste, noncupate cortegiane" (honest prostitutes, called *cortigiane*) – for the fifty women who provided erotic entertainment during a banquet organized by the Pope's son Cesare Borgia.[79] Initially, then, the word *cortegiana* denoted those prostitutes who were "honest" – a qualifier that in this context is meant to evoke not moral honesty or chastity but social standing and respectability.[80] A *meretrix honesta* was honest (in the sense of "honoured" or "honourable") because she kept company with men of high social and financial status.[81]

Just a decade or so after Burchard defined the *cortigiana* as an elite category of prostitute, the term lost its connotation of exclusivity and elevation, at least in Rome. In a census of the city dated between 1511 and 1518, *cortesana* (a variant spelling) was by far the most common word used for women who exchanged sex for compensation, indicating that by that time it had become a general term for prostitutes of all types.[82] The same census contains several instances in which *cortesana* is modified with various qualifiers: these include "cortesana putana" (courtesan-whore), "cortesana da lume" (courtesan by lamplight), "cortesana da la Candella [*sic*]" (courtesan by candlelight?), and "honesta cortegiana" (honest courtesan). Since Arturo Graf's essay on Veronico Franco brought these Roman terms to critical attention in 1926, they have sometimes been used to construct a taxonomy of prostitutes in early modern Italian cities that places the *cortesana putana/da lume/da la candela* at the bottom and the *honesta cortegiana* at the top.[83] Yet these formulations appear no more than twice each in the original Roman document, and they do not seem to have been used in sixteenth-century discourse on prostitutes outside of Rome.[84] Rather than interpreting these categories as part of a rigid hierarchy of prostitution, I suggest we read them as reflections of the perceived status of the women they describe – and regional ones, at that. In that sense, they complicate rather than simplify our understanding of the differences among Renaissance prostitutes.

As for the word *puttana*, it is interesting to note that this term was used both in speech and in legal documents to refer to prostitutes. Of course, then as now, such words were used not only to mark those women who actually practised prostitution, but also for women who were seen as sexually transgressive in a much broader sense. That said, the epithet *puttana* was understood as a serious insult to a woman's honour and reputation, whether or not she was a sex worker.[85] As Elizabeth Horodowich has demonstrated, *puttana* was one of the most common insults in accusations of verbal injury brought before the *Avogaria di Comun* from 1500 to 1625. In the minds of contemporary observers, what made a whore a whore was not her profession as sex worker, but the way she practised it. Whores, as imagined and feared, allowed their bodies to be used "dishonestly" – that is, indiscriminately and without regard for the social and economic status of sexual partners.[86] In that sense, the word *puttana* can be read as an expression of anxieties regarding male status.

The word's very etymology reflects its derogatory connotations: *puttana* probably came to Italian from the Old French *putain* or *pute* (both still common today), which likely derives from the Latin *putere*, "to stink" or "to be putrid."[87] This etymon is satirized in the *Ragionamento dello Zoppino*, a prose dialogue first published in 1539 by the Venetian printer Francesco Marcolini.[88] In 1584, the Zoppino dialogue was attributed to Aretino in a posthumous edition of his *Ragionamenti* printed in London by John Wolfe, who billed it as "Il piacevol ragionamento dell'Aretino" (The pleasant discourse of Aretino).[89] But Gino Lanfranchi, who edited the first modern edition of the Zoppino dialogue in 1922, would argue instead that it was the work of the Spanish priest Francisco Delicado.[90] The question of authorship has not been resolved, but it is not hard to see the thematic similarities between the Zoppino dialogue and other texts on prostitutes produced by Aretino and his circle during this period. The dialogue takes place between Zoppino, a recently converted whoremonger turned priest, and his friend Ludovico, who is pining for a courtesan named Lucrezia. When Ludovico asks Zoppino to explain the meaning of the word *puttana*, Zoppino responds with this pseudo-academic etymology:

> *Puttana* is a noun composed of both the vernacular and Latin: in Latin, that which we call *culo* [ass] in our language is called *ano* [anus], and thus [the

word *puttana*] is composed of *potta* [cunt] and *ano*; and in our vernacular *puttana* means "a woman whose cave stinks" and *cortigiana* means "courteous with the anus."[91]

Zoppino's claim that both *puttana* and *cortigiana* are derived from "anus" degrades both terms even as it blurs the boundaries between them. Earlier in the conversation, Zoppino had equated whores with courtesans even more explicitly, presenting the two terms as synonyms: "Well, my dear Ludovico, these *puttane*, or *cortigiane*, regardless of what you want to call them, are an evil thing."[92] Around the same time, an anonymous poet masquerading as Pasquino (the famed "talking statue" in Rome, a persona often adopted by Aretino) warned visitors to Rome that courtesans were simply whores with a higher price tag:

Lassa andare le cortesane
Se non voi disfarte al tutto;
Come l'altre son puttane;
Ma più caro vendon loro frutto

Leave the courtesans alone if you don't want to completely ruin yourself. They are whores, just like the others, but they sell their fruit at a higher price.[93]

In a similar vein, Sperone Speroni, a frequent interlocutor of both Aretino and Domenico Venier, lamented that "cortigiana comunemente non vuol dir altro che meretrice" (*cortigiana* in common usage means nothing but *meretrice*).[94] Strictly speaking, of course, Speroni was right. If we accept that the defining attribute of a prostitute is the exchange of sex for material compensation, then courtesans were indeed part of that category, in terms of both legal and social status. Yet the insistence in sixteenth-century legal and literary documents that courtesans were nothing more than prostitutes belies the fact that, at least for a select group of women, the opposite was true. The debate itself reveals the ways in which the status of the courtesan was intertwined with the performance of aristocratic Venetian masculinity.

So what made a courtesan a courtesan? Despite the inherent slipperiness of the terminology, there were important differences in wealth, social status, and lifestyle between women involved in the sex trade. The women we have come to think of as *cortigiane oneste*, honest or honoured courtesans, were at the top of what Guido Ruggiero has called the "social hierarchy of prostitution," at least for a time.[95] At the height of her career, a successful courtesan lived in relative luxury, employing household servants and tutors for her children and dressing in rich fabrics.[96] In her dress, manner, and clientele, she was careful to distinguish herself from the common prostitutes who could be found on the streets and in the taverns and brothels of most Renaissance cities. But what really set the *cortigiana onesta* apart was the fact that she was available only to the most worthy of men, at least as she was fantasized. As Ruggiero has argued, "the ideal was that … the 'honest courtesan' was an exacting mistress, a woman not unlike the court lady of Castiglione in her disciplining function, who judged honestly her suitors, accepting only the best."[97] It was precisely the courtesan's perceived power to judge and choose that made her so desirable, but this same power could also be a source of anxiety.

While Venetian law did not spell out what distinguished a courtesan from other prostitutes, a case involving a woman named Andriana Savorgnan suggests that there were important differences in contemporary attitudes towards these two groups.[98] In 1581, Andriana married the Venetian patrician Marco Dandolo in a private ceremony at her mother's home. Shortly thereafter, senior members of the Dandolo clan accused Andriana of having made use of love magic to ensnare her noble lover and brought her before the Holy Office for investigation. After the initial investigation, the Patriarch of Venice ordered the two lovers to separate. Instead, they fled to Padua, where they were eventually caught in bed together. With Marco's help, Andriana escaped the authorities, but what exactly happened afterwards (including the outcome of their marriage) is unclear.[99]

The proceedings from Andriana's investigation offer intriguing clues as to how sixteenth-century Venetians thought and talked about prostitutes of varying levels. An exchange between Andriana's mother Laura and one of the examiners suggests that both parties recognized the difference between a courtesan and a "public prostitute." To the examiner's request that she "chiariria se questa sua fiola è stata cortiggiana o publica meretrice qui in Venezia" (clarify whether her daughter was a courtesan or a public prostitute in Venice), Laura responded that Andriana "è stata cortiggiana con i suoi homini" (was a courtesan, given the men who had patronized her). She bolstered her claim at the examiner's request with a long list of high-ranking Venetian noblemen who had been among her daughter's lovers.[100] As this exchange makes clear, a distinguishing attribute of a courtesan, as opposed to a public prostitute, was the social status of her clientele. Andriana's patrician connections seem to have worked in her favour shortly before her marriage, when she was condemned by the *Magistrato delle Pompe*, probably for breaking one of the many sumptuary laws regulating the dress and self-display of prostitutes.[101] During the short period in which she was held in jail for questioning, she enjoyed private quarters and was allowed to keep a servant and entertain various noble visitors.[102]

These creature comforts are telling, since while Andriana certainly benefited from such preferential treatment, her patrician friends must have also appreciated access to her company. Yet while Andriana's refinements and her roster of noble clients made her an especially appealing companion for upper-class men, she was not and would never be acceptable marriage material in the eyes of those who sought to uphold the purity of the patrician class and its republic. Even her many ties to powerful men could not protect her from defamation when she transgressed clearly defined social boundaries and threatened to infiltrate the upper echelons of society. So it is not surprising that another nobleman named Aloisio Soranzo testified that he and the entire city found it very strange that Marco, "un giovene così honorato e ricco e nobile" (a young man so honoured and rich and noble), would marry "una donna mecanica, infame, et publica meretrize" (a lowly and infamous woman, and a public prostitute).[103] Other witnesses, when asked about Andriana's status, defined her as "una trista, cioè meretrice" (a wretched woman, that is, a prostitute) and a "putana publica" (public whore).[104]

The question of Andriana's status depended on careful adherence to and negotiation of societal codes that allowed her the role of companion but not that of wife. These codes were in place for men and women of all social standing, of course, but the stories of Cornelia Grifo and Andriana Savorgnan reveal the ways in which courtesans in particular were vulnerable to accusations of promiscuity – especially when their sexuality was seen as threatening to the social hierarchy. They also reveal how precarious the status of a courtesan could be, tied as it was to the men who patronized, protected, and loved her. The spectre of the disempowered, indiscriminate whore was always present for even the most successful courtesans.

Writing the Courtesan

Despite our modern tendency to draw fixed distinctions between *puttane, meretrici,* and *cortigiane,* the boundaries between these categories were fluid and ever-changing. The Renaissance *cortigiana* is a particularly elusive figure, since neither her legal nor her social status was clearly articulated – and both of these were tied to the status of the men who patronized her. Literary responses to the courtesan illuminate and negotiate this inherent ambiguity. Like her mythological alter egos – Venus, the goddess of love both sacred and profane, and Danaë, the virgin-whore – the courtesan was captivating because she embodied the tension between the idealized and the earthy, the divine and the sinful, the pleasurable and the painful.

Prostitutes of all social and economic levels were often figured in sixteenth-century discourse as the incarnation of sin, and especially the mortal sins of excess: lust, avarice, and gluttony. The parallel is clear in some of the earliest surviving records of the Venetian state, which refer to prostitutes as "femine de peccato" (sinful females) or "peccatrices" (female sinners).[105] By the first decades of the sixteenth century, prostitutes were also associated with the spread of syphilis, the so-called *mal francese* (French disease), which was believed to have been brought to Italy by the French troops who invaded Naples in 1495.[106] Over the course of the sixteenth century, the grotesque, disease-ridden body of the syphilitic prostitute, marked with the telltale pustules of disease, became a popular theme in text and image. Along with poetry and prose, broadsides and cheap pamphlets on this topic burgeoned in Venice, as well as the rest of Italy. These texts were often sold by vendors in markets, streets, and squares.[107]

A recurring theme in text and image is the ritual of the *carretta*, the cart in which the syphilitic prostitute was paraded through the streets, as onlookers jeered, on her way to the hospital where she would presumably die. Lorenzo Venier's *La puttana errante* culminates in a mock-triumphal procession that evokes this ritual: the whore-errant, her head adorned with a "corona di cazzi" (crown of dicks), makes her way through the streets of Rome on a cart pulled by "un'asina, una troia, una vacca, e una cavallaccia" (a female ass, a sow, a cow, and a broken-down old mare) to the Ponte Sisto, a bridge in Rome where the city's poorest prostitutes plied their trade.[108] As Deanna Shemek has pointed out, the ritual of the *carretta* recalls a phenomenon that was common in Venice and other early modern cities: the public shaming of those who had transgressed moral or legal boundaries.[109] Paradoxically, even as it purports to expose the prostitute's corrupt and diseased nature, the *carretta* also recalls the literary trope of the *donna angelicata*, the stylized angel-woman of *dolce stil novo* heritage. Petrarch's Laura and Dante's Beatrice, of course, both appear as heroines of elaborate triumphal processions. The image of the *carretta*, then, makes explicit the opposition between *donna angelicata* and syphilitic whore that was inherent in the figure of the prostitute – and especially in that of the courtesan.

Prostitutes, Pimps, and Bullies: Venetian Literature "alla bulesca"

The preoccupation with prostitution at the beginning of the sixteenth century is reflected in the particularly Venetian genre of literature that we now call "alla bulesca." This rather elastic category includes short verse comedies, poems in various metres, and dialogues, composed mainly in Venetian dialect.[110] Such texts circulated widely throughout the century, in manuscript, but also in print as cheap, short pamphlets or broadsides. They were important prototypes for later literary representations of courtesans. Literature "alla bulesca" gets its name from the *buli* that it features as protagonists.[111] These unsavoury types were professional armed thugs who roamed the streets of Venice and surrounding mainland cities looking for trouble. They often served as paid bodyguards and/or hit men for patricians and others able to afford such protection.[112] The term *bulo* was interchangeable with *bravo* in literary sources in the first decades of the sixteenth century, although *bravo* was used in official legislation regarding these men beginning in the 1570s.[113]

The Venetian literary *bulo/bravo* type can be traced back to the figure of the *miles gloriosus*, or braggart soldier, a stock character from ancient Roman theatre. The *miles gloriosus* figure got its name from the eponymous comedy by Plautus, which features a vain and boastful warrior who is duped by his clever slave and an equally cunning courtesan.

The leading lady in texts "alla bulesca" is usually a prostitute characterized by her insatiable desire for money. The formulaic plot structure of these texts highlights the avarice of prostitutes. Often the story is set in motion by the prostitute's rejection of a desperate suitor who lacks the cash she desires.[114] This is the case in the anonymous *Comedia dicta la bulescha* (hereafter *La bulesca*), a short comedy starring Bulle as the lovelorn *bulo* and Marcolina as the stubborn prostitute who resists his advances.[115] As the comedy begins, Bulle confesses his love for Marcolina to his friend Bio, lamenting that she has been ignoring him of late. The two decide to go to Marcolina's house, and when she refuses to comply with their wishes, they retaliate by showering first Fracao (her bodyguard and pimp) and then Marcolina herself with threats and obscene insults. All is resolved by the arrival of a gentleman identified only as "Misièr" (a title used for noblemen), who convinces the two *bravi* to make peace with each other. In the final scene, Fracao hands over the unwilling Marcolina to Bulle, exhorting him to take what she has promised him.

La bulesca is probably the comedy about "sbrichi venitiani" (Venetian *bravi*)[116] mentioned by Sanudo in an entry dated 8 October 1514: "This evening, in a house in the parish of Santi Giovanni e Paolo, a pleasant comedy about Venetian *bravi* was recited after dinner by the company called the 'Zardinieri.' It was lovely to see, and many went there to see it."[117] The "Zardinieri" (Gardeners) were one of the *Compagnie della Calza*, literally, companies "of the sock," so-called because of the distinctive emblems they wore on their stockings. These organizations for young male patricians often entertained themselves and onlookers by performing music, plays, and spectacles of various types. Whether or not Sanudo's description refers specifically to *La bulesca*, it does suggest where and how these sorts of comedies would have been performed. Sanudo's description of the performance is typical of its time; most performances by the *Compagnie delle Calze* took place in private palaces and were attended by an elite audience of Venetian nobles and their invited guests.[118] These gatherings often included prostitutes, as numerous entries by Sanudo show. On 12 June 1514, for example, the "Zardinieri" put on another comedy in the presence of "alcune meretrici" (some prostitutes) in a house owned by the Priuli family on the island of Murano.[119] In 1539 yet another comedy, this time "a la bergamasca" (in the style of Bergamo) was performed in the company of "molte putane suntuose stravestie" (many sumptuous whores in costume).[120]

For the Venetian noblemen who watched performances of comedies like *La bulesca*, the antics of the *bravi* and their prostitutes would have been amusing in part because the main characters represented a social class below their own. The scenario reinforces Venetian ideals of social order and harmony: it is the noble Misièr who resolves the conflict between the two *bravi*, demonstrating his superior wisdom along with his elite status. Distant as it may seem from the elite Venetian circles for which it was performed, the basic plot of *La bulesca* is in essence a low-level retelling of the time-honoured dilemma of the man in love with a woman who resists his advances, a theme that dominated the Petrarchist love poems that were written and read in Venetian literary salons. Yet the female protagonist of *La bulesca* is no noble, chaste lady but a prostitute who schemes to ensnare a rich lover in order to better her financial and social status. By mid-century, these lower-class characters – prostitutes, pimps, and bullies – would come to dominate the dialect poetry of the nobles associated with Domenico Venier's circle.

Although *La bulesca* is named for its two swaggering *buli*, its true protagonist is Marcolina, whose two defining characteristics are her "astuzia" (cunning) and her greed. In that sense, Marcolina is an important precursor to the hyperbolically avaricious courtesan figures represented in later Venetian texts. A scene between Bulle and Bio highlights Marcolina's avarice before she even appears on the stage. When Bulle laments that Marcolina has refused to see him despite her promises to the contrary, Bio retorts: "Compare, s'ti non tra' de là monzoia, / non sperar mai de averla" (My friend, if you're not prepared to get out your wallet, don't ever hope of having her!).[121]

Marcolina's greed is the subject of a hyperbolic invective by Bio that reaches its peak when he charges her with being so hungry for money that she is even willing to consort with a "sarasin" (a Saracen, or Turk).[122] Because Venetian law strictly forbade women to have sex with Muslims and Jews, this charge would have certainly resonated with contemporary spectators. The Venetian historian Pompeo Molmenti reports that in 1507 – seven years before *La bulesca* was probably performed – three women had been convicted of that crime and publicly flogged along the *Merceria*, one of Venice's main commercial streets leading to San Marco.[123] With its comic focus on Marcolina's potential relations with Turks and Jews, the comedy highlights patrician anxieties regarding the contamination of bloodlines through illicit sexual activities, foreshadowing the concerns we saw earlier about prostitutes marrying into the patrician class.

Bio punctuates his accusation with a few lines in Marcolina's voice, putting the finishing touches on his portrait of her as the consummate greedy prostitute who is willing to send her lover into bankruptcy in order to acquire material goods:

"Se ti non l'ha" – dise – "impegna el manto.
Non voio esser de bando to morosa,
e pur se debio far quel che te piase,
refondi, mare, una peliza tosa."

"If you don't have it" – she says – "hock your cloak.
I don't want to be your lover for nothing,
and if you want me to do what pleases you,
pay me back for my troubles, dear, with a nice fur."[124]

These lines, probably spoken in a mocking falsetto by the patrician dilettante playing Bio, would have brought smiles to the faces of the noble audience. The scene is funny precisely because it plays on commonplaces that would have been immediately recognizable to the *Cinquecento* listener. Marcolina's declaration that her love comes at a price tropes the historic greed of prostitutes even while emphasizing her status as a commodity available to the highest bidder. Here, too, there are deeper concerns at work. The trope of avarice is amusing, but it also reveals anxieties about male competition, since Bio implies that foreigners may be capable of outbidding Venetians.

The visual imagery offered to the spectator during the performance must have highlighted the courtesan's greed: when Marcolina first appears on the stage, she is flaunting triumphantly a bonnet she has received as a gift from her newest conquest. The short scene that follows reinforces this larger-than-life greed as well as Marcolina's other dominant quality, her cunning. As Marcolina boasts to her cousin Zuana that she has snared a wealthy lover, her words evoke the crass jingling of coins: "Che te par de custù? Te par che 'l sona?" (What do you think of him? Do you think his pockets jingle?)[125] Marcolina's deceitful scheme to convince her new client to marry her even requires that Zuana convince the wealthy gentleman that her cousin is not a prostitute but a chaste woman: "E, se 'l te domandase se io ho morosi, / dighe de no, e zura falsamente, / perché vogio far tanto che 'l me sposi" (And if he asks you if I have lovers, tell him no, and swear to it, though it is a lie, because I want to convince him to marry me).[126] But Marcolina's dreams of higher social status and independence are short lived. In the last scene, the pimp Fracao forcibly consigns the unwilling prostitute to Bulle, who has his way with her as his friends listen outside the door. For all her protests and her dreams of financial independence, by the end of the play Marcolina has been put back in her place as a sexual object to be bought and sold.

This formulaic presentation of prostitutes would be one persistent element in later satires. The long invectives launched against Marcolina by both Bio and Bulle, with their strings of insults targeting her transgressive sexuality, are another. And the time-honoured conceit that is the pretext for *La bulesca* – the scorned lover avenges his honour through violent invective – is a precursor to later satires on courtesans such as Lorenzo Venier's *La Zaffetta*. The following short monologue by Bulle has two features that would become commonplace in later Venetian dialect poems on courtesans: violent threats directed at the courtesan, and an almost catalogue-like list of obscene insults.

Adonca, la se trà de mi solazo,
questa putana, mamola deserta;
ghe voio far cusì groso el mostazo.
Se truovo un dì quella so porta averta
e' ghe voio tirar tanto i caveli
che ghe insegnerò ben darmi la berta.
Putana franzosà, pica bueli,
sta sera te voio dar la romanzina:
badia, che l'ha scovà centro bordeli.

Since this whore, this trollop rejected by all,
dares to amuse herself with me,
I'll beat her till her face is swollen,
if I find, one day, that her door is open.
And I'll pull her hair so hard
that she'll learn not to play tricks on me.
Syphilitic whore, who pierces men's insides,
this evening I'll get you back,
you great big slut, who has screwed a hundred bordellos full of men.[127]

Similar themes of invective and threats of physical violence are present in a contemporary form called the *bravata*, an extended monologue in the voice of a *bravo* who has been rejected by a prostitute.[128] Many of these texts circulated in pamphlet form, probably sold by street vendors. *Bravate* popularized commonplaces about courtesans that persisted in literature throughout the century and beyond: the mercenary, greedy courtesan character type, the hyperbolic references to syphilis and to sodomy, and the string of obscene epithets.

Textual Masculinity and Literary Fraternity

For Domenico Venier and his cohort, the whore trope was a site of negotiation not only for relationships between individuals but also for the creation of a specific type of textual masculinity that we might call literary fraternity. I use this term to describe relationships between men that were constituted through literary and social gatherings, companionship and conversation, and, especially, the practice of exchanging texts about women. This model of literary fraternity is front and centre in a letter written by Aretino in 1546 to the bedridden Domenico Venier. As Aretino's letter suggests, Venier's health crisis forced him to step down from an active role in Venetian political life, but it also gave him more time for literary pursuits:

> My delight was transformed into pain ... upon the news that illness estranges you from the business of the Republic ... And thus the bed where you rest has become both an office and a palace. When I say "palace," I mean that as far as affairs of state are concerned, your advice is no less important than your presence; by office I mean that your abundant intellect does not neglect a second, moment, or period of time that might be spent in imaginative pursuit, in composing verse, and in writing ... And so that you lack for nothing, the time you spend in erudite exchange and the grace of such noble discourse lightens the burden of your affliction, such that even your medicines must confess to not being so beneficial to you. Because, in truth, even two visits from a friend bring much more comfort during convalescence than a thousand of Galen's prescriptions, and the enriching of one's sight with the healing faces of loving sodality is a priceless treasure.[129]

For Aretino, discourse between men can have transformative, healing powers. Aretino hyperbolizes that gazing upon the faces of friends and engaging in "erudite exchange" with them is a much better medicine than any drug. My suggestion that exchanges of fictional women both reflected and created a sense of collective identity is meant to resonate with Foucault's notion of a "société de discours" (a society or fraternity of discourse).[130] For Foucault, such a fraternity served "to preserve or to reproduce discourse, but in order that it should circulate within a closed community, according to strict regulations ... It functions through various schema of exclusivity and disclosure."[131] The fraternity of discourse created by Venier and his circle worked in just this way, binding the group together through the repetition of specific themes (often erotic or obscene), poetic forms, and subject matter (the virtues and vices of women). At the same time, as we learn from Foucault, fraternities of discourse can exclude those who do not have access to the privileged themes, which work almost like a secret code.

When that code is based on the hypersexualized female body, it is difficult for women to become full members of such a fraternity. I will take up this subject in detail in the final chapter of this book, which focuses on the literary careers of two women who had ties to the Venier group,

Gaspara Stampa (c. 1523–1554) and Veronica Franco (1546–1591). Both women led what their contemporaries would have considered unconventional lives. Franco was a courtesan by profession, and Stampa was a *virtuosa*, a talented musician who performed in her own home and in various other *ridotti*, or salons, throughout the city. While Stampa was probably not a courtesan by trade, her free lifestyle and her performing career evoked similar judgment in terms of her moral reputation in a society in which patrician women's mingling with men was highly regulated. Both women sought to align themselves with Venier's group, and both were the targets of sexually explicit, defamatory satire – probably originating within the ranks of the salon – that used as its primary weapon the epithet "whore." In an anonymous poem in Venetian dialect that was probably addressed to Franco, the satirist imagines the courtesan humiliated in front of a roomful of men. When she offers to recite poetry, her colleagues respond only with the vulgar line "Mostra la figa!" (Show us your cunt!).[132] I read these defamatory poems as in part a reaction to the efforts of both women to negotiate a subject position for themselves within the fraternity of discourse. The stories of Stampa and Franco illuminate the push and pull between the discursive power of satire and pragmatic power – a tension that was integral to the discourse of male bonding.

Guido Ruggiero has argued that in the early modern period, sexual identity and identity in the broader sense were "'consensus realities': imagined realities, but no less real for that, which were shared within the various groups with which an individual lived and interacted."[133] In that sense, a man's identity was tied to the ways in which a given group perceived him. But, as Ruggiero points out, because consensus realities were "flexible and socially maintained" rather than fixed, early modern men could negotiate their social identities, at least to some degree, through skilful self-display and performance.[134] Also important in this regard is Ruggiero's work on the ideal progression of early modern male sexual identity from passive to active.[135] Especially for patrician men, the period of *gioventù* (youth, or adolescence) could stretch from the teens well into the thirties. During this period of transition and experimentation, a young man's sexual identity was perceived as both problematic and ambiguous. To enter adulthood, usually at the time of marriage, a man was expected to demonstrate an active and even aggressive sexual identity. With this in mind, we can read the sexually explicit texts exchanged by the male members of the Venier circle as crucial performances of virility and sexual maturity.

My readings here aim to take advantage of the productive friction between masculinity studies and feminist theory that has invigorated both fields since the 1970s, when feminist scholars began to see masculinity as an important theoretical concern.[136] In that sense, I mean to link an exploration of constructions of masculine identity to a feminist critique of how literary texts both reflect and shape early modern sexual politics. The dominant paradigm in studies of early modern masculinity has been the psychoanalytic model of anxiety, rooted in the Oedipal complex and castration anxiety, especially since Mark Breitenberg's *Anxious Masculinity in Early Modern England* (1996).[137] For Breitenberg, masculine subjectivity is inevitably anxious, since masculinity itself is "constructed and sustained by a patriarchal culture – infused with patriarchal assumptions about power, privilege, [and] sexual desire."[138]

Scholars of early modern Italy have continued in this vein to emphasize the crisis of the early modern masculine subject, casting masculinity as a deeply troubled and highly performative process.[139] Valeria Finucci's *Manly Masquerade*, published in 2002 and still one of the few monographs in the field of Italian Studies to focus on masculinity, uses this paradigm as a springboard to "investigate the performative nature of masculinity to show how problematic indeed it is for men to be virile, phallic, and active."[140] In response to work focusing on the cultural constraints imposed on early modern women, Finucci argues that men were equally constrained by gender expectations. In other words, like femininity, masculinity is ultimately a masquerade.

For Gerry Milligan and Jane Tylus, masculinity is both performative and anxious, haunted as it is by the "spectre of masculine gender failure."[141] Like Milligan and Tylus, I am interested here not only in literary representations of masculinity, but also in how textual strategies can create normative ideas of masculinity. An interesting counterpoint to these readings is offered by Patricia Simons, who argues that applying the concept of anxiety as a driving force only to men "reinforces the underlying ideological assumption that patriarchal masculinity is always in crisis yet forever triumphantly faces and overcomes every obstacle."[142] All of these critical approaches have informed the readings that follow, but I want to make clear from the outset that this is not a book that focuses exclusively on what masculinity meant for men. In the following pages, I explore how the circulation, creation, and exchange of fictional women consolidated homosocial bonds and constructed masculine identity. At the same time, my discussion analyses what the fictional female protagonists of these exchanges can tell us about what it meant to be a woman in Renaissance Venice.

Chapter One

Gang Rape and Literary Fame

The literary partnership between Aretino and Lorenzo Venier can be traced back at least to 1530, when Aretino sent Lorenzo's *La puttana errante* to the duke of Mantua. By that time, Aretino had been settled in Venice for about three years and was happily ensconced in the Palazzo Bollani on the Grand Canal.[1] It may well have been there, in one of the rooms looking out on the Rialto Bridge, that Aretino helped Lorenzo put the finishing touches on his poem. As we saw earlier, the sexual escapades of Lorenzo's fictional whore errant were instrumental in soliciting the financial support Aretino needed from Gonzaga. At the same time, through the circulation of the poem, Aretino could also shore up his connections with Lorenzo, the oldest son of one of the most powerful patrician families in Venice. Here, too, Aretino was successful: just two years later, Lorenzo declared his allegiance to Aretino in a dedicatory letter published with the first two cantos of Aretino's epic poem *Marfisa*.[2] Despite his superior social position, in the letter Lorenzo cast himself as disciple and Aretino as the literary mentor who had made of him "quello che né ero né potea esser" (that which [he] neither was nor was capable of being).[3]

Aretino, for his part, continually reaffirmed and publicized his friendship with Lorenzo in his own writings. In his six volumes of familiar letters (1538–1557), Aretino included multiple letters addressed to Lorenzo, as well as many passages that highlight his pupil's literary and political accomplishments.[4] Aretino was the first modern author to publish his own letters in the vernacular – an innovation that would prove to be extraordinarily successful. The first volume, published by Marcolini in 1538, was reprinted twelve times within two years, setting in motion a trend that other authors were quick to emulate.[5] Less than a century later, more than 130 letterbooks and 27 anthologies of familiar letters by various authors had been published in Italy alone.[6]

The familiar letterbook was by its very nature a particularly appropriate platform for authorial self-fashioning, because it presented itself as a collection of personal correspondence between the writer and his addressees. Aretino's reinvention of the familiar letter as a vernacular genre made it an even more useful form through which to solidify and publicize ties of patronage. Aretino's letters to Lorenzo Venier, scattered throughout the first five volumes of his letterbooks, emphasize the close bond between the two men, which Aretino portrays as based on both literary collaboration and friendship. In a letter published in the best-selling first book of 1538, Aretino addresses Lorenzo as "magnifico figliuolo" (magnificent [i.e., noble] little son), inaugurating an image of the two men as literary father and son that would figure prominently in their correspondence.[7] In a later missive, Aretino congratulates Lorenzo on the birth of his first son and casts himself once again as Lorenzo's symbolic father:

> I who because of the consanguineity of love dare to call myself your father, did not believe that any other kind of benevolence could ever take part in such affection; but that is not true, because now friendship, with its charitable confidences, unites itself with the tenacious bond (*copula*) of the sacred relationship of godfather … and, as if anything were missing, to that we can add the pleasure that I received in having held your little boy, as like you as you are like yourself, at his baptism ceremony.[8]

Here Aretino is careful to draw attention to the "tenacious bond" that connects him to his patrician patron. The word "copula," which has both erudite and sexual connotations, would have perhaps brought a smile to the faces of Aretino's readers. At the same time, this inside joke highlights the intimacy between writer and patron. The letter also broadcasts Aretino's role as *compare* (godfather) to Lorenzo's son, proof both of his close relationship with Lorenzo and of his privileged place in the highest echelons of Venetian society. Through this allusion to the honour of being chosen as *compare* in print, Aretino could both reinforce the ties that bound him to Lorenzo and make public his status as quasi-kinsman of the politically powerful Venier family.[9] Aretino would remind Lorenzo of their close connection a few years later in his fifth letterbook, addressing him as "Miser Lorenzo a me Padrone in la grandezza, compare nel batesimo, e figliuolo ne gli anni" (Sir Lorenzo, my patron in great-ness, *compare* in baptism, and little son in years).[10] While this reminder appears in the guise of private correspondence, in its published form it is intended not only for Lorenzo but also for Aretino's wider readership, who would have certainly taken note of his friends in high places.

Aretino was notoriously hotheaded, and his relationships with other writers often ended badly. Such was the case with Niccolò Franco, a writer born in Benevento to a family of decidedly humble origins.[11] Shortly after his arrival in Venice in 1536, Franco lived under Aretino's roof and collaborated with him on various literary projects, most nota-bly the first book of Aretino's letters. But around 1538, for reasons that are still unclear, their partnership came to an explosive end. In contrast, Aretino's relationship with Lorenzo Venier, at least as represented in their correspondence, remained warm and affectionate until Lorenzo's death at the age of forty in 1550. Like Niccolò Franco, Lorenzo seems to have worked for a time as Aretino's personal secretary and literary assistant. Aretino suggests as much in a letter of 1546 to the Venetian patrician Francesco Zeno, whom he thanks for having recommended Lorenzo for the job years before: "My obligation to you, to which I want you always to hold me, began when it occurred to you (by the authority of your friendship with him) that Lorenzo Venier, a young man of noble talent, take up the responsibility of my affairs. Because of your idea, his aspiration, and my belief in what you said, His Magnificence has man-aged to acquire the esteem apparent to all; such that your opinion, his loyalty, and my belief merit praise, commendation, and honor."[12] Are-tino's account of the beginning of his relationship with Lorenzo Venier, which as he points out occurred thanks to Zeno, showcases his connec-tions to both men and his impressive patrician network. At the same time, the letter broadcasts Aretino's fundamental role in the "esteem" (i.e., fame) acquired by his protégé.

In fact Lorenzo's literary fame, such as it was, seems to have been largely an invention of Aretino. Shortly after finishing *La puttana errante*, Lorenzo wrote *La Zaffetta*, a poem on the alleged gang rape of a Vene-tian courtesan known as Angela Zaffetta. Both poems were circulated and promoted primary by Aretino as part of his own publicity machine. Not coincidentally, both are in *ottava rima*, mirroring Aretino's *Marfisa*, which he was drafting and revising at the time. Other than a few let-ters (to Aretino), *La puttana errante* and *La Zaffetta* represent the extent of Lorenzo's literary activity, at least in print.[13] In that sense Lorenzo

Venier truly was Aretino's "creation" – as Aretino himself had emphasized in his *capitolo* to Federico Gonzaga.[14] In Lorenzo, Aretino found a *figliuolo*, a literary son whose writings reflected and amplified his own stylistic and thematic interests.[15] At the same time, Lorenzo's status as *magnifico*, a member of the patrician elite, provided Aretino with the political and social support he needed in Venice. Through the circulation of the fictional whores featured in *La puttana errante* and *La Zaffetta*, and later in his own writing, Aretino created a niche in the literary market that helped create and publicize his own unique authorial persona.

The topos of the whore would become emblematic not only of the literary partnership between Aretino and Lorenzo Venier, but also of Aretino's own stylistic stance. From the beginning of his career, Aretino had positioned himself as an iconoclast in terms of style. Already in his first publication, a collection of poetry published in 1512 when he was just twenty years old, Aretino had begun to experiment with alternative ways of writing about women and love.[16] This early collection was a mishmash of popularizing poetic forms – *strambotti, capitoli, desperate*, and *barzellette* – that would later be echoed in the Venetian dialect poems of Domenico Venier and his circle. In these early poems, Aretino presents the theme of love as decidedly comic – a vehicle through which to lampoon conventional ways of representing women and to fashion his own authorial persona. In the *sonetti lussuriosi*, composed around 1525, this element of parody as self-fashioning is still present. But we also see – still in embryonic form – the articulation of the whore trope for which Aretino would become known later in his career, and for centuries to come.

One of the first things to be said about Aretino is that he was a remarkably versatile writer. His literary production includes an astonishing variety of forms and genres, from religious tracts to letters to literary pornography. Here I focus on his use of the whore trope, not to reduce him to the status of literary pornographer or to discount his many other rhetorical strategies, but instead to underscore the ways in which this particular image was fundamental to his self-fashioning, especially during the mid-1530s as he was establishing a social and literary home in Venice. In a literary scene crowded with Petrarchist poets who represented women as chaste and virtuous, writing about whores, pimps, and ruffians was a declaration of stylistic difference. For Aretino and his followers, the body of the whore, represented not as closed off and remote but instead as accessible to all, was an emblem of what they saw as a new way of writing that supposedly rejected the mandates of

Petrarchism. But of course Aretino's embracing of bawdy subject matter was also a shrewd business strategy, as he declared openly in print. When his friend Vittoria Colonna exhorted him to focus his talents on religious subjects, Aretino explained that he wrote secular works for two reasons: first, to satisfy the desires of his patrons, and second, out of economic necessity: "The source of these evils can be found both in the desires of others and in my own necessity ... and so I deserve to be forgiven for my gossip, which I compose to make a living and not from evil intent."[17] To drive home his point, Aretino reminds Colonna (and the readers of his letters) that while Antonio Brucioli has been waiting for years for a response to his translation of the Bible from King Francis I, Aretino has already earned a heavy golden chain from the King in exchange for his comedy *La cortigiana* – a more entertaining, if less spiritual, gift. The play is not graphically sexual, but it does feature some racy plotlines, as well as detailed descriptions of the beauty of the Florentine courtesan Camilla Pisana.

It was not until after he had settled in Venice that Aretino would create Nanna, the most famous fictional whore of the Renaissance. Despite his many other contributions to literary culture, the two dialogues in which Nanna stars are the texts for which Aretino is remembered. The first of these, *Ragionamento della Nanna e della Antonia*, appeared in print in 1534. As the dialogue opens, Nanna and her friend Antonia ponder the fate of Nanna's adolescent daughter Pippa. Should the girl become a nun, a wife, or a whore? Nanna, who has experience in all three areas, devotes one day of conversation to the life and sexual experiences of each. As the dialogue draws to a close, Antonia argues that Nanna should make Pippa a whore, because at least the whore is honest about what it is she does: "The nun betrays her sacred vows and the married woman murders the holy bond of matrimony, but the whore violates neither her monastery nor her husband; indeed she acts like the soldier who is paid to do evil, and when doing it, she does not realize that she is, for her shop sells what it has to sell."[18] In the end, Nanna resolves to take Antonia's advice and prepare Pippa for a career in prostitution.

In the second dialogue, *Dialogo nella quale la Nanna insegna alla Pippa l'arte puttanesca* (1536), Nanna teaches Pippa the "whorish arts" and warns her against "the betrayals that men wreak on the wretched girls who trust them."[19] Part of Pippa's training includes tips on how to behave at gatherings hosted by her noble clients. Because such men are "used to grand ladies and they nourish themselves on chatter and discourse above all else," Pippa must know how to tell a good story (*favellare*). She should also take special care to stroke the egos of any literary types: "If there's a scholar there, approach him with a cheerful face, showing that you appreciate him more – yes, even more – than the master of the house. Why all you need is for one of these fellows to start writing books against you, and to have the gossip spread everywhere, with those slanderous things they are so good at saying about women!"[20]

Through Nanna's words of warning, Aretino was calling his readers' attention to a literary trend in which he had a vested interest – texts featuring prostitutes of all levels, from the lowliest whores to the most celebrated courtesans. His interest would pay off. Aretino's "dialoghi puttaneschi" (whorish dialogues, as he himself would call them) would become notorious, first in Italy and then across Europe.[21] The dialogues went to press in 1534 and 1536, but Aretino had begun work on them as early as 1530, about the same time he met Lorenzo Venier and supervised the writing of *La puttana errante* and *La Zaffetta*.[22] If Aretino's sponsorship of Lorenzo's writing was advantageous in terms of securing patronage both in Mantua and in Venice, it was also an efficient means for publicizing Aretino's own literary projects. Even contemporaries sometimes believed that Lorenzo's poems were the work of the teacher rather than the master.[23] Aretino, for his part, would continue to cite and celebrate Lorenzo's fictional whores in his own publications. In the following pages, I focus on the collaborative relationship between Aretino and Venier, tracing the intertextualities between them to examine the ways in which tropes of sexual availability and collective violence functioned as sites of negotiation and display of masculine identity, literary fraternity, and fame.

La puttana errante: The Whore-Errant between Men

La puttana errante and *La Zaffetta* appeared together for the first time in print in a cheap octavo pamphlet, undated but probably produced in 1531.[24] The two poems were reprinted several times over the course of the century, a fact that suggests they must have sold well. A fascinating hint at how the poems may have circulated is provided by a second edition, now lost, that seems to have been commissioned in 1538 by the street performer turned publisher Ippolito Ferrarese and printed by Venturino Ruffinelli in Venice.[25] Ferrarese had also commissioned a short poem entitled *Opera nova del superbo Rodomonte* in 1532, a work that turns out to be a roughshod adaptation of an episode taken from Aretino's epic poem *Marfisa*.[26] The details of just how Ferrarese got his hands on the writings of both Lorenzo and Aretino are murky (and warrant further study), but these curious connections between a Venetian patrician, a famous *poligrafo*, and a charlatan bring interesting questions to mind about the blurriness between elite and popular culture.

The 1531 pamphlet begins with a preface to the reader, which is immediately followed by two sonnets penned by none other than Aretino. The sonnets are public endorsements of Lorenzo's literary debut, but they also link Aretino's name to that of his patrician pupil–patron in print. In the first sonnet, "Pasquino alli lettori" (Pasquino to the readers), Aretino writes in the voice of Pasquino, the satiric alter ego he had developed in Rome.[27] As Pasquino, Aretino defends the obscene content of Lorenzo's poems by arguing that they were written to save other young patricians from sure ruin at the hands of the whores of Venice: "Non perché sia 'l poeta disonesto ... Ma perché vede dietro al sporco e incesto/puttanil stuolo, a questa ria semenza, / Fallir tutta la sciocca adolescenza, / A commun beneficio ha scritto questo" (The poet has written this not because he is indecent [*disonesto*] but for the common good, because he has seen that other foolish young men are ruining themselves by running after this filthy, corrupt whorish coven, this evil race).[28]

Aretino's second sonnet echoes the poem he wrote for the duke of Mantua, praising Lorenzo for his ability to speak the truth: "Perché in dir ben male, *id est* ben vero, / Son le muse massare, e Apollo e fante, / E facchine le rime tutte quante / De lo stupendo ingegno del Veniero" (In speaking ill [of others] well – that is, in speaking the truth well, the Muses are servants, Apollo is a pageboy, and all rhymes are porters of Venier's stupendous talent).[29] This portrayal of Lorenzo as truth-teller recalls Aretino's own motto "Veritas odium parit" (Truth begets hatred). Aretino cultivated his reputation as truth-teller not only through visual imagery but also through his letters, poems, and dedications. As early as 1527, Aretino declared as much in a sonnet he sent to Federico Gonzaga along with a portrait by Titian (now lost): "Son l'Aretino, censor del mondo altero/ et de la verità nuncio et propheta" (I am Aretino, censor of the prideful world, messenger and prophet of truth).[30] As Raymond B. Waddington has argued, this motto was integral to Aretino's strategies of self-presentation throughout his career.[31] But the motto, as Aretino invokes it, has a double meaning. Sometimes

Aretino's insistence on truth is meant to remind his readers of his power to expose politicians and patrons for what they truly are. But the motto of truth also appears as a cipher for the literary trope of the whore and her sexuality, which in turn can be a metaphor for unexposed human frailty and vice. Tellingly, as late as the eighteenth century, Aretino's motto on the power of truth was still being associated with Lorenzo's poems, which purport to expose the true nature of their courtesan protagonists.[32] Lorenzo's ability to "dir ben male" (speak ill well) of his fictional whores echoes and publicizes Aretino's own powers of speaking ill of his powerful patrons.

To return to the pamphlet, Aretino's endorsements framed and legitimized Lorenzo's poems, making public his status as Aretino's literary heir and collaborator. For his part, Venier paid homage to his mentor in the opening lines of *La puttana errante*. Instead of invoking the Muses, as had been traditional in epic poetry since Homer, Venier calls upon Aretino's "diabolical and divine spirit" for inspiration:

Io non invoco ser Giove o don Marte,
Come i poeti pecore ogn'or fanno,
Per impiastrar le lor coglione carte,
Ch'odor né sapor in sé non hanno.
Tirati, Apollo ciaratan, da parte,
Con donne Muse, e non mi date affanno,
Se i versi miei non vi chiaman rimando
Ch'a chi può più di voi mi raccomando.
Supplico te, grandissimo Aretino,
Plus quam perfetto, da ben e cortese,
Pel tuo spirto diabolico e divino
Che tienti al nome eterno torcie accese,
Ch'a me, ch'oggi t'adoro a capo chino,
Presti tanta di lingua, che palese
Faccia dall'Arsenal fin alla Tana,
L'opre poltrone d'una gran puttana.

I do not invoke Sir Zeus or Don Mars,
as many poets, like sheep, constantly do,
in order to dress up their ridiculous papers,
which, in and of themselves, are odorless and tasteless.
Move aside, Apollo, you charlatan,
with the lady Muses, and don't give me any trouble

if my verses don't call out to you,
since I entrust myself to someone who can do much more than you.
I beg you as a good and courteous gentleman,
most illustrious Aretino, *plus quam perfetto*,
for your diabolic and divine spirit
that keeps eternal flames burning along with your name,
that you lend me your tongue,
I who adore you with head bowed,
so that I might make known,
from the Arsenal to the Tana,
the evil works of a true whore.[33]

This allusion to poetic fame casts Venier as Aretino's adoring disciple but also declares Venier's adherence to his mentor's stylistic choices. In the final canto of *La puttana errante*, Lorenzo parodies the chaste *donna amata* glorified by the Italian lyric tradition through a rewriting of the appearance of Laura in Petrarch's *Triumphi*. Petrarch's Laura arrives on a golden chariot as part of a procession celebrating the defeat of Love by Chastity, accompanied by virtuous allegorical figures such as "Honestà" (Honour) and "Vergogna" (Modesty).[34] In the parallel scene, Venier's whore enters on a lowly wooden "carretta" (cart), escorted by "Disonestà sfacciata" (cheeky Deceit) and "sfrenata Foia" (frenzied Lust). Crowned with thorns, artichokes, and borage leaves and infected with syphilis, she is hauled off to the Ponte Sisto, the notorious bridge in Rome where only the poorest prostitutes ply their trade. That we are meant to read the *puttana errante* as a sort of anti-Laura is evident in Venier's adaptation of Petrarch's text. Venier follows Petrarch's rhyme scheme as closely as the different metres of the two poems permit, transposing Petrarch's elegant *terza rima* down to the register of his satiric octaves.[35]

1. Francis Petrarch, *Triumphi*, II, vv. 79–87:

Honestate e Vergogna a la fronte era,
nobile par de le vertù divine
che fan costei sopra le donne altera;
Senno e Modestia a l'altre due confine,
Habito con Diletto in mezzo 'l core,
Perseveranza e Gloria in su la fine;
Bella-Accoglienza, Accorgimento fore,

Cortesia intorno intorno e Puritate,
Timor-d'infamia e Desio-sol-d'onore.

Honor and Modesty were in the lead,
those noble, divine virtues that set her high above all other women;
Prudence and Moderation were nearby,
Habit and Delight deep in her heart,
Perseverance and Glory brought up the rear,
Graciousness and Foresight were on the outskirts,
Courtesy and Purity were all around,
and Fear-of-Infamy and Desire-only-for-Honor.

2. Lorenzo Venier, *La puttana errante*, canto II, octave 43:

Disonestà sfacciata a la fronte era,
condegna par di sue virtù divine,
che la fa andare sopra le vacche altera,
Imprudentia, Ignorantia, a lei confine,
sfrenata Foia, vaccamente fiera,
ch'ella ha sempre per mille concubine,
habito di puttana in mezzo 'l core,
disio d'infamia e sol timor d'honore.

Cheeky Dishonor was in the lead,
the worthy equal of her divine virtues,
which makes her go proudly among all other whores,
Imprudence and Ignorance were nearby,
Unrestrained Lust, whorishly proud,
who always has a thousand concubines,
the essence of a whore deep inside her heart,
Desire-for-Infamy and Fear-only-of-Honor.

Venier's early modern readers would surely have appreciated his obscene parody of Petrarch's chaste lady, which turns the text into a witty joke for the literary elite. This is not the only instance in the *Puttana errante* in which Lorenzo comments on the Italian lyric tradition. In the preface, addressing his fellow *letterati*, he points an accusing finger at Petrarch himself: "Blessed are they who open their hearts to the great trumpet of the fifth Evangelist, Giovanni Boccaccio, and may those who

follow the mad ravings of Sir Petrarch be damned, because while Boccaccio's words are the light that illuminates the path of Righteousness,
Petrarch's are the darkness of one who stupidly believes that his Lady
Laura pissed Holy Water and shat ambergris."[36] While Bembo's *Prose
della volgar lingua*, published in 1525, had promoted Petrarch's *Canzoniere* as the supreme model for Italian lyric poetry, Lorenzo wryly urges
his fellow poets to adopt Boccaccio's misogynist manifesto, the *Corbaccio*, as their new Bible: "il sacro-santo *Corbaccio* è quello che non lascia
intrare in tentatione coloro che gli credono" (the sacrosanct *Corbaccio* is
the book that keeps those who believe in it from temptation).[37]

Lorenzo's criticism of Petrarch and Petrarchism debases the idealized, immaculate female beloved and replaces her with a sexually
voracious whore who leads the poet into temptation. Yet this virulent
invective against Petrarch does not quite ring true, since it underscores
and promotes the importance of the very thing it satirizes. At the same
time, Lorenzo's self-conscious anti-Petrarchism recalls that of Aretino,
who satirized Petrarchan diction and conceits as a matter of course in
his own work. Like his mentor, Lorenzo uses the figure of the whore
to make a stylistic choice that sets him apart from the "poeti pecore"
(sheep-like poets) who cling blindly to boring literary conventions.

La Zaffetta: Rape as Literary Fraternity

Like its sister text, Lorenzo Venier's *La Zaffetta* is composed in *ottava
rima* and features a famous Venetian courtesan as its protagonist. *La
Zaffetta* recounts the alleged *trentuno* (a euphemism for gang rape) of
Angela del Moro, also known as "La Zaffetta," on 6 April 1531.[38] If we
are to believe the poet, the *trentuno* was organized by the courtesan's
noble lover as a vendetta for an offence against his honour. The nobleman lures the courtesan into his gondola with the promise of a sumptuous afternoon feast at Malamocco, a tiny town on the island of Lido
in the Venetian lagoon. After lunch, instead of returning to Venice, the
nobleman takes the courtesan even farther from the city, to the fishing
town of Chioggia. There, as her scorned lover looks on, Angela is raped
by no less than eighty men. Afterwards, she is sent back to Venice in
disgrace on a boat piled high with melons, a fruit with obvious sexual
connotations.

The punishment of a resistant courtesan by her scorned lover echoes
the formulaic conceit of the anonymous comedy *La bulesca* and other
dialect texts we saw earlier. But while the *bulesca* comedies featured

prostitutes and their pimps, in Lorenzo's poem the organizer of the gang rape is a Venetian patrician and his unfortunate lover is a celebrated courtesan. Even so, the poet is careful to specify that while his noble protagonist is responsible for organizing the gang rape, he is only a spectator to the *trentuno* itself. The rapists themselves are not patricians but riffraff with decidedly non-noble origins: the cast of characters includes a fisherman, a drunken boatman, a lazy servant, and a porter, among others. The scene of the crime is the fishing town of Chioggia, far outside the confines of Venice and the seat of patrician power, as if to leave untouched the city's idealized reputation for social and civic concord.

No one has been able to establish whether Lorenzo Venier's tale of the rape of Angela Zaffetta reflects historical reality in Renaissance Venice. Although some have argued that Venetian courtesans were regularly subjected to gang rape, there is little hard evidence that this was the case. That said, of course the lack of evidence for such crimes does not prove they did not happen. On the contrary, as Guido Ruggiero has argued, group assaults on women were probably not uncommon in Venice, and may well have involved patrician men as well as the lower social classes.[39] In early modern France, where group sexual assaults have been most studied, gang rape was often perceived as a way of disciplining women who had transgressed societal rules of sexual conduct.[40] Similarly, the *trentuno*, whether literary or historical, was an instrument of social discipline and community judgment.

In that sense, the *trentuno* was much like the various public shaming rituals that were conducted throughout Europe in response to transgressions of social norms.[41] Known as *mattinate* in Italy and *charivari* in France, these rituals involved the public humiliation of the transgressor through raucous and often lewd singing or noise making.[42] In Italy, the *mattinata* ritual could sometimes have festive, celebratory connotations. It often took the form of a raucous serenade, offered to couples who were marrying for the first time and especially to those who remarried. At the same time, it could also be a vehicle for public censure. Christiane Klapisch-Zuber has highlighted both of these functions, describing the *mattinata* as "a public display centered on love; it also proclaimed the formation of a new couple, the guarantee of social reproduction; finally, it expressed reprobation of certain members of the community, particularly those who contracted an atypical marriage."[43]

Like the rituals of the *chiaravari* and *mattinata*, Lorenzo Venier's *trentuno* puts the unruly Angela Zaffetta, and other courtesans who dared transgress societal boundaries, back in their place, at least in the world of the text. This is made clear near the end of the poem, when the narrator tells the whores of Venice that Angela's punishment was intended to teach them respect for their noble patrons:

Se, quando un gentilhuom vi vol chiavare,
De la Zaffa pensaste al dishonore
Dicendo voi di sì l'osservereste,
Et le vie d'ingrandirvi sarian queste.

If, when a gentleman wants to screw you,
you were to remember Angela and her dishonor,
by saying "yes" you would honor her example,
and you would be on the road to bettering yourselves.[44]

La Zaffetta is a particularly unsettling poem for modern readers, in part because its graphic sexual violence is imbedded in a comic frame that invites the reader to laugh along with the teller of the tale. Even before the *trentuno* begins, the men assembled underneath Angela's bedroom window laugh in anticipation of what is to come: "Come la turba, che l'aspetta, il vide, / Dal gran diletto ismascellando ride. / Dopo le risa, si conchiude ch'uno gentil giovane vada a cominciare / il meritato honorevol Trent'uno" (When the crowd, awaiting [the signal], saw it, they began to laugh and lick their chops in delight. After the laughs, it was decided that a noble youth begin the well-deserved and honourable *trentuno*).[45] The laughs continue with the first rape, presented as a comic spectacle that will make Chioggia the envy of the lagoon. After the "giovanotto amico" (young friend) has ordered Angela to turn over ("Voltate in là, sporgete il tondo!" – Turn over, and stick out your butt), and begun to rape her, he pauses to proudly display his penis, which is adorned with the oysters the courtesan had greedily eaten earlier in the evening. This grotesque spectacle prompts more riotous laughter from the group of men looking on: "Le risa che di ciò fur fatte alhora, / Non le racontarebbe un calendaro" (It would take more than a year to recount all of the laughs that this prompted in that moment).[46] While the group continues to laugh, the courtesan weeps in fear as another rapist arrives: "E mentre le reliquie la Signora / tenea scoperte, e facea pianto amaro, / eccoti un pescator pazzo e bestiale, / che grosso e lungo havea il pastorale" (And while the Signora, with her "relics" exposed, wept bitterly, a crazy, brutish fisherman arrived, and his rod was thick and long).[47]

The collective laughter of the mob of rapists is important, since it points us to the poem's function as a site of homosocial bonding. Indeed the story of the rape of Angela Zaffetta would be told and retold by Aretino, always in a comic key. In Aretino's comedy *La cortigiana*, the procuress Alvigia invokes the *trentuno* as a warning to the young and beautiful Tonna. Her words of caution are interspersed with the *pater noster* for comic effect: "And you'll be wise – *pater noster* – and come out dressed as a man, because these groomsmen – *qui es in celis* – get a little crazy at night – *santificetur nomen tuum* – and I wouldn't want you to wander into a *trentuno* – *adveniat regnum tuum* – like Angela del Moro – *in cielo et in terra*."[48] Alvigia's warning invokes the very real spectre of the dangers, for women, of the streets of the Renaissance city. Yet it is not hard to imagine how this juxtaposition of the sacred and the profane would have incited laughter from male readers and spectators. At the same time, *La cortigiana*, which Aretino revised and published in 1534 from the safety of Venice, targets the corruption of the Roman court that Aretino had experienced first hand. In that context, the potential threat of the *trentuno* can also be read as an exposé that reveals the truth – the beastly and violent natures of the courtiers Aretino targets.

Aretino's own writing is peppered with scenes depicting the gang rape of prostitutes. Most of these occur in the second day of the *Dialogo*, during which Nanna tells her daughter Pippa stories of "le poltronerie degli uomini inverso le donne" (the nasty tricks that men play on women).[49] One of these tales features an unnamed whore "non-ci-fosse-mai-nata" (who never should have been born).[50] After two years of being abused by her pimp, she decides to leave him. He gets his revenge by tricking her to come to the countryside with him, where she is "data per merenda a la fame di più di quaranta contadini" (given as a snack to satisfy the hunger of more than forty peasants).[51] In another, a Roman courtesan called "Madonna nol-vo' dire" (Madame-I-won't-say-who) is lured out into the countryside for a banquet and raped by a parade of stable boys.[52] Her coy nickname is a blasphemous pun on a hymn to the Virgin Mary by the thirteenth-century friar and poet Jacopone da Todi, in which the poet appeals to the Madonna to heal his wounded heart.[53]

Setting aside whether such accounts are rooted in reality, the tales of rape recounted by Aretino and Venier are characterized by hyperbolic literary violence. Both authors use the rhetorical strategy of *ecphrasis* to describe first the rapes themselves and then the physical after-effects of sexual violence on the female body in minute detail. After her all-night ordeal in the countryside, Aretino's unnamed whore is left "more dead than alive … her eyes blood red, her cheeks swollen, her hair disheveled, her lips dry and cracked, her clothes torn to shreds."[54] And after Venier's Zaffetta has been raped by eighty men, the narrator paints a disturbingly realistic picture of her violated body, seen through the eyes of her mother: "Quando la madre gl'alza i panni, e vede / il suo quadro, e 'l suo tondo rosso, e rossa, / E l'uno e l'altro enfiato, certo crede / Fra due hore d'andarsene in la fossa" (When her mother lifts up her skirts and sees her crotch and butt red and raw, and both so swollen, she is certain that Angela is not long for this world).[55] Both accounts present the raped woman as near death, as if to emphasize the potential power of literary sexual violence to neutralize the threat of unruly female sexuality.

And then there is the mocking laughter on the part of both rapists and onlookers. What is so funny about rape? What are we to make of such juxtapositions of sexual violence, literary and religious parody, and comedy? One way of approaching this puzzle is through Freud's investigation of the pleasures of the smutty joke. According to Freud, men tell smutty jokes as a "defensive reaction" to female resistance.[56] Leaving aside Freud's problematic characterization of such resistance as a positive attribute in women, his essay is useful for its discussion of how the telling of dirty jokes can create bonds between men:

> Generally speaking, a tendentious joke calls for three people: in addition to the one who makes the joke, there must be a second who is taken as the object of the hostile or sexual aggressiveness, and a third in whom the joke's aim of producing pleasure is fulfilled … When the first person finds his libidinal impulse inhibited by the woman, he develops a hostile trend against that second person and calls on the originally interfering third person as his ally. Through the first person's smutty speech the woman is exposed before the third, who, as listener, has now been bribed by the effortless satisfaction of his own libido.[57]

In light of Freud's analysis, we can read the comic sexual violence of these texts as a site of mutual homosocial satisfaction. Through the representation of exposed and violated female flesh, Aretino and Venier satisfy the libidos of their male readers, who repay them by welcoming them into the fraternity of discourse. In Aretino's case, at least, the satisfaction he offered translated directly into both literary fame and financial support from his wealthy and powerful male patrons. In fact, in sixteenth-century Italian literature, both the euphemism *trentuno* and the scenes of gang rape it stood for were almost exclusively the domain of Aretino and his circle.[58] In that sense, the topos of the *trentuno* was both a touchstone for the relationships between the men who wrote about it and a means for publicity and literary success. The representation of rape, then, celebrated the power of male collaboration even as it attracted the attention of readers and commentators.

Angela Zaffetta, *cortigiana da vero*[59]

What would have made Lorenzo's poem all the more titillating for its contemporary readers is that its protagonist was Angela Zaffetta, one of the most famous courtesans in Venice in the 1530s. Historical evidence regarding Angela's life is scarce, but if we are to believe Lorenzo, she claimed to be the daughter of a nobleman from the Grimani family who was a procurator of San Marco (one of the most prestigious political appointments in Venice).[60] By 1532, as documented by Marin Sanudo, Angela was famous enough to have spent the night with the Cardinal Ippolito de' Medici.[61] Most of what we know about Angela is filtered through Aretino, who alluded to her often in his own writing. Aretino addressed two of his published letters to Angela Zaffetta and mentioned her in at least two more. From these we can glean that at least for a time, the two of them were neighbours, and that it was probably Aretino who introduced Angela to his friend Titian. In a letter dated 1548, Aretino wrote to invite Angela to dinner with Titian and the architect Jacopo Sansovino. Here he emphasizes his great affection for the courtesan, which he compares to his love for his two daughters, Adria and Austria:

> I do not need to express in words the extreme desire of a father to see his daughter to someone who is the mother of her own children. So do not put any more wood on the fire of my desire to enjoy you right now, you who are just as much to me in love as Adria is in flesh. In case envy wishes to silence this display of benevolence towards Milady Angela, I will let your gracious goodness respond to her. Because, although I have been your minister and rector and Lord since you were a tender little girl, you have never known any other charity from me than that which Austria, born from my blood, has known. But, if this observance of the affection that I have for you was always contained within the required limits during my

lascivious youth, let it be known that the respect I have for your honour is twice as great now that I feel so very honest in my old age. Come, then, tomorrow evening to dinner with the eternity of your ancient advocates: Titian, Sansovino, and me. Their love for you has doubled since you have transformed your licentious life into a continent one.[62]

Aretino's letter to the courtesan plays on the same tropes of paternal affection he had used to describe his relationship with Lorenzo Venier. His deployment of these tropes both neutralizes and highlights the erotic charge of his relationship with Angela, which he represents as a thing of the past. Whatever that relationship was in life, the fictional Angela that Aretino constructed in his writing drew her power from the tensions inherent in the lived life of a courtesan. Aretino's assertion that Angela has undergone some sort of conversion adds another layer of complexity to the character he has created. The courtesan's transformation mirrors his own: just as she has left her "licentious life" behind, he has become "honest" in his old age. All of this is tongue-in-cheek, or at least it reads as such. Yet Aretino's use of the fictional Angela as an avatar for himself offers interesting insights into how the figure of the whore could also stand in for the authorial self of a man who depended on satisfying the whims of those more powerful than himself to make a living.

Elsewhere, however, Aretino's fictional Angela appears as an echo of Lorenzo Venier's raped whore and a reminder of the perils of female unruliness. The same Angela Zaffetta is mentioned multiple times in Aretino's second whore dialogue, the *Dialogo nel quale la Nanna insegna alla Pippa* (1536). On the third day of conversation, Nanna and Pippa listen as the midwife and the wet nurse discuss the ins and outs of being a procuress. The midwife, an ex-procuress herself, recounts the tale of a young priest who came to her house in search of a beautiful girl with whom to satisfy his sexual desires. The midwife gives the priest a book to read as he waits, as part of her plan to arouse his lust and thus "cavargli de l'anima cento ducati" (draw from his soul one hundred ducats).[63] The book contains, among other things, "una [poesia] terribile, fatto in laude di una signora Angela Zaffetta, il quale ancora vado cinguettando quando non ho che fare, o vero nel darmi noia i miei guai" (a terrible poem, in praise of a certain lady Angela Zaffetta, which I go around chirping when I don't have anything better to do, or when my cares annoy me).[64] In this context, the allusion to Angela's "terrible" fate is presented as simultaneously arousing (for the priest) and terrifying (for Pippa, the young courtesan-in-training).

The midwife's book also contains a series of madrigal texts, all variations on the same theme: a lover desperate for the attentions of his beloved. In registers from high to low, the madrigal texts poke fun at conventional tropes of courtly love. One madrigal mirrors such courtly laments in its opening line, but instead of a courtly lady, the woman addressed is a whore. She is invoked not through her golden hair or ruby lips, but through her lice-infested vulva and large anus:

Madonna, per ver dire,
S'io vel facessi, che possa morire:
Perché so che ne la vulva vostra
Sovente Amor con le piattole giostra;
Poi sì grande ano avete,
Che v'entrarebbe tutta l'età nostra.
E tu, Amor, senza giurar mel credi,
Che ugualmente le puzza il fiato e i piedi.
Adunque, per ver dire, s'io vel facesse, che possa morire.

Milady, to tell you the truth,
if I were to do it to you, just kill me.
Because I know that in your vulva
love often jousts with crab lice;
And you have such a wide anus,
that our entire generation could fit in there.
And you, Love, believe me without my swearing on it,
that her breath and her feet are equally smelly.
So, to tell you the truth, if I do it to you, just let me die![65]

After Aretino's priest finishes reading the madrigal, he begins to laugh heartily. But the joke is on him; he does not notice that "la Comare smascellava perché la robba che egli doveva toccare era simile a quella della canzone" (the midwife was laughing her jaw off because the stuff he was going to touch was similar to that in the song).[66] The comic tone of this madrigal brings to mind Lorenzo Venier's presentation of the courtesan's violated body in *La Zaffetta*, which is also accompanied by laughter. The verb "smascellare," used by Lorenzo to describe the laughter of Angela's assembled rapists and here by Aretino for the laughter of the midwife, reinforces the textual and homosocial connections between the two poems. The reference to Angela is more than skin deep; a manuscript now in the Biblioteca Nazionale Marciana contains an early variant of the poem that names Angela as its addressee.[67] Like

Lorenzo Venier's tale of rape, Aretino's madrigal denigrates the courtesan's body, exposing her and deconstructing her as first the midwife and then the priest burst into laughter. Like the hypersexualized body of Elena Ballarina in the guise of *puttana errante*, in Aretino's madrigal the body of Angela Zaffetta is transformed from a site of pleasure into a smutty joke for the amusement of Aretino and Venier, as well as for that of their readers.

It may seem paradoxical that in Aretino's writing Angela was represented as daughter and lover, courtesan and whore, but such oppositions only underscore her literary role as muse and mediator between men. As a courtesan, Angela was the ideal inspiration for such a creation, since her profession required her to walk the line between sexual availability and exclusivity. Part of her ideal role as courtesan was to judge and choose only the worthiest of men as her suitors. But this power was a double-edged sword, since it was a source of anxiety for the very men who imagined it.

Intertextuality, Masculinity, and Fame

David LaGuardia has argued in his study of masculinity in French Renaissance literature that "reading and writing for men throughout the Middle Ages and Renaissance was in large part both a continuous reflection upon the relation of texts to other texts, and a constant consideration of what it meant to *be* a man and to *read* as a man within the social context that was defined by those texts."[68] If the construction of normative masculinity was a fundamentally intertextual process of reading, writing, telling, and retelling stories, what do we learn about what it meant to be a man in early modern Venice from Aretino and his followers? The gang rape trope features hypersexual, promiscuous women who transgress social boundaries and are disciplined as a consequence. On the one hand, the texts negotiate anxieties about the fragility of male authority over women. But they are also preoccupied with men's authority over one another. In that sense, we can read the intertextualities between Aretino and Venier as a way of constructing a masculine subject that is both individual and collective. As they tell and retell stories of men who judge and then dominate prostitutes, they affirm and strengthen the bonds between men.

Bibliographers disagree about the date of the first edition of Lorenzo Venier's *La Zaffetta*, which may have been composed as early as 1531 or as late as 1534.[69] Although the poet claims that the *trentuno* occurred on 6 April 1531, that date may well be invented: 6 April, as every good

Petrarchist knew, was the day that Petrarch claimed to have encountered Laura, and the year 1531 is a an obvious echo of the *trentuno* that unfolds in the poem. In any case, what is clear is that Lorenzo did not begin work on his poems until after he met Aretino. A 1536 letter from a poet named Alessandro Zanco requests that Aretino send *"la Zaffetta corretta e la Errante"* (the corrected *Zaffetta* and the *Errante*).[70] This letter is important for our purposes because it suggests that Venier was still working on the poems in 1536. Even more interesting, in terms of the collaboration between Aretino and his protégé, is that when addressing Aretino, Zanco refers to the poems as "le opere vostre" (your works), seemingly ignorant of the fact that they were not written by Aretino, but by Lorenzo.

These logistical details may help explain why there are such obvious parallels between Lorenzo's tale of the rape of Angela Zaffetta and Aretino's story of the *trentuno* experienced by the Roman courtesan "Madonna no 'l so dire" in his *Dialogo*. Although we cannot know which rape tale was composed first, the similarities between the two texts are certainly not coincidental. They are essentially variations on the same theme, set in two different locations (Lorenzo's *Zaffetta* in Venice and the lagoon islands, Aretino's in Rome). In Venier's poem the courtesan feasted with her noble lover and his friends as a prequel to the *trentuno* – the oysters she consumed greedily, as we recall, were the catalyst for the earthy, comic violence of the rape scene that followed. In Aretino's version, a group of men invite the courtesan to partake in a sumptuous banquet at a vineyard in the countryside. After the meal, she asks for permission to be on her way, explaining that she is expected that night by one of her regular clients. But, like Angela, she is detained unexpectedly, and the scene soon becomes both comic and violent:

> Then the drunks, fools, and scoundrels gave their answer via a farting buffoon, who said: "My lady, this night is owed to us and our stable boys, and we hope that you will happily double the simple thirty-one. And thus, thanks to you, they will be called *arcitrentuni* [super-thirty-ones], and there will be as great a difference between them as between bishops and archbishops."[71]

Before the rapes take place, the buffoon sings the first few lines of a popular folk song: "La vedovella quando dorme sola / lamentasi di sè: di me non ha ragione" (The young widow when she sleeps alone, laments to herself – of me she has no right to moan).[72] This song provides a concrete textual link to Lorenzo's poem, where it is sung by the "nunzio gentile" (the noble young messager) just before the rapists begin their assault on Angela Zaffetta.[73] In both texts, the song signals the beginning of the rapes, conferring a ceremonial quality to the ritual of the *trentuno* that it initiates, and recalling the shaming rituals mentioned earlier. These moments of public discipline could be administered to men whose behaviour was out of line, as well as to women.[74] Perhaps the obsession with the literary disciplining of transgressive prostitutes can be read, in part, as a response to anxieties not only about sexual performance but also about the regulation of male behaviour.

The song about the lusty young widow was something of a calling card for Aretino; it also appears in his comedy *Il marescalco*, first published in 1533 but probably written much earlier.[75] Its incipit recalls a popular song of uncertain origin that was still being sung in Venice at the end of the nineteenth century: "La vedovela, co' la dorme sola / La pianze 'l morto e 'l vivo la consola: / La pianze 'l morto, perch'el ghe rincresse, / E la ga 'l vivo che ghe fa carezze" (The little widow, when she sleeps alone, cries for the dead man, but the live one consoles her. She cries for the dead man, because she misses him, while she has a live one who caresses her).[76] The song plays on tropes of women's inherent inability to control their sexual appetites even as it encourages male readers to laugh along with the text at the comic association of a lusty widow with a Roman prostitute about to be raped. At the same time, the ceremony marks a rite of passage for the prostitute, who is forever changed by the *trentuno*, as well as for the male rapists, who affirm their own place in the social hierarchy as they put her back in her proper place.[77] In the *Marescalco* the same song is sung at a pivotal moment of transition by the pageboy Giannicco, who has begun to progress from a passive sexual relationship with his (male) master to the more active, adult sexual role he will assume with his female partners in the future.[78]

Both Aretino and Venier represent the *trentuno* as a collective ritual and group display of power. In Venier's poem, in particular, the gang rape of Angela Zaffetta is represented as a religious ritual that is transformative for both the courtesan and the mob of rapists. The *trentuno* culminates in the arrival of two priests, who insist that Angela must first confess her sins "acciò che non sia l'anima vostra scritta tra i dannati" (so that your soul will not be written among the names of the damned).[79] After she has confessed, the two priests "alla Zaffa divota / cacciar dietro e d'innanzi una carota" (shove one carrot in the pious Zaffetta's behind, and one in front).[80] The juxtaposition of the ceremony of confession with the colloquial and humorous euphemism for both anal and vaginal sex is jarring to our modern ears but would likely have been an occasion for raucous laughter for Renaissance (male) readers. After this comic moment, the mob of rapists gathered around the violated courtesan is likened to a crowd of parishioners at Good Friday mass awaiting their chance to confess their sins:

Havete visto la del Vener Santo
Quando ch'ogni plebeo vuol confessarsi
A star la turba su l'ali da canto
Che al confessor il primo vuol lanciarsi?
Così, mentr'un la chiava, l'altro in tanto
Sta desto, e vuol con la diva attaccarsi
Son sempre cinque o sei ch'hanno il piè mosso
E vorria ognun saltarle il primo adosso.

Have you ever seen a Good Friday mass,
when every plebe wants to go to confession,
and the crowd gathers in the aisles,
each one wanting to be the first to throw himself upon the confessor?
In the same way, while one is screwing her, the other
is on the ready, and wants to do the goddess himself.
There are always five or six of them with one foot forward,
and each one would like to be the first to jump her.[81]

The blasphemous comparison of the *trentuno* to confession makes the smutty joke even funnier in its irreverence, but through its humour it reveals the rite of passage that the poem envisions for both courtesan and rapists. The ceremony is meant to correct the unruly Angela, who transgressed social and gender hierarchies when she refused to comply with her patrician lover's wishes. After her mock-confession, the poet hopes, she will have learned her lesson. For the rapists, on the other hand, the rite of the *trentuno* marks the symbolic restoration of masculine power and authority, at least in the literary world of the text. At the same time, the comparison of the rapes to the religious rite of confession, and the description of Angela as a "diva," or goddess to be worshipped, reveals something more complex. Even as they violate the courtesan, the rapists seem to be seeking something from her, whether absolution or some other type of transformation, that only she can offer.[82] This tension between the sacred and the profane perhaps reveals anxieties regarding the courtesan's power to judge the worthiness of men.

Lorenzo's comparison of the gang of rapists to an unruly mob of plebes waiting for confession also highlights the group dynamic of competition for the desired object, whether that object is the courtesan or the holy sacrament. Like parishioners who push to the front of the line in order to be first to arrive at the confession booth, Lorenzo's rapists are egged on by the presence of other men. Moreover, the description of the rapes turns both the eager crowd of men and the reader into voyeurs, inviting them into the text and bribing them through the effortless satisfaction of their own libidos – to recall Freud's explanation of the power of the smutty joke.

Aretino's dialogues, too, are full of self-consciously blasphemous parallels between religion and illicit sex, often as a means for anti-clerical satire. These are especially prevalent during the first day of conversation, when Nanna tells Antonia about the sexual escapades she enjoyed during the first phase of her life as a nun. The rape of the Roman courtesan begins with an announcement by a farting buffoon, who informs her that she is about to be the victim of an *arcitrentuno* (super-thirty-one) rather than a simple *trentuno*. He explains the difference between the two types of *trentuni* by comparing them to figures of religious authority: a *trentuno* is like a bishop, while an *arcitrentuno* is like an archbishop. The comparison degrades the authority of these religious figures but at the same time confers on the *trentuno* some of their power. Like an archbishop, the *trentuno* has the power to judge and regulate the behaviour of prostitutes. Aretino's description of the rape scene that follows emphasizes both the ceremonial aspect of the *trentuno* and its function as a display of collective male power. After the buffoon signals the beginning of the ritual with his song on the lusty widow, the rapes begin:

> Then the dirty swine pulled her to the stump of a chopped-down almond tree, and propping her head against it, he flung her underclothes over her head, and after plunging his stake wherever he wished, thanked her for her services with two of the most painful spanks that ever stung a beautiful bottom. And this was the signal for the second bully, who turned her over on the stump and did it to her the right way up, and got great delight from the jagged pieces of the badly trimmed stump that pricked her ass so that, despite herself, she rose up to meet him. And as he finished, he made her take an ape-like tumble, and her yells brought the third jouster at the run.[83]

Here, as in Venier's poem, the narrator focuses on the rapists' perspective rather than that of the courtesan. Aretino's narrator is female, and a prostitute herself, and her account does briefly acknowledge the courtesan's pain. But Aretino's appropriation of the female voice privileges both the gaze of the mob as it waits for its turn and the pleasure the men feel as they violate the courtesan, who is likened to an animal as her body is forced to assume a posture of female pleasure. Aretino's description also highlights the collective enterprise of raping the courtesan. When the first man has finished, he slaps the courtesan's rear end as a signal to the second man, who takes over, and then in turn summons the third man when he makes the courtesan cry out in pain. This display of collective sexual violence mirrors the literary collaboration between Aretino and his followers, who create rape tales, express their pleasure, and pass them on to the next poet.

After her *trentuno*, Aretino's raped courtesan is paraded down the Via dei Banchi in shame, "seated on a pack horse," and eventually dies "of sorrow and hardships."[84] Venier's Zaffetta, on the other hand, resists the disciplining power of the *trentuno*. Only six days later, the poet tells us, she is back on her balcony trolling for men, "più sfacciata di prima, ladra e ghiotta" (more cheeky than before, that thief and glutton).[85] This image of female resistance hints at the ways in which masculine power, even in these tales of domination and sexual violence, was not perceived as unproblematic. Yet in the end, at least in the text, the joke is on Angela, Madame-I-won't-say-who, and the other prostitutes who are represented as victims of gang rape. We will never know if Angela Zaffetta was physically victimized, but the poet's words achieve what the rapes would have: the public defamation and humiliation of the courtesan, foreshadowed twice in the text itself. In the first instance, Angela weeps in despair after the last man has finished with her. In a transparent parody of Livy's Lucretia, the chaste heroine *par excellence*, the humiliated courtesan considers committing suicide in order to avoid the gossip that she knows will circulate as a result of her ordeal:

> La Signora fottuta a capo basso
> piangeva ad alta voce sì dolente,
> ch'havrebbe umiliato un Satanasso,
> e un bulo 'n bizzaria fatto clemente.
> Dicea: Deh! Perché il petto non mi passo,
> acciò non senta cianciar fra la gente,
> a San Marco, a i Frari, e da ciascuno,
> ch'io degnamente avuto habbia il Trent'uno?[86]

The fucked Lady, with her head bowed,
cried loudly, and with a voice so full of pain
that she would have made even a demon humble,
and rendered a *bulo* in one of his crazy fits merciful.
She said, "Ah! Why don't I just stab myself through the heart,
so that I won't hear people gossiping
from San Marco to the Frari, and everywhere else,
that I was the deserving victim of a *trentuno*?

Later, the poet reports with delight that "già per Venetia il Trent'un divulgato / Della Zaffetta è pieno ogni bordello, / Ne pur un sol s'è in la città trovato / Che non esalti chi gl'ha dato quello" (Every brothel is full of talk of Angela, and the news of her *Trentuno* has spread throughout Venice. In the entire city, not one man can be found who does not praise the man who did it to her).[87] In Venier's poem, the courtesan's shame is cause for celebration both by the collective of rapists who victimized her and by the poet himself. At the same time, the poem's insistence on the diffusion of gossip regarding the humiliation of Lorenzo's literary "Zaffetta" foreshadows the slur on the historical Angela's reputation.[88]

As late as 1540, Aretino was still celebrating and circulating Lorenzo Venier's fictional whores. In his *Orlandino*, an unfinished burlesque parody of the *Orlando furioso*, Aretino invokes the violated bodies of Elena Ballarina and Angela Zaffetta.[89] On the battlefield, Aretino's Turpino comforts his master by pointing out that if the two men die in combat, they will be showered with praise, just as Elena and Angela have been vilified. In the masculine realm of epic poetry (recall that Lorenzo's poems were both in *ottava rima* as well), Aretino explicitly connects the writing of rape to literary fame:

Glori', a tua posta! Morti che noi siamo,
può sonar mona Fama con la piva,
che in polvere di Cipri ci posiamo
con lauro, con mirto e con l'uliva,
e tanto de le lodi ci sentiamo
quanto de le vergogne Elena diva
o la Zaffetta, a ben che 'l sappia ognuno
del dato benemerito trentuno.

Glory, in your place! When we are dead,
Lady Fame can play her bagpipes,

and we'll cover ourselves in scented powder
and laurel, myrtle, and olive leaves.
And we'll hear ourselves praised
just as much as Elena was shamed,
or the Zaffetta – but this was for the best,
so that everyone would know about her well-deserved *trentuno*.[90]

Turpino's prediction seems to have come true, at least in terms of literary fame. Aretino's campaign to circulate Lorenzo's text – and, along with it, to promote his own reputation as master pornographer – was so successful that the use of the term *trentuno* as a euphemism for gang rape became commonplace in erotic texts even outside of Italy. In England, the term can be found in *A Worlde of Wordes* (first edition 1598), the famous Italian–English dictionary compiled by John Florio. Florio likens the Italian practice of the *trentuno* to an English shaming ritual called "pumping," which involved dunking the offending women in a vat of water multiple times:

> *Dare un Trentuno* is a punishment or revenge that Ruffianly fellows and Swaggerers use to punish and inflict upon rascally whores in Italie, who (as some use to pumpe them, or duck them in the water in England) cause them to be iumbled one and thirtie severall times by so many base rascals one after another without stop or stay.[91]

Florio's definition emphasizes the *trentuno*'s disciplining function as a punishment for "rascally whores," echoing Lorenzo Venier's literary revenge on Angela del Moro as well as Aretino's tales of the gang rapes of defiant courtesans. Fourteen of the seventy-two books listed as sources in Florio's preface are Aretino's, making it quite likely that he learned the term from the master himself.[92] The *trentuno* even made it into Shakespeare's comedy *The Taming of the Shrew*, where Bianca and Kate are threatened by Tranio's tales of Petruchio's taming school: "Petruchio is the master; That teacheth tricks eleven and twenty long, To tame a shrew and charm her chattering tongue."[93] The telling of dirty jokes, then – and the circulation of the exposed, violated bodies of fictional women – was an extraordinarily successful vehicle for homosocial bonding, and as a consequence, for literary fame.

Chapter Two

Fictional Ladies and Literary Fraternity

And then Count Alessandro said, "Praise be to God that we are gathered here without the company of women, since they are usually the absinthe, or rather, the toxin, that embitters and poisons even the sweetest and most lively group." At that, Benetto Corner came forward and said, "Count, what are you saying? On the contrary, the one thing missing here that would bring perfection, sweetness, and liveliness to our amusement is a lovely group of ladies." To which the count responded, "Corner, go ahead and defend them, that way they'll always pick you as a dance partner above all the rest, those ingrates."

Girolamo Parabosco, *I diporti*, c. 1551.[1]

The whore trope that Lorenzo and Aretino had deployed so successfully would become an important vehicle of literary sodality for the group of writers that gathered around Lorenzo's brother Domenico Venier. From the 1540s to the 1570s, Domenico's circle produced an astonishing number and variety of texts on women and sexuality, from hyperbolic encomia exalting their chastity to pornographic, obsessive retellings of their sexual promiscuity. This chapter focuses on the decorous, stylized images of women in the Petrarchan poems that constituted the salon's public identity; the following chapter will move instead to the group's pornographic dialect production. Here I consider how Venier and his group displayed their literary and social connections through the medium of print, and especially in the anthologies of lyric poetry that dominated the Venetian literary scene at the middle of the sixteenth century. Printed anthologies not only reflected the discourse and intellectual exchange carried out in the salon, but also were an important vehicle for publicity, displaying connections of patronage and friendship.

Girolamo Parabosco's *I diporti*, printed in Venice by 1551, offers a literary portrait of the Venier salon. Set during a fictional fishing party on the Venetian lagoon, the dialogue features many of the "valorosi, e nobili spiriti" (valorous and noble spirits) who were frequenting Venier's salon at the time. Parabosco's long list of interlocutors gives pride of place to the Venetian patrician poets in the group: Domenico Venier, Girolamo Molino, Federico Badoer, and Benetto Corner, among others. Also present are the humanist scholar Sperone Speroni from Padua and the notorious satirist Pietro Aretino, not patricians but celebrated nonetheless for their widespread literary success.[2]

As the dialogue begins, the men are forced by an impending storm to take shelter in a fisherman's hut in the middle of the lagoon.[3] To pass the time, they decide to take turns telling stories, an echo of the *lieta brigata* in Boccaccio's *Decameron*. But while Boccaccio's group of storytellers included both men and women, Parabosco's idealized portrait of the Venier salon self-consciously excludes women from the conversation. The first line of direct discourse in the book, spoken by the Bolognese count Alessandro Lambertino, highlights women's conspicuous absence: "Praise be to God that we are gathered here without the company of women, since they are usually the absinthe, or rather, the toxin, that embitters and poisons even the sweetest and most lively group!"[4] The Venetian poet Benetto Corner steps in to defend the fairer sex, arguing that "the one thing missing here that would bring perfection, sweetness, and liveliness to our amusement is a lovely group of ladies."[5] Lambertino's riposte, which accuses Corner of defending women in order to win their approval, hints at the troubling potential of male desire of women to disrupt homosocial bonds – a theme that will continue to bubble up during all three days of conversation. Towards the end of the second day of storytelling, the gentlemen digress long enough to debate four *questioni d'amore*, recalling the thirteen questions on love elaborated in Boccaccio's *Filocolo*. On the third day, a bawdy novella on female desire is followed by a discussion of the fine art of the *motto* (loosely translated as "witticism"), as well as various poetic forms such as the madrigal, the *capitolo*, the sestina, and the sonnet. The book concludes with a series of hyperbolic encomia in praise of the beauty and virtue of the women of Venice, Ferrara, Bologna, and Viterbo.

That Parabosco's book is preoccupied with women and love is not surprising, since the literary debate on the merits and vices of women known as the *querelle des femmes* was still in great vogue at the middle of the sixteenth century and would continue to be discussed for centuries to come.[6] But the exclusion of women from Parabosco's frame story is telling, especially since this represents a departure from the two most important literary models for Parabosco's book, Boccaccio's *Decameron* and Castiglione's *Cortegiano*.[7] While Castiglione's duchess Elisabetta and her lady-in-waiting Maria Pia have a largely decorative role in his dialogue, they are at least physically present during the men's conversation, which takes place in the domestic, feminine space of Elisabetta's private rooms.[8] In contrast, Parabosco's dialogue unfolds during a fishing party on the lagoon, creating an active, outdoor, masculine rhetorical space that excludes even the possibility of women's participation in the discussion.

Despite this idealized portrait of the Venier salon as an exclusively masculine realm, the interlocutors of *I diporti* cannot seem to stop talking about women. In that sense, Parabosco's dialogue articulates the dialectical relationship between the act of writing and the representation of women that is at the centre of the Venier salon's literary production. This underlying tension is spelled out at the beginning of the first day of storytelling through the ironic voice of Alessandro Lambertino, whose role as spokesman for the anti-woman side of the debate is a gloss on Signor Gasparo, Castiglione's misogynist interlocutor in the *Cortegiano*. Goaded by Aretino, who mocks him for his devotion to an unknown lady, Lambertino declares that the only reason he and the other men in the group write poetry in praise of women is to show off their own poetic talent (*ingegno*): "As far as praising [women], I do the same thing as the rest of you, who sing their praises in order to better exercise your talent, which you show to be even greater through your ability to depict such a lowly [*vile*] and sinister [*tenebroso*] subject as a noble one."[9]

After much back and forth, Domenico Venier interrupts the quarrel between his two friends, as if to demonstrate his role as group leader and literary adviser. Tellingly, Venier does not take sides. Instead of defending women, he defends the men who praise them, pointing out that Girolamo Ruscelli is so talented in this regard that he has "almost convinced the entire universe to believe that women are much more perfect and worthy than we are."[10] Here Parabosco, through the voice of Venier, is invoking Ruscelli's famous *Lettura di un sonetto dell'illustrissimo signor Marchese della Terza alla divina signora Marchesa del Vasto* (1552). In his *Lettura*, Ruscelli had glossed his patron's own sonnet in praise of the noblewoman Maria d'Aragona. The book also included a discourse on the perfection of women and a catalogue of virtuous ones.[11]

The conversation takes an even more interesting turn when Lambertino retorts that "while Ruscelli is alive, because he is friends with all the literati, everyone will show respect – if not for him, then for his friends – and no one will ever write anything to contradict him."[12] Aretino steps in once again to contradict Lambertino, saying that in fact "Ruscelli will be the reason that someone decides to write something against women, not so much to offend them, but to make a name for himself by daring to have written against a great man."[13]

I begin with this literary debate because it is a fascinating window onto the politics of writing about women in the context of Venier's circle. Parabosco, like Girolamo Ruscelli, was neither Venetian nor of aristocratic origins. His interpretation of Ruscelli's literary success is telling in its concern in regard to how texts on women could serve as currency in the relationships of non-noble men with their more elite patrons. As Parabosco sees it, Ruscelli writes in praise of women to please his powerful patrons and secure the support he needs. Indeed, Ruscelli's *Lettura* with its discourse on the perfection of women was an encomium in praise of his patron's own praise of female beauty and virtue. But as Parabosco has Aretino point out, the exchange of texts on women could also serve as an agonistic arena for competition and one-upmanship. Another man might decide to contradict Ruscelli by defaming women instead of praising them for the purpose of "daring to have written against a great man," thus displaying the appropriately masculine quality of bravado.

Even as Parabosco's dialogue foregrounds the woman question as the centre of the Venier group's poetic discourse, it is concerned, above all, with relationships between men. In Parabosco's view, men write about women primarily to display and negotiate relationships with one another. At the end of his dialogue, Parabosco practises what he preaches in a long series of encomiastic "lodi di donne" (praises of women), which focuses on the women nearest and dearest to his aristocratic patrons. The women of the Venier, Corner, and Badoer families are given special attention and praised for their "gentilezza e bellezza" (nobility and beauty).[14] For Parabosco, a man of middling status, such praise was a way to secure his own connections to Venier's elite group of powerful patricians and literary luminaries.

In its representation of the Venier group as engaged in conversation, storytelling, and literary analysis, *I diporti* also dramatizes the process of literary collaboration itself. We might think of Parabosco's book as a virtual salon, similar in many ways to the lyric anthologies in which the Venier circle appeared for the first time in print as an ensemble.[15] In such anthologies, poets could advertise their collective identity through clusters of poems, which often included paired sonnets in which the group members addressed one another by name.[16] As Diana Robin has argued, this form of group publication "imitates the salon, whether real or imaginary, in its interactivity, face-to-face style, variety of actors and themes, and mix of personalities."[17] Such anthologies reflected the discourse and intellectual exchange carried out in the salon and displayed the social and political ties among salon members; in this way, a discourse community was created that was an extension of the physical salon. In other words, anthologies and other group publications opened up a space where writers could "write themselves in" to the more porous boundaries of the virtual salon. Parabosco's *I diporti* is a particularly bold example of this practice, since it is not actually an anthology but Parabosco's own representation of the Venier circle's discourse and literary exchange. Parabosco modestly does not cast himself as an interlocutor, yet his portrait of the salon and its inner workings, however mediated or idealized, broadcasts to his readers that he is part of Venier's inner circle.

Academies, Salons, and Other Sodalities in Sixteenth-Century Venice

By the time Parabosco published *I diporti*, the Venier group had firmly established its reputation as an elite collective of writers with shared stylistic interests. Already in 1548, Aretino wrote to the wealthy Venetian statesman Girolamo Cappello describing the group of literary men who had begun to gravitate around Domenico Venier as "the Academy of the good Venier" (l'Accademia del buon Veniero).[18] Aretino's use of the word *accademia* to describe Venier's circle may be misleading to some, since we tend to reserve this term for the more formalized literary academies that would become common in Venice only later in the sixteenth century.[19]

Such groups invariably had most if not all of the following: an official name, an academic *impresa* or emblem,[20] a written constitution and/or by-laws, an official list of members, formal minutes, and regular meeting times. Venier's group had none of these formalities. Nevertheless, Aretino's reference to the group as an *accademia* is perfectly concordant with sixteenth-century usage, when the word was regularly used to denote any regular gathering of literary men, with or without the formalities mentioned above.[21] In this respect, Aretino's definition of Venier's group as an academy is important, since it points to the fact that it was regarded as a collective by members and observers alike. What is clear is that, like more formally organized academies, the Venier circle had a strong sense of group identity. Moreover, as with later academies, the gatherings at Venier's house were characterized by conversation, debate, and intellectual exchange.

The picture that can be pieced together from scattered correspondence and literary references suggests that meetings at Ca' Venier were often held on an impromptu basis, in part because several of the Venier group's most illustrious participants lived outside Venice. In one literary account of the salon, we learn that Sperone Speroni, who lived in Padua, organized his trips to Venice so that "all the free time left over after his errands" could be "spent in pleasant and honourable conversation with the Magnificent Messer Domenico and the rest of the gentlemen that often meet at his house."[22] The informal structure of the Venier circle was much like that of other drawing-room salons in Venice. One of the most celebrated of these was the salon held at the home of another Venetian patrician named Antonio Zantani (d. 1567). Zantani and his famously beautiful wife Elena Barozzi are known to music historians as patrons of musical gatherings at their home.[23] Some of the musicians who took part in the Zantani gatherings can also be linked to the Venier circle, including Parabosco and his composer friend Perissone Cambio.[24] Cambio, like Parabosco, was a protégé of the illustrious Flemish composer Adrian Willaert. That he was also acquainted with Domenico Venier is suggested by a sonnet exchange between Venier and Girolamo Fenaruolo another musician friend, lamenting Perissone's death.[25]

Until later in the century, most literary gatherings in Venice were of the informal, private type, like the salons presided over by Venier and Zantani. However, there were some notable exceptions. The named, formalized academies that would flourish in Venice only later in the sixteenth century may have had a precedent in a group founded by the printer Aldo Manuzio (1449/50–1515). The Neacademia, ostensibly active from about 1496 to Aldo's death in 1515, was established to promote the study of Greek language and letters. Although Aldo refers to his academy in no less than eight colophons and prefaces, the scholar Martin Lowry has cast doubt on its existence, suggesting that it may have been simply a "Renaissance dream."[26] Following in Lowry's footsteps, David S. Chambers has argued that Aldo's references to the Neacademia were little more than a "stylish description of his officina."[27] Even the discovery of the academy's constitution, which declares that members were required to speak Greek during meetings on penalty of fines, and which lists the Greek pseudonyms used by some members, does not convince Chambers that the Aldine Academy existed; he suggests instead that the document could be the expression of a "playful in-house fantasy."[28] Such reluctance to define Aldo's Neacademia as a true academy points to the existence, in modern critical discourse, of what I see as a false dichotomy between early, less formal literary groups and later, formalized academies. Even if Aldo did dream up the Neacademia as some sort of a publicity stunt, he must have believed that his books would sell better if they were presented as the result of a collective effort. Aldo's academy, regardless of its level of formality, is interesting as a manifestation of the perceived pay-off of group membership. For Aldo, affiliation with such a group was a way to present his press as a collective enterprise in a city whose patriciate valued civic concord and a shared, group identity.

Another formalized academy that should be mentioned because of the close links of some of its members to Venier is the Paduan Accademia degli Infiammati (Academy of the Burning Ones), founded in 1540 by Leone Orsini. This group had all but completely disbanded by the time Venier's circle began to meet regularly in the late 1540s. Yet several members of the Infiammati would eventually become regular visitors to Venier's house. One of the most influential members of the Infiammati, who would become a regular visitor to Venier's house, was Sperone Speroni. Speroni served as *principe*, or president, of the Paduan academy from November 1541 until March of the following year. Just before Speroni became *principe*, Pietro Aretino had been elected as a member of the academy under the leadership of the Ferrarese poet Galeazzo Gonzaga. Another one of Venier's closest adherents, the Venetian *poligrafo* Lodovico Dolce – a humanist, poet, and incredibly prolific editor – also became a member of the Infiammati in the early 1540s.

The academy most closely connected to Venier's circle was the Accademia della Fama (of Fame), also known as the Accademia Veneziana.

Founded by Venier's longtime friend Federico Badoer in 1557, the Accademia Veneziana was defunct by 1561. As Feldman has pointed out, there is no direct evidence to support the oft-repeated hypothesis that Badoer's academy was a direct offshoot of the Venier circle, nor that Venier's salon was subsumed into Badoer's academy in the late 1550s. This is not to say there were no connections between the two groups. Indeed, there are several literati who can be linked to both, and because of their shared interest in vernacular prose and poetry, it does not seem unlikely that writers and ideas flowed from one group to another. Among these writers were Torquato Tasso's father Bernardo, who became *cancelliere* (chancellor) of Badoer's academy in 1559,[29] and the young Venetian *cittadino* writer Celio Magno, who is listed as a founding member in the academy's *Instrumento* (charter or constitution) in 1557.[30] Both Tasso and Magno were portrayed as regular visitors to Ca' Venier in *Il diamerone*, a dialogue by Valerio Marcellino published in 1564 to which I will turn shortly. A further connection is Venier's musician friend Girolamo Fenaruolo, who signed the academy's *capitoli* (bylaws) in 1559.[31]

That said, there is plenty of evidence that both Venier and his old friend Girolamo Molino were supportive of Badoer's new academy, at least initially. Domenico Venier was among the signers of a 1557 letter to "our dearest friend, Messer Camillo Vezzato" that invited Vezzato to join the ranks of Badoer's academy.[32] Moreover, a notarized document printed with the academy's original charter in 1557 records that Domenico Venier agreed to supervise Marcantonio Vallaresso in his position as editor of the group's publications.[33] Molino, too, seems to have lent a hand in recruiting new members and works for publication. In 1558, it was Molino who wrote a letter to Bernardo Tasso inviting him to entrust the academy with the publishing of his epic poem, the *Amadigi*, and assuring him that Paolo Manuzio (the son of the illustrious Aldo) would be entrusted with the job of printing it. In the closing lines of the letter, Molino claims that he has been asked to write Tasso by "these Signori [the members of the Academy], my friends, and several of their protectors, including the Clarissimo Messer Federico Badoaro and Messer Domenico Venier."[34]

Despite their initial efforts to assist Badoer with the formation of the academy, neither Venier nor Molino is mentioned as a founding member in the academy's original *Instrumento*, and neither signed the *capitoli*. As Pietro Pagan has pointed out, there are several good reasons why Venier may not have wanted to become an official member of Badoer's academy.[35] From a purely practical standpoint, Venier's health problems, which kept him housebound, would have prevented him from being a regular presence at the academy's meetings. Also, given his prominent role in Venetian society, it is not surprising that Venier may have felt more comfortable participating in the academy only indirectly.[36] Finally, I am inclined to agree with Feldman, who argues that "Venier's academic tastes were better accommodated in the atmosphere of the informal *accademia*, thriving in the slippery space between private elitism and public fame that drawing rooms could provide."[37] The formalized structure and political agenda of the Accademia Veneziana must have left little room for the informal sorts of exchanges that enlivened the discussions in Venier's drawing room.

Meanwhile, there is a particularly Venetian phenomenon that offers a suggestive prototype for both the informal, private gatherings like those held at Venier's palace and the more formally structured academies. The late fifteenth century saw the formation of the *Compagnie della Calza*, literally, "Companies of the Stocking" (in the sense of clubs for the silk-stocking crowd), so named for the finely embroidered emblems they often wore on their stockings to identify themselves as members of a particular group. The *Compagnie della Calza*, whose activities in Venice have been documented from about 1487 to 1565, have been defined by Lionello Venturi as "private societies that were temporarily constituted between young men, mostly noble, who united their energies with the goal of entertaining themselves."[38] In balder terms, these *compagnie* were clubs consisting of young Venetian noblemen who gathered on a regular basis to eat, drink, and be merry and to organize music, plays, and various entertainments for special occasions such as marriages or Carnival.

In 1533, the Venetian diarist Marin Sanudo listed thirty-four individual *Compagnie della Calza*.[39] Very little information has been uncovered regarding specific *compagnie* and individual members, so it is difficult to determine what may have drawn the groups together. However, based on the membership lists recorded in Sanudo's diaries, we can hypothesize that these groups often fostered extra-familial ties among the patriciate. In most cases, membership lists seem to have included only one son from each family that participated, although one group did include three or more men with the same family name.[40]

The *Compagnie della Calza* shared many characteristics with the formalized academies that would become commonplace later in the sixteenth century. Like academies, the *compagnie* fostered a sense of group identity by giving themselves a name. As Lodovico Zorzi has noted, the names can be divided into several categories: self-aggrandizing (*Immortali* [Immortal Ones] and *Sempiterni* [Eternal Ones]), rustic or Arcadian (*Ortolani* and *Zardinieri* [Gardeners]), or self-deprecating (*Sbragazai* [Raggedy Ones]).[41] The *compagnie* also had written statutes, called *capitoli*, that were similar to the notarized by-laws of formalized academies.[42] The by-laws of the *compagnie* were approved by the Consiglio dei Dieci (The Council of Ten), a governing body responsible for maintaining the security of the republic and preserving the government from overthrow or corruption. Once the groups were organized, the government no longer regulated their activities. Many *compagnie* had a full administrative staff that included an appointed leader or president known as the *priore* (a position that foreshadows the *principe* of later academies), one or more *consiglieri* who acted as advisers to the *priore*, a *signore* who served as the master of ceremonies for the festivities organized by the group, a *sindaco*, who oversaw the group's finances, and a *camerlengo*, who served as treasurer and was in charge of day-to-day spending.

The *Compagnie della Calza* were highly visible to the rest of the community; their sense of collectivity was promoted and sanctioned by the church as well as the Venetian government. After its statutes had been approved, each *compagnia* organized a lavish inauguration ceremony, displaying its newly acquired group identity to the entire city. Dressed in their distinctive uniforms, the members proceeded together to their parish church, where they heard high mass and swore their allegiance to their group leader, the *priore*. The mass was followed by an audience at the Doge's Palace with the *Maggior Consiglio* (Great Council), the highest-ranking body of the Venetian magistrature, which included all patrician men over the age of twenty-five (numbering over 2,500 by the end of the sixteenth century). The day of festivities concluded with a banquet offered by the *priore*, often enlivened by music and dancing.

The *Sempiterni*, constituted in 1541, had ties to at least two men associated with Domenico Venier's salon. The first was Bartolomeo Vitturi, a Venetian patrician who was among the twelve founding members of the *Sempiterni*[43] and appears in Parabosco's *I diporti* as an interlocutor.[44] The second was Aretino. Although he was not an official member (it was rare for *Compagnie della Calza* to admit members who were not Venetian patricians – this only happened in the case of foreign dignitaries), in 1542 the *Sempiterni* commissioned a play from him for their Carnival festivities. The play was *Talanta,* a bawdy comedy loosely based on Terence's *The Eunuch* and starring a greedy courtesan (for whom the play is named). Splendid *apparati* (sets) were designed by Aretino's friend Giorgio Vasari and set up in an unfinished palace somewhere in the Venetian neighbourhood of Cannaregio.[45]

The *Sempiterni*'s statutes, drawn up on 15 March 1541, emphasized the sodality's function of reinforcing and formalizing the bonds of friendship among its members. It did so in strikingly sentimental terms:

> Considering that our love for one another as brothers began at a tender age, and that all during our tender youth we have maintained this unity and benevolence, we feel we should not neglect to demonstrate this to everyone, as a manifest sign of the unbreakable bond of our eternal friendship, without which states, empires, and republics cannot endure.[46]

As the company's statute makes clear, one of the most important functions of these groups was to make public the bonds between their members. These bonds between men are cast here as fundamental to the survival of the Venetian Republic itself. Although these clubs were certainly sites of entertainment, they were also training grounds for the Venetian senators of the future, who were expected to put the collective good before their own individual desires.

The practices detailed in the *capitoli* of the *Sempiterni* were designed with two main functions: first, to create a sense of homosocial collective identity, and second, to display their homosocial bonds to the rest of the city. For example, all members of the *Sempiterni* were required to buy and wear the company's distinctive *calza* (stocking), as well as a "veste di seta" (silk cassock or gown), to be worn first at the ceremony that marked the group's official inauguration and for twenty days afterwards. Also, when a *compagno* (as members of these groups were called) married, the rest of the group was required to wear a "veste di scarlato" (a red wool cassock) to commemorate the occasion. In the event of the death of a *compagno,* the group was to display its collective mourning by wearing a "mantello" (mantle, or cloak).[47]

A letter to the duke of Ferrara from one of his agents in Venice recounts an incident in which the *Sempiterni* had expressed their *esprit de corps* in a very public manner. Just a few days after the group's official constitution, several *palazzi* scattered throughout the city were adorned with the phrase "W. i Sempiterni (Long live the *Sempiterni!*)." Several days later, unknown rivals – most likely members of another *Compagnia della Calza* – cleverly defaced the *Sempiterni*'s self-aggrandizing graffiti so that it read instead "W. i sempii eterni!" (Long live the eternal fools!).[48] As Venturi recounts, this sort of competition among various companies was fairly common – a fact that emphasizes the degree to which these groups served as sites of masculine solidarity for the patricians who participated in them.[49] By displaying their affiliation with a particular group, and by engaging in competition with other groups, the young members of each company were also demonstrating their own status and power.

The Virtual Salon

The practice and performance of homosocial bonds also occurred in the Venetian salon. Like the spaces of the city where the Compagnie della Calza gathered to display their collective identity, the salon was a performative space. It was also, as Parabosco's *I diporti* suggests, a space of agonistic play in which men could demonstrate their literary, poetic, and verbal prowess. Through these displays of literary *virtù*, even a man of lower status could establish social space.[50] Nowhere was this truer than in Domenico Venier's salon, held at his family's private palace in the parish of Santa Maria Formosa.[51] Centrally located between the Rialto and San Marco, Venier's home became a gathering place for an eclectic crowd of literary luminaries, musicians, artists, and theorists of diverse backgrounds and social classes. A plethora of literary references to the Venier salon document its fundamental importance as a centre for intellectual and literary exchange and give us a tantalizing glimpse of the group's activities.

Secondary sources have disagreed as to the exact year in which Venier's circle began meeting regularly, but what is clear is that Venier's literary activities escalated in the mid-1540s, after health problems forced him to take a break from the civic duties normally required of a nobleman of his age and rank.[52] About twenty-five years later, Giovan Mario Verdizzotti, the author of a posthumous biography of Venier's close friend Girolamo Molino, would describe Venier's house as "a continuous salon of virtuous people, both noblemen from Venice and men of any other sort, rare and excellent for their skill in the letters or otherwise."[53] Verdizzotti's remark regarding the presence of non-nobles ("men of any other sort") at Ca' Venier points to a certain social heterogeneity that, as Feldman has argued, was a defining characteristic of the Venier group and other private salons in Venice.[54] While many of the poets who frequented Venier's house were aristocratic Venetians – Federico Badoer, Girolamo Molino, and Giacomo Zane, for instance – Venier also welcomed with open arms social climbers of decidedly humble origin such as Girolamo Parabosco and Pietro Aretino. Not surprisingly, authors of bourgeois background are responsible for many of the most informative literary allusions to Venier and his circle; after all, they had the most to gain from publicizing their connections.

The two contemporary sources that provide us with an insider's view of the Venier salon were both written by non-nobles. We have already encountered the first of these, Girolamo Parabosco's *I diporti*, published in 1551. Parabosco's book features many poets who were frequent visitors to Ca' Venier and offers a suggestive albeit fictional portrait of its members and literary activities at mid-century. The second source is *Il diamerone*, a philosophical dialogue by a Venetian poet named Valerio Marcellino, who seems to have frequented Venier's group in the late 1550s and beyond. While the conversations in Parabosco's book take place during an imagined fishing trip on the Venetian lagoon, Marcellino's *Il diamerone* (published in 1564 but completed in 1561) takes place in Venier's private palace.

Parabosco was born in Piacenza to a bourgeois family, but came to Venice while still in his teens – presumably to study with the Flemish composer Adrian Willaert.[55] By the time he published *I diporti* in 1551, Parabosco had been appointed First Organist of San Marco, one of the most prestigious musical positions in all of Europe, and was an intimate of numerous circles of literati, both noble and non-noble. Parabosco's connections to Domenico Venier can be traced back at least to 1549, when Aretino wrote him a letter praising his literary talent and highlighting their mutual ties to Venier:

> The works you have published at such a young age promise to make you very famous and honoured, since even the works of those who find themselves writing at a more advanced age are not so desired. But, because I love you as much as anyone else might envy you, I will leave this matter to Venier, so that my praise of you will not be attributed to benevolence. He, the magnificent Domenico, who knows and understands so much (since he introduced me to you), will, in testifying to the talent that you demonstrated even as a babe in arms, prove it by believing in it himself, since cultured men listen to what he says and respect his taste.[56]

Aretino's letter casts himself as loving father to Parabosco even as it highlights the subtle dynamic of competition between the two writers for the approval of their mutual patron. Although Aretino's friendly tone can be explained in part by the standard literary codes associated with the genre of the familiar letter, there is other evidence to suggest that Aretino and Parabosco were well acquainted. In 1551 Parabosco included a letter to Aretino in his own book of letters, the *Lettere famigliari*.[57] And in 1545, Parabosco sent the first two books of his *Lettere amorose* to Venier's close friend Girolamo Molino. The letter Parabosco sent Molino along with his new books makes use of the predictable rhetoric of self-deprecation to praise his Venetian patron. At the same time, Parabosco artfully underscores both his social ties to Molino and his patrician patron's belief in his literary talent:

> I am sending [the *Lettere amorose*] to you with some amount of shame, being certain of diminishing in large part the hopes that you always say you have for me, which cannot be small, given the loving and wise reminders and advice that you deign to give me all the time.[58]

By 1551, if we are to believe Parabosco, he was a regular visitor to Ca' Venier and was well-acquainted with Venier himself, Aretino, and other members of the salon. In a long *capitolo* published in 1551 and addressed to Alessandro Lambertino, the Bolognese count cast as the misogynist in *I diporti*, Parabosco claims to have been frequenting Venier's house for four years.

> Andarò spesso spesso a ca' Venieri,
> ove io non vado mai ch'io non impari
> di mille cose per quatr'anni intieri,
> Per ch'ivi sempre son spiriti chiari,
> et ivi fassi un ragionar divino
> fra quella compagnia d'huomini rari.
> Chi è il Badoar sapete, e chi il Molino,
> chi il padron della stanza, e l'Amalteo,
> il Corso, lo Sperone, e l'Aretino.
> Ciascun nelle scienze è un Capaneo,
> grande vo' dire, et son fra lor sì uguali,
> che s'Anfion è l'un, l'altro è un Orfeo.
> Mi vogliono ben questi huomini immortali;
> chè li ha il senno e 'l valore immortalati,
> e oltra il termine human spiegato han l'ali.

I'll go as often as possible to Ca' Venier,
where, for four whole years, I have never gone
without learning a thousand things,
because there are always illustrious spirits there,
and there is always divine discussion
among that company of extraordinary men.
You know who Badoer is, and Molino,
the lord of the house [= Venier], and Amalteo,
Corso, Sperone, and Aretino.
Each one is in learning a Capaneus –
great, I mean, and they are so on par with one another,
that if one is an Amphion, the other is an Orpheus.
They love me, these immortal men –
they have been immortalized by their wisdom and valour,
and they have spread their wings beyond human limits.[59]

All of the literary men Parabosco lists here as members of Venier's salon are also cast as interlocutors in *I diporti*, with the exception of Giovanni Battista Amalteo, a poet from Oderzo renowned for his skill in both Italian and Latin verse.[60] Parabosco's encomium to the Venier salon serves also as a means of self-promotion, of course, since he elevates himself through his praise of the illustrious company of writers at Ca' Venier. His portrait of the salon casts his mentors as illustrious men and the salon as a place where men know how to "ragionar divino" (speak divinely), showcasing both the salon's literary fame and his own association with such a group of extraordinary men. But his declaration that all of these great poets are equal to one another belies his lower status within the group, since he needs to ensure that he does not offend any of his illustrious mentors by implying that some are more talented than others. Even as he praises Venier and the other illustrious members of the salon, Parabosco highlights the affection that binds him to his mentors, and them to him. Because they love him, their immortal qualities of wisdom and valour reflect Parabosco's own worth as the friend and protégé of such an elite group of men and suggest that he, too, is capable of spreading his wings beyond mortal limits and attaining the heights of literary fame.

Parabosco deployed similar strategies of self-promotion in *I diporti*. The third day of the dialogue includes a discussion of the required qualities for a variety of poetic forms: madrigal, *strambotto*, *capitolo*, sestina, canzone, and sonnet. Except for two sonnets by Domenico Venier, all of the examples of poetic perfection put forth by the group are Parabosco's own. Through the fictional discourse on poetic form and technique, Parabosco advertises both his own poetic skill and his connections to the elite group of writers he portrays in his dialogue. Parabosco quite literally writes himself into the group's discussion, crafting a scene in which such luminaries as Speroni and Aretino wax enthusiastic about the talent of the unnamed author of the poems they are critiquing (Parabosco, of course). Although absent from the discussion as interlocutor, Parabosco has fashioned a literary salon of which he is the focal point and star.

All of the poems discussed are variations on the theme of amorous distress, featuring pale, weepy male lovers who lament the resistance of cold-hearted ladies and threaten suicide. In that sense Parabosco has returned to the problem he had articulated in his frame story – the disruptive and dangerous potential of love. This is highlighted in Speroni's comment on Parabosco's madrigal, "Donna, s'io resto vivo" (Lady, if I survive):

"Just look at how much grace this one has … it was written by a young man who, if he were not often derailed from his studies and his thoughts by certain other things, would have some hopes for success. This madrigal was written about his breakup with one of his ladies."[61]

Speroni's comment presents Parabosco as a talented poet who would be even more successful if he were not sidetracked by his preoccupation with women and love. The problem with uncontrolled desire, Parabosco seems to be saying through Speroni, is not just its potential for disrupting relationships between men, but also its power to render the poet unable to write.

As the discussion continues, one by one Parabosco's mentors praise his poetic prowess as they analyse his poems. Through the mouth of Aretino, Parabosco makes public a defence of the excellence of his own verse:

If I weren't afraid of going overboard and losing all modesty, since the author of these compositions is so close to my heart, I would certainly say more than I am saying now in his favour. And I'd also say to those to whom having whole woods full of laurel trees encircling their temples would mean very little (since they consider themselves to be such excellent drinkers of the waters of Parnassus) and who insist on judging this, that, and the other, without ever saying anything positive about anyone ... I would say, I mean, that I would like to see them write such compositions![62]

Parabosco has Aretino emphasize their ties of friendship even as he defends himself from pretentious poets who have criticized him and attempted to keep him on the margins of the literary scene in Venice. Through the mouths of his friends and literary mentors, Parabosco constructs an image of himself and his own poetic production as central to the group of elite writers he has represented in his book without violating principles of authorial modesty. At the same time, this very performance of literary fraternity and identity is tied to the representation of women. For in the end, Parabosco's book represents the Venier circle as a group of men engaged in the collective effort of talking and writing about women.

Just over a decade after Parabosco published his literary portrait of the Venier salon, the Venetian lawyer and poet Valerio Marcellino[63] published another work casting Venier and his coterie as interlocutors, a short philosophical dialogue titled *Il diamerone di M. Valerio Marcellino, ove con vive ragioni si mostra, la morte non esser quel male, che 'l senso si persuade* (The *diamerone*, by Messer Valerio Marcellino, where, with lively reasoning, death is shown not to be as bad as our senses would persuade us).[64] *Il diamerone* was first published by Giolito in 1564 but was probably complete by 10 April 1561, when Marcellino signed the dedicatory letter to the Venetian nobleman Pietro Zane that precedes the dialogue. Pietro's brother was Giacomo Zane (1529–1560), acclaimed by his contemporaries as a gifted poet, who had passed away less than a year earlier. Giacomo Zane, too, had close ties to Venier and may have participated in the group's meetings before his death. In the dedicatory letter to Pietro Zane, Marcellino claims that he wrote *Il diamerone*, a philosophical discussion on the meaning of death, to comfort Pietro for the recent loss of his brother. Marcellino's letter also highlights his connection to Venier's prestigious salon, presenting his book as a reconstruction of a meeting in Venier's house: "the discourse that is the subject of this product of my labour took place over two days in the house of the Magnificent Domenico Venier (as you will see when you read it)."[65]

Despite its billing as a philosophical dialogue on death, *Il diamerone*, like Parabosco's dialogue, is also concerned with the business of writing about women. As the first day begins, both themes are introduced when a servant of Giorgio Gradenigo arrives with a letter from Bernardo Capello accompanied by two sonnets lamenting the untimely death of Irene di Spilimbergo. Renowned as a talented musician and painter, Irene was the daughter of the Friulian count Adriano di Spilimbergo and his Venetian patrician wife Giulia da Ponte. When Irene died suddenly at the age of twenty-one in 1559, Dionigi Atanagi organized an ambitious memorial volume that contained poems in Italian and Latin by over 140 authors. Atanagi, a native of the Marches, had arrived in Venice the year of Irene's death and quickly found employment as the secretary of Federico Badoer's Accademia Veneziana. But the real promoter of the Spilimbergo volume was the Venetian nobleman Giorgio Gradenigo, a friend of both Badoer and Venier.

That Marcellino chose to use Irene's death as a springboard for the fictional conversation in *Il diamerone* is certainly not coincidental: Venier and many other members of his circle contributed poems to the volume compiled in her memory by Atanagi.[66] In that sense, Marcellino's text highlights the salon's collective enterprise of praising Irene. Many of the poets who contributed to the volume were of non-noble status – Celio Magno, Lodovico Dolce, and Giovanni Battista Amalteo, to name a few. In writing sonnets in honour of Irene, these men ingratiated themselves to the patrician commissioner of the volume even as they displayed their elite connections. For the patrician poets in the group, Irene was an ideal muse for Petrarchan praise because of her aristocratic background. Especially in death, she was remote and unattainable enough to inspire irreproachably chaste collective mourning, uniting the group as they lamented her loss and displayed their poetic skill in elegant rhyme.

Like Parabosco's *I diporti*, Marcellino's book provides us with detailed descriptions of the various personalities who may have frequented Venier's house and of the kinds of activities that went on there. *Il diamerone* was completed in 1561, approximately ten years after Parabosco's *I diporti*. By then, several of the interlocutors featured in Parabosco's book – including Parabosco and the influential Pietro Aretino – were dead.[67] What's more, a new crop of younger writers had started to frequent the salon. That said, several important figures we have already encountered in Parabosco's book are also featured in *Il diamerone*. Parabosco had divided his catalogue of interlocutors according to city of provenance, introducing first the Venetian noblemen and then the *foresti*, or foreigners (a term used by Venetians to denote anyone, even an Italian, not a native of the Venetian Republic). Marcellino, by contrast, organizes his catalogue of literary men according to age. The older men (*uomini gravi*), who spend their time discussing important matters (*cose importanti*), are naturally presented first. These include two of Venier's long-time acquaintances also featured in *I diporti*, Speroni and Molino. Also classified as *uomini gravi* are Atanagi, Torquato Tasso's father Bernardo, and the Venetian patrician poet Giorgio Gradenigo. After the older men have been introduced, Marcellino points out that Venier's house is a place where "many young and very worthy men of the happiest intellect" also gather. These include Alvise Belegno, Girolamo Fenaruolo, and the Venetian *cittadino* poet Celio Magno.

Another distinguishing feature of Marcellino's book is its attention to physical details of people and settings. Parabosco had made only a brief mention of Venier's health problems in *I diporti*.[68] But Marcellino's description of Venier's crippled body here becomes occasion for praise of the patrician's spirit and intellect:

> The magnificent Messer Domenico Venier, a gentleman of rare valour (as everyone knows), was given a very strong and very elevated spirit by the heavens. In the same way, Nature gave him a languid body that is not very healthy, due to the cruel misfortune of infirmity. It is possible, however, that Nature did this with the same judgment with which she is wont to do many other marvellous things. Indeed, having given him an intellect that is so sublime, it was perhaps lucky that to that soul more angelic than human, she gave a body that was slight and thin – and besides being thin, it was reduced by illness to even greater thinness – so that the size and the softness of the body might not impede the spirit's flight towards the heavens, where [Venier] can often be seen resting with his lofty concepts giving flight to his wings.[69]

Venier's slight body, according to Marcellino, enables rather than impedes his poetic talent, allowing him to fly freely towards the heavens bolstered by his "lofty concepts." This portrayal of Venier as a divine creature, elected by both Nature and the heavens to a position of intellectual superiority, echoes and amplifies Parabosco's descriptions of Venier and the other elite poets of his circle. Through this adept rhetorical strategy of praise, Marcellino transforms Venier's wasted body into a display of poetic *virtù*. His praise affirms his patron's prowess as an indicator of masculine superiority, an especially effective strategy given Venier's inability to conform to ideals of masculine strength and physical virility.

These two books, penned by eyewitnesses to Venier's inner circle, offer intriguing clues to the sort of discourse and discussion that took place during these gatherings, however mediated. Of course, both Parabosco and Marcellino, as members of Venier's circle, would have had a vested interest in how the group was perceived by outsiders, as well as how they themselves were perceived within it. But as idealized representations of the process of literary collaboration, *I diporti* and *Il diamerone* align their authors with Venier and his prestigious circle of writers in the public medium of print. Both texts also reveal the ways in which the practice of writing about women constituted and publicized relationships of patronage, friendship, and literary partnership.

Petrarchan Praise and Literary Fraternity

For all of Domenico Venier's renown as a literary patron and adviser, barely half the poems he composed were published during his lifetime. His unpublished poems, however, circulated widely in manuscript form, as demonstrated by the forty-nine extant manuscripts preserving them.[70] Yet a full-length *canzoniere* of his collected poems was not published until the middle of the eighteenth century, almost two hundred years after his death. Many of the elegant sonnets he wrote and exchanged with his coterie of vernacular poets are scattered throughout the poetry anthologies that began to flow from Venetian presses in the middle of the century. In 1545, the Ferrarese printer Gabriele Giolito sparked what would become a literary phenomenon with the publication of *Rime diverse di molti eccellentissimi autori*.[71] This volume is the first printed anthology to focus mainly on lyric poems by authors who were alive at the time of publication (although it does include a handful of poems by Dante and Petrarch that would be eliminated in later volumes). It was so successful that Giolito printed a second edition in 1546 and a third in 1549. The series would eventually grow to include nine distinct volumes – or ten, if we accept the argument by Diana Robin that Domenichi's *Rime di illustre donne* should be included.[72]

The printed lyric anthology burst onto the scene just as Venier's group was beginning to consolidate in the late 1540s. In fact, the first two volumes in the *Rime di diversi* series contain poems by writers who would later come to be associated with the Venier salon, including Aretino and Parabosco. Venier's own poems did not appear in print until 1550, when Andrea Arrivabene published the third volume of the series, *Libro terzo delle rime di diversi nobilissimi et eccellentissimi autori nuovamente raccolte*. In addition to nineteen poems by Venier, the *Libro terzo* contains verses by many of the writers who by this time had become part of Venier's inner circle: Aretino and Parabosco (again), Giovanni Battista Amalteo, Fortunio Spira, and Giovanni Battista Susio, among others.

By the time Arrivabene took over Giolito's *Rime di diversi* series in 1550, the Venier group had been meeting informally for about four years. In fact, many contemporary sources from around this time refer to the group as a formed entity, and as we saw earlier, comments by members of the group such as Parabosco and Aretino suggest that they themselves had developed a sense of collective identity. This may be one reason why Arrivabene's *Libro terzo* contains so many poems by writers with close ties to Venier. Although it was certainly not conceived as a means to showcase the Venier group, the new anthology form made it possible for the group to appear in print as an ensemble for the first time. In that sense the book can be thought of as a virtual salon, a reflection of the heterogeneous mix of personalities who frequented Venier's house and a public display of the poetry they exchanged there. The poems also give us a fascinating glimpse into the dynamics of sixteenth-century poetry exchange, characterized by tropes of courtesy, gamesmanship, modesty, and pride, among other things.

Aretino's contribution totals thirty-four poems, seemingly arranged according to the relationships among their dedicatees. The first group of poems, placed prominently near the beginning of the book, contains many verses addressed to rulers and heads of state, in addition to a few poems commemorating the death of Bembo in 1547. In the second group, consisting of five poems by Aretino, all of the dedicatees can be linked with the Venier circle. In order of their appearance in the anthology, they include Antonio Mezzabarba, a Milanese poet whose presence at Ca' Venier is documented by several contemporary sources; Lodovico Dolce, a Venetian writer and editor who was a frequent correspondent of Aretino; and Giovanni Battista Susio, a poet friend of Venier who hailed from Mirandola but studied medicine at the University of Ferrara. Aretino's fourth sonnet is addressed to Domenico Venier himself,[73] while the final one laments the death of Trifone Gabriele, an aristocratic Venetian poet in whose house Venier and his friends often gathered in the 1540s.

All five of these sonnets refer to Aretino's addressees by name, a practice that was widespread in occasional sonnets. That these poems function as a public declaration of the writer's connections with those he addresses is underscored by the fact that the printer has set each proper name in capital letters, a convention also followed in Giolito's first volume of the *Rime di diversi* series. This convention emphasizes the fact that the poems made relationships between writers public. From the reader's point of view, even the visual layout of each page emphasizes the importance of the collectivity of names. A hurried or inattentive reader, skimming through the pages, might pick out only the web of names thus printed but could still place each name within the discourse community highlighted by the pages.

We cannot know, of course, whether Aretino or any of the other poets in the volume had any influence or input as to this typographical arrangement. Yet whether arranged by the writers or by the editor, the group of Aretino poems as printed serves to align his name with those of the poets he addresses, thereby reinforcing his connections to Venier and his circle. Four of the sonnets in Arrivabene's *Libro terzo* (those addressed to the living poets Mezzabarba, Dolce, Susio, and Venier) had appeared in Aretino's fifth book of letters, first published by Comin da Trino at Venice in 1550. Unlike in the poetic anthology, Aretino's letters frame the sonnets with his own commentary. In that sense, Aretino is creating his own virtual salon within the pages of his letter book.

The same poets addressed by Aretino in the *Libro terzo* are among the various personalities mentioned in a *capitolo in terza rima* to Domenico Venier penned by Anton Giacomo Corso and published in Corso's collected poems the same year as Arrivabene's *Libro terzo* (1550).[74] Originally from the seaside town of Ancona, Corso was a well-connected poet who lived in Venice and Ferrara in the 1540s and corresponded with both Aretino and Parabosco, who cast him as an interlocutor in *I diporti*. Corso's exact birth and death dates are unknown, save that he had died by 1555, when Parabosco published a *canzone* lamenting his death.[75] Corso's connections to the Venier circle are further confirmed in his letter to Belliardo Belliardi, which was printed in 1551. In the letter, Corso claims to have been a frequent visitor to Domenico Venier's house: "It is our custom to meet often, for our own benefit, in the house of that divine spirit the most illustrious Messer Domenico Venier."[76]

Corso wrote his *capitolo* to Venier in 1548 during his stay at a villa just north of Padua.[77] He begins by extolling the pleasures of the company and conversation of friends, a theme that dominates the poem. As the poem closes, Corso asks Venier to give his regards to their mutual friends in Venice who may come to visit Venier in his absence. This conceit becomes the pretext for a list of names of poets that provides us with yet another testimony as to the heterogeneous group of poets who frequented Venier's house at the middle of the century. Poets mentioned by Corso include Aretino, Mezzabarba, Dolce (the "sweet signor Lodovico," a pun on his last name), and Susio, in addition to many of the figures we have already encountered as interlocutors in Parabosco's *I diporti*.

> Signor Veniero, io non credo che sia
> altra felicitade in questo mondo
> che ritrovarsi spesso in compagnia.
> [...]
> Di gratia intanto se 'l Vitturi viene
> a visitarvi, quel Vitturi io dico
> che del mio cuor tutto l'imperio tiene,
> fategli fede ch'io gli sono amico.
> E similmente s'altri per lui manda
> farete al Dolce Signor Lodovico.
> Se 'l Badovaro, o 'l Molin vi dimanda
> del fatto mio, piacciavi dir loro,
> "il Corso vostro vi si raccomanda."
> Al gentil Gradenico, al Susio, al Goro,
> al Mezzabarba, al Divin Pietro, al nostro
> medico, proprio dal età del oro,
> O ditegli "questa carta e questo inchiostro
> vi saluta, via piu di cento volte
> per nome d'un ch'e tutto quanto vostro."
> Al Parabosco ancora, e a quel che molte
> fiate parla co i Re senza rispetto
> et ha di man le rime a Phebo tolte.
> In somma a tutti, in sin oltre al traghetto
> vostro, a quelle tre fie raccomandeme,
> se voi non sete, come penso, in letto. [78]

> Signor Venier, I don't believe there is
> anything that makes me happier on this earth
> than being often in the company of friends.
> [...]
> Please, in the meanwhile, if Vitturi
> comes to visit you (the Vitturi, I mean,
> who reigns over my heart),
> assure him that I am his friend.
> And, in the same way, if he sends others to you,
> I hope you will greet the sweet signor Lodovico.
> If Badoer, or Molin ask you
> about me, may it please you to tell them,

"Your Corso sends his regards."
To noble Gradenico, to Susio, to Goro,
to Mezzabarba, to the divine Pietro, and to our
doctor, truly from the Golden Age,
oh, tell them: "this paper and this ink
greet you, more than one hundred times over,
in the name of one who is entirely devoted to you."
To Parabosco again, and to the one who many
times speaks to kings without respect,
and has snatched verses from the hand of Febus.
To everybody, I mean, even those beyond your *traghetto*,
including those three girls, give my regards,
if you are not, as I believe, confined to your bed.

Corso's catalogue of poets functions in much the same way as Aretino's little *réseau* in the *Libro terzo*. Through the web of names, Corso publicly declares his membership in the fraternity of discourse that had its physical nucleus at Venier's palace. Tellingly, Corso's poem begins with an encomium to friendship and conversation. Through the rhetoric of literary fraternity, he simultaneously praises Venier and his circle and reinforces his homosocial bonds to the group. Corso concludes the poem by asking Venier to pay his respects to "quelle tre fie" (those three girls), a mysterious reference but one that hints at the role that women played in the creation of literary fraternity. Whoever the three girls may have been, in Corso's poem they become collective muses whose presence energizes the exchange between men.

In the same vein, female beauty is the pretext for a paired sonnet exchange between Domenico Venier and the *cittadino* poet Celio Magno. Venier's sonnet to Magno begins by describing a portrait of a beautiful lady, now dead, whom Venier once loved. Venier praises the portrait as an example of the power of art to represent nature, deploying a string of Petrarchan oxymora to praise the portrait's remarkable similarity to its subject. The portrait is so lifelike that it "muta parla, ode sorda, e cieca vede" (speaks though mute, hears though deaf, and sees though blind), and sometimes Venier is not sure if "l'opra è d'arte, o di natura" (if it is a work of art, or nature). For Venier, the portrait is a comfort, although looking at it reminds him of what he has lost: "Io, quando quel veder non m'è permesso, / Questo contemplo; e 'l ben ch'allor m'è tolto, mi rende il pinto a par del vivo istesso" (Because I cannot look at [her face], I look at [the painting] instead, and the gift that is taken from me in that moment, makes the painting equal to the living image).[79]

Magno's response deftly reworks Venier's praise of the portrait to focus instead on his patron's poetic talent:

Dentro al tuo cuor più viva e bella siede
Colei, che rassembr'io nobil pittura;
E più da morte in lui regna secura,
Mentre al mondo ne fai sì chiara fede.
O qual grazia è la tua darle in mercede
Eterno onor d'un ben, che 'l tempo fura.
Omai più non la punga invida cura
Del grido, che 'l gran Tosca a Laura diede.
Né men ti debbo anch'io del pregio colto
Dal tuo divino stil; che spiro in esso
Di corpo finto in viva forma volto.
Ma pria ne lodo amor, che al ver sì presso
Fa gir il falso: onde in me credi accolto
Quel, ch'hai negli occhi, e più nell'alma impresso.

Inside your heart, more alive and beautiful resides
she whom I, noble picture, resemble.
And, being dead, she reigns there more securely,
while in the world you speak so illustriously of her.
Oh, how gracious you are to give her eternal honor
in exchange for a treasure that time has stolen away.
Now she is no longer pricked with envious worries
of the fame that the great Tuscan gave to Laura.
And I owe you no less for the praise .
received from your divine style, since it breathes
living form into my counterfeit body.
But first I praise Love, who makes what is false
seem so close to the truth, so that in me you think you see
the image that is engraved in your eyes,
and even more so in your soul.[80]

Magno's response was designed to circulate along with Venier's sonnet on the same theme. Its rhyme scheme matched Venier's (like all such *risposte*), displaying Magno's poetic talent even as it highlighted his connections to his patrician friend. The "great Tuscan," of course, is Francis Petrarch, whose *Rime sparse* created a monument to his own poetic genius even as they immortalized lady Laura, his poetic beloved. Through the conceit of the beautiful lady – codified by Petrarch himself – Magno aligns Venier with Petrarch, the ultimate poetic authority. This strategy seems rather conventional until we notice that Magno writes his sonnet in the female voice of the portrait, casting himself as the ghost of Venier's dead lover. Because Venier's dead lady can no longer respond to his poems of praise, Magno steps in and assumes the feminine role. In the voice of the portrait, Magno thanks Venier for breathing living form into his/her "counterfeit" body. Here Magno's appropriation of the feminine voice functions as a vehicle for literary fraternity. Magno's poem hints at the homoerotic potential of his relationship with his patrician patron, transforming and adapting tropes of heterosexual desire. Venier is represented in the masculine role of poet and active creator of verse; Magno represents himself in the feminine role of poetic muse.[81]

That Venier and his coterie wrote Petrarchan sonnets praising female beauty is not surprising, since love poetry was an important part of any sixteenth-century poet's rise to fame. The elegant love sonnets the Venier group published in the *Rime di diversi* series, as we have seen, were one way in which these writers could demonstrate both their individual talent and their connections to one another. Following in the hallowed footsteps of Petrarch and then Bembo, Venier and his contemporaries constructed exquisitely stylized images of chaste, blond ladies whose very unattainability was the inspiration for their songs. Love poetry and encomia were important vehicles through which the Venier group forged relationships, publicized their connections to one another, and attempted to circumscribe the boundaries of their fellowship of discourse. Yet there is another side of the salon's literary production that has remained virtually unexplored by scholars of Italian literature. If Venier and his circle promoted Bembist canons in their printed sonnets, they exchanged poems of quite a different sort in the semi-privacy of the salon. Written in Venetian dialect and scattered throughout manuscripts in Venice, Rome, London, and Paris, these poems foreground the figure of the sexually available woman – often, but not always, a courtesan.

Chapter Three

The Erotics of Venetian Dialect

In 1553, a group of thirty-four poems by Domenico Venier appeared in the sixth volume of the *Rime di diversi* series of lyric anthologies. Three of these are scattered throughout the book as responses to other authors, but the rest (thirty sonnets and a madrigal) appear as a group.[1] As Massimo Frapolli has argued, Venier's poetic sequence can be read as a *micro-canzoniere* for its thematic and structural affinities to Petrarch's famous songbook.[2] Venier's poet-protagonist, echoing the fourteenth-century model, recounts the story of his love for a beautiful yet unattainable lady who will not respond to his sighs and tears.[3] Like Petrarch's Laura, Venier's poetic beloved is evoked as a series of ethereal, fragmented body parts, which are represented through metaphors that highlight her exquisite remoteness: her eyes are like two stars, blindingly beautiful; her lips are of rubies, her teeth of pearls; her hair is sweet knots of the finest gold.[4]

Venier's *micro-canzoniere* culminates with a sonnet lamenting the premature death of the poet's beloved. Since no amount of tears or suffering will bring his lady back to life, he resolves to immortalize her through his verse:

Poi che pianti, e sospir gravi, e dolenti
Sì, ch'in più parti il cor sentia spezzarsi,
Per la bocca, e per gli occhi indarno ho sparsi
Nè tornan vivi i due bei lumi spenti.
A che trar più dal sen sospiri ardenti,
A che pianger' in van tanto, e lagnarsi,
Che non far' anzi lei, perch'io tutt'arsi,
Conta in perpetuo a le future genti?

Lei, ch'al sembiante a gli occhi, e a le chiome
De l'antica figliuola alma di Leda
Le bellezze non men tenea, che 'l nome.
Lei, che fea del mio cor continua preda,
Dolce già nodo a le mie care some,
Nè l'harà Morte ancor sciolto, ch'io creda.

Since I have spilled in vain from my mouth and from my eyes
tears, and such deep and painful sighs
that my heart felt as if it was breaking into pieces
and those two beautiful lights have still not returned to life.
What good is drawing more burning sighs from my breast,
what good is crying in vain, and lamenting,
unless I ensure that she for whom I burned
will be remembered for all eternity?
She, who possessed the beautiful features, eyes, and tresses
of the noble, ancient daughter of Leda,
no less than her name.
She who made of my heart continuous prey,
and was the sweet knot that bound me to this grateful burden [= body]
that I doubt will ever loosen, even in death.[5]

The daughter of Leda to whom the poet compares his lady is of course Helen of Troy. Helen, born from her mother's famous union with Zeus in the guise of a swan, has been a problematic example of female beauty since the time of the *Odyssey*. As Mihoko Suzuki has argued, Helen is "always present … but as a myth – either an emblem of doubleness or of duplicity on the one hand, or a trivial cardboard figure on the other – to be scapegoated and repudiated."[6] Helen was celebrated for her spectacular beauty, but she was also imagined and feared as a destabilizing force – a sower of discord between men. By the time her story made its way to medieval Italy, Dante had placed her in the circle of the lustful with the likes of Semiramis, Dido, and Cleopatra. For Renaissance readers and writers, the disruptive power of Helen's beauty was the root cause of the Trojan War. As Marlowe's damned Faustus would exclaim in the early seventeenth century, hers was "the face that launched a thousand ships."[7]

Venier's allusion to the beautiful but dangerous mythological Helen points to the ambivalence with which female beauty is represented in his own poetry. At the same time, the figure of Helen makes his lady's name explicit to the writers who were part of his inner circle and would have known that the woman Venier was mourning was Elena (i.e., Helen) Artusi. Artusi's premature death in 1550 was lamented by several poets with close ties to Domenico Venier.[8] Among these was a Venetian patrician poet named Giacomo Zane, a member of Federico Badoer's Accademia della Fama.[9] Because Zane and Venier had so many friends in common, it seems likely they knew one another. In any case, they had in common a poetic appreciation for the beauty of Elena Artusi.[10] In Zane's *canzone in morte* dedicated to Artusi, "Surgea nel mezzo de' tuoi prati, Amore, così chiara fontana" (A clear fountain flowed in the middle of your meadows, Love), he figures her as a "limpido, vago, lieto e fresco fonte" (clear, lovely, happy, and refreshing fountain).[11] Zane's poetic *senhal*, or signal, for Artusi plays on the phonetic similarities between her name and that of the mythical nymph Arethusa, who in Ovid's *Metamorphoses* was transformed into a fountain to escape her suitor Alpheus.[12] The seventeenth-century Venetian historian Alessandro Zilioli would later romanticize that Artusi's death was the cause of Zane's own premature demise: "Giacomo Zane, a noble Venetian patrician, sang sweetly of his loves, and in particular of the lasting love he had for lady Elena Artusi, a gentlewoman from Venice celebrated for her beauty. But this love turned out badly, since when Artusi died in the flower of her youth, the poet was so pained that just a short while afterwards, consumed by illness while he was still young, he too went to find her in the afterlife."[13]

Girolamo Molino, Venier's old friend, wrote a *canzone* on Artusi's death that figures her as the adored favourite of a group of bereaved lovers.[14] Written in the third-person plural (*noi*), the *canzone* is characterized by a sense of collective loss: "Lasso chi sia, che più d'amor n'invoglie / Con sì dolci desiri, / E ne insegni a languir lieti e contenti?" (Alas, who will incite us to love, with such sweet desires, and who will teach us to languish happily and contentedly?). Molino's commemoration of Artusi figures her as "un'angeletta pura, e 'n atti e in favella" (a pure little angel, in her deeds and in her words), echoing a sonnet by Venier on an "angioletta" (little angel) descended from heaven to earth and then called back to her rightful place at the moment of her death.[15] At the same time, the poem highlights Artusi's power to inspire love in the hearts of men:

Sola una piaga fe mille ferite:
Ch'ella mill'alme havea

Vaghe di se, ch'egual dolor portaro
Et con la sua fur le lor doglie unite;
Ma l'empia ben dovea
Per non darne a sentir piu lungo amaro,
Se n'affligea di paro,
Cosi finirne adun; che se gia tante
Fidi servi & amanti
Secon attendean d'honesto amor gioire,
Potean felici ancor seco morire.

With a single wound, [Death] created a thousand wounds,
since [Artusi] had a thousand souls
in love with her, who felt equal pain,
and with hers, their wounds were united.
But cruel death should have
wounded us all equally,
so that we wouldn't have to suffer so bitterly for so long,
and so that all of her faithful servants and lovers
who were hoping to delight in chaste love with her,
could have happily died with her again.[16]

Here Molino exploits the traditional associations of death with sexual climax to create a portrait of Artusi that emphasizes both her sensuality and the danger it represents for the men who love her.[17] Death is personified as a female archer – Cupid's cruel alter ego – who wounds Artusi with her arrow, simultaneously piercing the flesh of her (multiple) lovers. That the wound is an erotic one is underscored in the last two lines of the stanza, in which Molino imagines that Artusi's "faithful servants and lovers," no longer able to fulfil their hopes of enjoying "chaste love" with her on earth, hope to "die with her again."[18] In this context, the death Molino is imagining is clearly a sexual one.

That Venier and his friends used Petrarchan conceits and paradoxes to eulogize Artusi is not particularly surprising, since such love poetry was an important vehicle for any sixteenth-century poet's rise to fame. Through the stylized poems they sent to print, Venier and his group constructed the public face of the salon even as they negotiated their relationships with one another. But the veiled eroticism of Molino's *canzone* mourning Artusi's death hints at another aspect of Venier's literary production, one that operated in the liminal space between public and private: the creation and circulation of sexually explicit Venetian dialect poems in manuscript.

One of the richest examples of this phenomenon is a lengthy collection of dialect poems exchanged between Venier and his friend and fellow patrician Benetto Corner, whom we encountered briefly as Parabosco's defender of women in *I diporti*.[19] The dialect collection, now held in the British Library, is preserved in a sixteenth-century codex of 208 pages.[20] It contains 144 poems (89 by Venier and 55 by Corner) that chronicle the vicissitudes of the relationship between the two poets and a woman who turns out to be none other than Elena Artusi. In print, Artusi was figured as a remote *donna angelicata*, but in the dialect manuscript she is cast as a "puttana di natura" (whore by nature) and "cagnazza traditora" (traitorous bitch).

The exchange on Elena Artusi is only one example from the vast amount of dialect poetry preoccupied with women, sex, and love. These poems have received little sustained critical attention,[21] yet their influence on literary culture in Venice and beyond was considerable, as evidenced in manuscript collections all over Italy and as far afield as London and Paris. The flourishing print industry in mid-sixteenth-century Venice did much to foster the rich and vivacious intellectual exchange that took place there. But the advent of print only strengthened the already thriving tradition of manuscript circulation of poetry in Venice. As Harold Love has argued for seventeenth-century England, manuscript circulation in and of itself had the function of "bonding groups of like-minded individuals into a community, sect, or political faction, with the exchange of texts in manuscript serving to nourish a shared set of values and to enrich personal allegiances."[22] This was particularly true among poets who chose to write in Venetian dialect. The reason for this was not only linguistic but also thematic: the erotic themes and imagery with which dialect poetry had become associated were particularly congenial to the negotiation of relationships between men.

The Uses of Dialect

By the sixteenth century, literary Tuscan had become the language of mainstream love poetry, while Venetian and other regional vernaculars were increasingly associated with the low textual register of popularizing genres.[23] Ironically, it was a native Venetian, Pietro Bembo, who sealed the fate of his mother tongue. In his *Prose della volgar lingua* (1525), Bembo devoted an entire chapter to the superiority of what he called "Florentine" or "Tuscan" to Venetian. The first part of the argument, presented by Bembo's younger brother Carlo, hinges on the particular sound (*suono*) of each language: "Tuscan words have a better sound than Venetian words – sweet, lovelier, more fluent, and more vivid. And they are not apocopated [i.e., they do not omit the final syllable] and defective like most of ours, which never double any of the letters."[24] As the argument progresses, Carlo points to the dearth of famous Venetian writers, in contrast to the plethora of famous Florentines, as proof of the inferiority of Venetian to Tuscan. Near the end of the chapter, the scholar and cardinal Federigo Fregoso seconds Carlo's opinion, declaring that "the Florentine language is used not only by Venetian poets when they want to be read by everyone, but by all other Italians as well."[25]

Bembo's observation that Venetian writers write in literary Tuscan "when they want to be read by everyone" is worth exploring here, since it sheds light on the ways in which Venier crafted his public image. Domenico Venier's poems in literary Tuscan, published in multiple print anthologies, maintained and reinforced his impeccable image as a skilled poet and arbiter of literary taste. At the same time, Venier was lauded as a prolific writer of risqué Venetian poetry among the writers who were part of his inner circle and who read, copied, and circulated his dialect poems. When Venier "wanted to be read by everyone," then, he wrote in the Tuscanized Italian promoted by Bembo. When he had a specific readership in mind, he chose to write in Venetian, his mother tongue and the true vernacular of the Venetian Republic.

The love sonnets published by Venier and his cohort were intended for the wider public with access to printed books; their dialect poems were meant instead for a limited circle of trusted friends and colleagues with similar literary tastes. An obvious advantage to writing in Venetian dialect was that it implied a limited readership of Venetians only. Against the backdrop of the *questione della lingua*, the superiority of Venetian was a common if somewhat tongue-in-cheek motif in dialect poetry. One anonymous sixteenth-century dialect poet went so far as to declare that his poems were meant only for "venetiani naturali" (native Venetians).[26]

Domenico Venier's salon was frequented by a vibrant mix of writers from diverse geographic and social backgrounds; however, the group was dominated by Venetian aristocrats whose native spoken language was the Venetian dialect. Notwithstanding Bembo's marginalization of Venetian as a literary language, it was the primary idiom of spoken communication in all situations, from home and street to courts of law, and among all social classes.[27] In that sense, Venetian remained the language of power – in the sense of social capital – within the confines of the Venetian Republic. During the sixteenth century, *venexian* (the dialect spoken within Venice itself) held sway over the dialects of towns on the mainland (such as Padua, Vicenza, and Treviso) as the language of prestige. Speakers of *venexian* were immediately identified as privileged residents of Venice, the commercial and cultural capital of the region.

Among salon members, the Venetian dialect was a sort of secret code, a group language that signified belonging in both spoken and written exchanges. Tellingly, even non-Venetian writers participated in this aspect of the salon's literary activity. Among these was Aretino, who in a letter to Domenico Venier of 1549 – when the exchange on Elena Artusi would have been at its apex – praises the dialect poetry composed by Venier, Corner, and others in his circle:

> Just as the crudeness of food fit for peasants, oh magnificent signor Domenico, incites the appetite to gluttony in such a way that the delicacy of noble foods never could, so too, the coarseness of lowly subjects can sometimes sharpen the intellect with a certain eagerness for quickness that never shows itself in any kind of heroic material. Thus, in composing to divert the intellect in the Venetian language, style, and fashion, I praise to the highest degree the sonnets, *capitoli*, and *strambotti* that I have seen, read, and heard – composed by you, by others and by myself. Because within [these] there are some spirits that awaken the ears of those who hear them with outbursts of laughter – it's not possible to say more. Your brother Girolamo and my patron Corner are very skilled at (besides the excellence that appears in their most noble writings) the gallantry of such sweet jokes; and as I believe I may have already told you in writing, the other day I was overcome with ecstasy, so unexpected was the pleasure that completely invaded my sentiments upon hearing a poem on *buli* (*"un non so che bulesco in canzone"*) recited to me by one of the above-mentioned gentlemen in a boat.[28]

Aretino's suggestion that he himself has written in the "Venetian fashion" is tantalizing – is he implying that he wrote in dialect, or simply that he wrote in the Venetian style? – but too vague to take as proof of his direct participation in Venetian poetic exchange. That said, it does seem relevant that so many of the dialect poems penned by Domenico Venier and his circle are either *sonetti caudati* or *capitoli* – forms that Aretino wittily deployed as vehicles of pornography (in the *sonetti lussuriosi*) or satire. While both of these poetic forms have a long history before Aretino, the notoriety that Aretino acquired through their use would not have been lost on Domenico Venier, who must have had the *sonetti lussuriosi* in mind as he composed his own pornographic poems.

Aretino's account of the recitation of a "non so che bulesco in canzone" (a poem on the subject of *buli*, or braggarts) is suggestive for several reasons. First, the subject of the poem recalls a poem by Benetto Corner – Domenico Venier's interlocutor in the exchange on Elena Artusi – eventually published as *L'arcibravo veneziano* (The Venetian *arcibravo*, or superthug), which will be discussed below. What's more, Aretino's description of the performance itself provides us with a likely context in which Venetian dialect poetry was recited aloud for the amusement of groups of literary men.

The playful and irreverent salutation with which Aretino closes the letter, "vi bascio il seder con le mani" (I kiss your bottom along with your hands), offers an important clue as to how to read the letter. That Aretino should express such familiarity with his Venetian patron in the same letter in which he discusses the dialect poems cannot be mere coincidence. As Aretino suggests here, part of the pay-off of communicating in a lower register is the figurative intimacy it creates between writers and readers. The same can be said of the erotic and often graphic sexuality that by the sixteenth century was associated with Venetian dialect poetry. In that sense, Venetian dialect – and the erotic and rustic themes that had become associated with it – was a particularly congenial medium for writers seeking to solidify their relationships with members of the Venetian patriciate.

Suggestively, even some writers who were not native Venetians sometimes wrote in Venetian dialect. One of these was Anton Giacomo Corso, a poet originally from Ancona.[29] Earlier we saw how Corso's *capitolo* addressed to Domenico Venier in 1548 publicized the bourgeois writer's connections to the powerful Venetian patrician and the group of elite writers who frequented the salon. The same poem contains evidence that Corso wrote in Venetian dialect. He composed the *capitolo* in question during an extended absence from Venice, while he was a guest at a villa in the Paduan countryside. After criticizing, at one extreme, those "savi mezzi matti" (half-crazy intellectuals) who do nothing but read, and at the other, those men "che spendon tutt' i loro giorni in diletto" (who spend each day in the pursuit of pleasure), Corso praises Venier and his friend Federico Badoer as examples of literary men who have found a middle ground and live a balanced life. Corso's hyperbolic praise of Venier, conventional among writers of the time, is reinforced by a strategy of linguistic appropriation. When he left Venice for the villa, Corso worried that he would be surrounded by strangers and forced to spend his days writing only love poetry. While describing his anxiety at leaving his literary community in Venice behind, the poet suddenly switches from Tuscanized Italian to Venetian:

Senza ch'io m'affatichi in raccontare
tutti i meriti suoi, io dico infine
che 'l star fra buon compagni è un dolce stare.
Io pensava (per Dio) fra margemine
e pignole e verdici e simil uve,
in queste bande far la mala fine,
e fra gente da mi non conosue
passar i zorni in gran malanconia
con sier Apollo, e le Muzze fottue.
In Vinesia ho lassà, savè, la fia,
che vù savè, che pur me dava affanno,
benchè alla fè me se de cao insia.

Without troubling myself to recount
all of your merits, I'll sum up by saying
that being among good friends is a sweet way to be.
I thought [by God], that things would not end well for me
in these parts, among *marzemino*
and *pignolo*, and *verdicchio* and other such grapes,
and that, among strangers,
I would spend my days in deep melancholy
with Mister Apollo and the fucked Muses.
In Venice, you know, I left my girl behind,
and, as you know, that pained me,
even though, in truth, she is out of my mind [now].[30]

Corso's use of dialect in a poem addressed to his Venetian patrician patron is significant for several reasons. Through his playful appropriation of the Venetian vernacular, Corso creates a sense of intimacy and familiarity with Venier. Quite literally, he speaks Venier's language. Corso is not Venetian, but he demonstrates his membership in the fraternity of discourse by using the Venetian language, which for the Venier group functioned as a sort of insiders' code. This strategy of linguistic camaraderie is bolstered by thematic camaraderie: the section of Corso's poem that is in Venetian makes reference to the "fia" (girl) he has abandoned in Venice; this echoes the theme of amorous distress often adopted by Venier and others in their dialect poetry. Furthermore, the lady muses are "fucked" rather than elegant inspirers of conventional verse. As we shall see, the trope of the "fucked" woman is commonplace in the dialect poetry penned by Venier and his cohort. Finally, the twice-repeated phrase "as you know," addressed to Venier, emphasizes the friendship between the two poets by implying that Venier is privy to Corso's secrets.

Another non-Venetian writer in Domenico Venier's orbit who may have participated in these sorts of exchanges was Parabosco. The first piece of evidence regarding Parabosco's connections to dialect poetry is a short madrigal found in a manuscript collection of Venetian poetry now held in the Biblioteca Nazionale Marciana. This madrigal, written in the voice of a lover lamenting the cruelty of his beloved (evidently a courtesan) who has requested compensation for her services, is preceded by a rubric that reads "Del Parabosco" (By Parabosco):

> Madona, a un tempo, mi ve ho soportao
> e sì di cuor ve ho amao,
> che alegramente tuto el tempo ho perso.
> Ma xè forza che 'l diga
> che vu se, più crudel che non xè un orsa
> dopo che volè tuorme anche la borsa.
> Questa è quella fadiga
> che tuti i afari intriga,
> e in tel regno d'amor
> non ghe de questo el più crudel dolor.

> My lady, I once put up with you,
> and loved you so with all my heart,
> that I happily wasted all of my time on you.
> Now, however, I must say

that you are crueller than a she-bear,
since you want to take even my purse from me.
This is that tiresome thing
that makes all such business complicated,
and in the empire of love,
there is no pain more cruel than this one.[31]

Although it would be very easy to take the copyist's identification at face value and assume that it was indeed Parabosco who wrote "Madona a un tempo," we should be cautious about jumping to such a conclusion. In fact the dialect madrigal is essentially a translation of "Donna, un tempo di voi l'ira soffersi," a madrigal in literary Tuscan that Parabosco first published in his *Primo libro* in 1551:

Donna, un tempo di voi l'ira soffersi
senza dolermi mai,
e sì di cuor v'amai,
che lietissimamente il tempo persi.
Ma or forza è ch'io dica
Che siate più crudel che tigre od orsa,
che straziar mi volete anco la borsa.
Non vo' questa fatica,
ch'io non potrei soffrire
così acerbo martire,
che nel suo regno Amore
non ha fra tante sue pena maggiore.

Lady, I used to suffer your anger
without ever complaining,
and I loved you so deeply,
that I happily wasted all of my time on you.
But now I must say
that you are crueller than a tiger or a she-bear,
since you want to take even my purse from me.
I don't want this burden,
since I couldn't take
such cruel torment –
in his entire reign, Love
does not have a greater punishment.[32]

The content of the Tuscan version has been rendered faithfully by the author of the Venetian madrigal, although the Venetian version is shorter – ten lines to the Tuscan's twelve. The Venetian poet has repeated the *orsa/borsa* rhyme from the Italian version – an important pairing that emphasizes the mercenary nature of Parabosco's courtesan lover. Did Parabosco translate his own madrigal into Venetian, as at least one scholar has assumed?[33] Perhaps he did, but given the tendency among poets writing in Venetian, pavano, and other regional dialects to translate Tuscan poetry into their own vernacular, the poem may be a translation by someone else of Parabosco's original.

A ready example of this kind of translation can be found in Domenico Venier's famous sonnet in Italian, "Non punse, arse, o legò, stral, fiamma, o laccio" (No arrow, flame, or tie ever pierced, burned, or bound).[34] This sonnet was rewritten in pavano (a dialect associated with the Paduan countryside and most famously employed by the playwright Angelo Beolco, also known as "il Ruzante") by Marco Thiene – a noble poet from Vicenza – not once, but twice.[35] Whether "Madona a un tempo" was composed by Parabosco himself or by one of his Venetian friends, its presence in the Marciana manuscript suggests that Parabosco's poetry was circulating among dialect poets.

Parabosco was one of several members of Venier's salon who had ties to Andrea Calmo (1510–1570), a prolific Venetian-born actor and writer of poems, letters, and comedies in Venetian dialect. While it seems unlikely that Calmo was a regular visitor to Ca' Venier, literary sources suggest he was in contact with many of the writers and theorists in Venier's circle. His dialect letters, the *Piacevoli et ingeniosi discorsi* (1547–60), include missives to Aretino and Parabosco as well as to Domenico Venier's brother Francesco and his friends Federico Badoer and Lodovico Dolce. Calmo's collection of Venetian poems, *Le bizzarre, faconde et ingegnose rime pescatorie*, was first published in 1553. The volume includes a sonnet addressed to Parabosco in which the poet recounts his symptoms of lovesickness and requests his friend's advice: "Parabosco mio bello, inzucaròo, / déme un coseio, dolce frar e fio, / perch'ho 'l cervello un puoco descusìo, / vu che havé l'intelletto ben fermào" (My dear Parabosco, sweet as sugar, give me some advice, my sweet brother and boy, because my brain is coming apart at the seams; oh you with your firm intellect).[36]

Calmo's sonnet, like many of those exchanged between Venier and his friends, recalls the tradition of the *tenzone*, a form of poetic correspondence and debate inherited from early Provencal poets and in the Italian tradition used most famously by Dante in an exchange with Forese

Donati. In these exchanges, the first author proposed the subject of the debate and set the rhyme scheme, and the second author responded in like rhyme. Calmo's sonnet seems designed to elicit a response: the exhortation "déme un conseio" (give me some advice) in the first quatrain is echoed in the last line, in which the poet pleads "aiuteme in sti gran accidenti!" (help me with these unfortunate events!). Although a response by Parabosco has not turned up, tradition would have dictated that he respond to Calmo's challenge. In any case, Calmo's address of letters and poems to non-Venetian writers like Parabosco and Aretino provides us with important evidence as to the circulation of Venetian poetry at mid-century. Even if Parabosco and Aretino did not write in Venetian, they certainly read it.

Parabosco's participation in exchanges of Venetian poetry, at least as a reader, is confirmed by still another sonnet in dialect, ignored by previous scholars (extant in a manuscript held at the Biblioteca Marciana of Venice). Here, the unidentified poet praises Parabosco for his poetic skill, exalting him as a "gran 'huomo" (great man) and "gran poeta" (great poet):

Pota son deventao una zuetta
al sangue de la Verzene Maria
a veder l'arte, e la filosofia
che dentro a i vostri versi havè restretta.
Vu se un gran'huomo, vu se un gran poeta
E ve dirò, no per coionaria,
no credo che sia zoia d'hostaria
ch'al vostro gran cervello non fosse stretta.
Ma quanto atorno i banchi si ha trovao
lauro sto nadal dal citronato
no sarave bastante al vostro cao.
Parabosco da ben, notè sto tratto:
no studiè così che m'ho pensao
ch'un zorno vu possè deventar matto.

I have become an admirer of yours,
I swear on the blood of the Virgin Mary,
upon seeing the art and the philosophy
that you have contained in your verse.
You are a great man and a great poet
and, I tell you – I'm not kidding –
that I don't believe that there are any joys of the tavern

that don't adorn that great brain of yours.
And even all the laurel leaves
found in the stalls this Christmas
would not be enough to encircle your head.
Parabosco, old chum, pay attention to this bit:
don't keep studying like this, because if you do,
I think one day you might go mad.[37]

The hyperbolic encomium to Parabosco in this sonnet recalls the tradition of paired sonnet exchanges in literary Tuscan that were standard among sixteenth-century poets and a privileged form in Venier's circle. A typical example of this phenomenon can be found in the many "proposte e risposte" (challenges and responses) exchanged between Venier and various friends and contemporaries in the higher register of Tuscan.[38] Collected and published as a group by Pierantonio Serassi in 1751 as an appendix to Venier's *Rime*, these paired sonnet exchanges reveal the ways in which sixteenth-century poets used strategies of praise to forge bonds of friendship and patronage.

In fact, the Marciana manuscript mentioned above also contains a series of six dialect sonnets (all with identical rhyme scheme) exchanged between two unidentified poets.[39] Like the sonnet addressed to Parabosco, the exchange is based on the conceit of encomiastic praise. Even as they congratulate each other for their poetic skill (each supplementing his praise of his interlocutor with a conventional posture of self-deprecation), the two poets are engaged in a playful battle of one-upmanship.

Ogni saor: The Flavours of Dialect

An important advantage to writing in dialect was that it offered freedom to write on themes perceived as unconventional or inappropriate. In part, this feeling of freedom must have been a reaction to Bembo's linguistic principle of *decoro* (propriety), which required that literary style be concordant with its subject. Dialect poets often celebrated the poetic licence accorded them when they wrote in Venetian, especially on the subject of love. Maffio Venier (Lorenzo's son and thus Domenico's nephew) argued that writing in Tuscan limited his subject matter to "Amor" – Love, in the stylized sense. Venetian, by contrast, was a medium with "ogni saor" – literally, every flavour – that was more appropriate for the openly erotic themes favoured by Domenico Venier and his circle. This is not to say that members of Venier's group did not deal with sexuality in their works written in literary Italian. Aretino, for example, made a career of it, as did his disciple Lorenzo Venier. But for some high-profile Venetian patricians like Domenico Venier, the very marginality of dialect offered freedom from the conventions of mainstream literature.

As Franco Brevini has argued, Bembo's elite linguistic model was particularly attractive to the "middle class of humanists" who adopted and defended it fiercely in their search for social prestige and status.[40] A prime example is the *poligrafo* Lodovico Dolce, a friend and follower of Domenico Venier who was born into the *cittadino* rather than the patrician class.[41] In the preface to his comedy *Il Ruffiano* (1552), Dolce informs his audience that they will not hear any Venetian, which he defines as "da buffoni" – for buffoons. A few years earlier, Dolce had enthusiastically reiterated Bembo's linguistic ideology in his own literary treatise, *Osservationi della volgar lingua*. Dolce's treatise praises Venier and several other aristocratic Venetian poets for perfecting their skills in Tuscan, the proper literary language.

Dolce, then, was careful not to associate himself (at least in public) with the lowly connotations of dialect literature. But for Venetian patricians like Domenico Venier and Benetto Corner, writing in dialect upheld social status rather than undermining it. The same can be said for the subjects and themes that had become associated with dialect poetry, which often played on parodies of the lower-status world. We might call one strain of dialect poetry "poesia alla bulesca" because of its thematic affinities to the comedies produced in Venice earlier in the century. Like the comedies before them, *bulesca* poems featured *buli* (also known as *bravi*), Venetian thugs-for-hire who wandered the streets looking for trouble. One of the best-known examples of this type was penned by Benetto Corner, Venier's interlocutor in the dialect exchange on Elena Artusi. Corner's poem "Potta mo posso pur rengraziar Dio" (Damn, now I can surely give thanks to God) features a character known as the *arcibravo*, or superthug. It appears in at least three different manuscript copies, and during the sixteenth century it was published anonymously in an undated pamphlet titled *Cinquanta stanze de Arcibrauo venetiano, ne le quali egli narra cose oltra modo terribili et grandi, non mai più intese, della sua destrezza, gagliardia, et fatti ...* (Fifty stanzas of the Venetian *arcibravo*, in which he recounts things extraordinarily terrible and great, and never heard before, regarding his skill, bravery, and deeds).[42]

In the form of a monologue in octaves, the poem features a Venetian braggart who boasts about his superhuman strength and his reputation as a violent bully, claiming that "gh'è nessun ch'osa vardarme in fazza; / tuti se caga soto de paura" (nobody dares to look me in the eye, everyone shits on themselves for fear of me). He sleeps on a cushion made from the beards and hair of his victims, which he has torn from their heads with his bare hands:

> Tra l'altre cose, e' dormo s'un stramazzo
> ch'è tuto pien de barbe e de cavei
> ch'ho tirà o dal cao, zò dal mostazzo
> a pì d'un milion con sti mie dei;
> e ho sì forte man, sì forte brazzo
> che co un pugno frantumo i cervei;
> dar, po, d'un pè in tel cul a qual che sia
> tel betterò da qua fin in Sorìa.

> Among other things, I sleep on a mattress
> that's all full of beards and hair
> that I have ripped from the head or the face
> of more than a million men with these fingers of mine.
> And I have such strong hands and such strong arms
> that with one punch I shatter people's brains.
> And if I were to kick someone in the ass,
> I would throw him from here to Syria.[43]

The braggart's self-aggrandizing narration continues for forty-four octaves, during which he recounts various far-fetched anecdotes. Many of his tales have a particularly Venetian flavour: he claims that during the *caccia al toro* (running of the bulls) through the *calli* of Venice, he grabbed a furious bull by its horns and spun it around as if it were a child's toy; and that after he was insulted by a fish vendor in the Rialto market, he drowned the poor man by spitting on him.[44] In the final octave, the *arcibravo* takes leave of his listeners, a device that emphasizes the orality of the poem: "mo vago via, no ve metè in scatura, / che no voi che morì mo de paura" (I'm leaving now, don't be frightened, since I don't want you to die of fear).[45]

Like other *bulesca* characters, Corner's *arcibravo* is hyperbolically masculine – he brandishes his sword, spits and swears, and recounts far-fetched tales of his superhuman strength. The violent, crass thugs featured here reflect the fascination among Venetian nobles with the underbelly of Venetian society; they also make a striking contrast with the cultured, refined gentlemen exalted in early modern comportment literature like Castiglione's *Book of the Courtier*. On the one hand, poems featuring such low-life characters must have been amusing to Venier and his circle because they represented difference – the coarse, unmodulated speech and actions of the *arcibravo* demonstrated the opposite of the refined decorum to which a Venetian aristocrat should aspire. On the other, writing in the hyperbolic masculine voice of the *arcibravo* would have been exciting to young nobles like Corner, whose speech and actions were expected to conform to Venetian ideals of aristocratic refinement.

"Bella istoria": Helena Artusi, Dialect Whore

The feminine incarnation of the superthug is the sexually voracious whore, a character type we first encountered in the invectives directed against Venetian courtesans penned by Lorenzo Venier. The figure of the whore dominates sixteenth-century Venetian dialect poetry on women, whether she is evoked literally or through the whorish behaviour of the female protagonist/love object. On the surface, the dialect whore appears to be an inverted parody of the unattainable, chaste beloved of the mainstream love lyric. But the binary opposition of angel and whore, here as elsewhere, is a reductive lens through which to read these texts. A more fertile way of thinking about them is to notice instead the ways in which they exploit the tensions between these two poles.

We saw earlier how Domenico Venier experimented with these paradoxes on a more subtle level in his Tuscan love poems for Artusi – through, among other things, casting her as a Renaissance Helen of Troy. Similar tensions are at work in the dialect manuscript, but in the lower register of dialect poetry these tensions are negotiated explicitly through the trope of the whore and her sexual availability. This quality is emphasized in the sonnet that opens the British Library collection, from Venier "a i Lettori" (to the readers). Here the poet boasts that while he has "za chiavà" (already screwed) Artusi, his friend Corner "adesso la chiava" (is screwing her now). The sonnet also articulates the fact that the whore trope is just that, since Venier explains that the poets accuse her of being a whore when they are angry with her, while when they are "in control" of their emotions, they "pardon her":

Questo si se un bel libro, che tratta
d' una donna, c' ha nome Helena Artusa,
fatto in sta nostra lengua, che se usa,

da do zoveni bravi a posta fatta,
Un d'essi haveva za chiavà sta matta:
l'altro adesso la chiava; ora i l' accusa,
che l' è massa puttana: hora i la scusa;
cussi co la ghe monta, o co i se catta.
Un ha nome Domenego, e Benetto
l'altro. Questo si se da ca Corner,
l'altro è da ca Venier, ch' è gramo in letto.
Lezello, c'haverè gran apiaser,
e se ghe trovessè qualche deffetto,
sappiè, ch'i no g'ha messo altro pensier.

This is a beautiful book about
a lady whose name is Helena Artusa,
written in our language, that we use,
and crafted by two fine young men.
One of them has already screwed this madwoman,
the other is screwing her now. Sometimes they accuse her
of being a consummate whore, and sometimes they pardon her,
depending on whether they are angry with her, or in control of themselves.
One is named Domenico, and Benetto
is the other; this one is from the house of Corner,
while the other is from the house of Venier, and is sick in bed.
Read it, because it will bring you great pleasure.
And if you should find a few defects in it,
you should know that they don't really care.[46]

The description of Venier as "sick in bed" suggests that the two poets probably began their exchange sometime after about 1546, when Venier's health declined and he lost the use of his legs. Since the collection is presented as a diary of the poets' daily interactions with Artusi, we can assume that the poems were composed while she was still alive; the exchange can be dated, then, to the period between 1546 and 1550. The only trace of Artusi in the archives records that her death, which occurred on 6 September 1550 in the Venetian parish of San Pantalon due to an unspecified illness, "za diesi giorni amalà" (after having been sick for ten days).[47] The death record also confirms several details of Artusi's lived life that appear in the dialect poems, including the fact that she was married to a man named Francesco Novello, who hailed from Castelfranco. The couple lived in the parish of San Marcuola for a time before moving across town to San Pantalon, where they were living at the time of her death.

As the fictive chronology of the dialect exchange unfolds, we learn that it was Venier who initiated the poetic dialogue with Corner. When he learned of Corner's relationship with his ex-lover, he proposed to his friend that they make her the centrepiece of a collaborative project. Each time Corner saw Artusi, he was to write Venier a poem recounting the details:

> O che bel rasonar
> Vogio, che femo insieme el primo di;
> Mi riderò de vù, e vù de mi;
> E tutti do de chi
> N'haverà dà materia de sta cossa;
> Morsù vegnì pi presto, che se possa;
> Che mi vago in angossa,
> Che me disè la cossa co l'andò
> Ponto per ponto, e giusto co la fò.

> Oh, what a lovely conversation
> I want us to have that first day.
> I will laugh at you, and you at me;
> and both of us will laugh at
> the people who have given us our material;
> now, come as quickly as you are able,
> because I am in agony
> to hear exactly how things went –
> point by point, exactly as it happened.[48]

If we are to believe Domenico Venier, he met Artusi before he lost the use of his legs, and shortly thereafter the two of them began a romantic relationship. Their meeting, along with the early days of their affair, is the subject of Venier's nostalgic *capitolo* addressed to "Madonna Helena":

> Vustu, mo, che te diga, Helena, fia,
> per dirte a la desmestega ogni cossa,
> co feva avanti la mia malattia?
> Ch'al primo aspetto andì quasi in angossa,
> co t'intrassi in mezzado, e me n'accorsi,

che anca ti ti diventassi rossa.
Me tremava la man, co te la porsi,
e so ben mi che ti te n'accorzessi,
e se n'accorse anca to mare forsi.
Per tante donne, ohimè, ti no podessi
basarme, nè mi ti per sto rispetto,
mo che ciera, ohimè Dio, che ti me fessi!
Ciera da farme mo levar de letto,
san de le gambe e senza mal a i piè,
mo da resuscitarme in caeletto!

Do you want me to tell you, Helena, my girl,
everything, without any pretence,
and how it was before my illness?
That, at the first sight of you, I was almost overcome with anguish
when you came into the mezzanine, and I noticed
that you, too, were blushing.
My hand was trembling as I offered it to you,
and I'm certain that you noticed,
and maybe your mother noticed, too.
Alas, you were surrounded by so many women that you couldn't kiss me,
and I couldn't kiss you, for the same reason.
But what an expression – oh God! – you showed me.
An expression that could make me get out of bed right now,
heal my legs, and take away the pain in my feet,
or even breathe new life into me in heaven![49]

Venier's *capitolo* is modelled on the conventional theme of "innamo-
ramento" – the life-changing moment when the poet fell in love with
his lady. Here, the dialect poet's trembling hand at the sight of Helena
recalls Dante's trembling heart at the first sight of Beatrice in the *Vita
nuova*. The reference to Dante is reinforced by the description of Helena
among "tante donne" (so many women), which recalls another iconic
moment in the *Vita nuova*. As Dante recounts, the first time Beatrice
greeted him she was walking down a street somewhere in Florence, "in
mezzo a due gentili donne, le quali erano di più lunga etade" (between
two noble ladies, who were older than she).[50] But the references to Dante
are juxtaposed with the nostalgic eroticism of the middle section of the
capitolo. Here Venier recalls the first time he kissed Helena ("la prima
volta siando nu do soli, / che ve basì zaffandove da drio" [the first time

we were alone, that I kissed you, grabbing you from behind]), as well as the rumpled sheets on the bed after they made love ("quel piegar de tovaglioli").[51] But the poem's tone changes from nostalgia to comedy when Venier describes Helena's gluttonous husband, for whom he claims to have purchased food in exchange for time alone with Helena: "Perché saveva ben mi, dal mio canto, / che sto manzar non ghe farave pro / e che 'l me zoverave a mi altratanto" (Because I knew well, from my point of view, that this food would not do him any favours, and that it would be just as beneficial to me).[52]

Direct evidence that Elena Artusi was a prostitute by trade has not surfaced, despite the many allusions to the contrary in the dialect poems. According to a law passed by the Venetian Senate in 1543, as a married woman who lived under her husband's roof, Artusi would not have been considered a prostitute in the legal sense.[53] But during this time period, many courtesans and higher-level prostitutes married and flouted this and other laws intended to regulate their behaviour; Artusi may or may not have been one of them.[54] Whatever the truth about Artusi's lived life, she is represented as hyperbolically promiscuous in the manuscript. This, we recall, is the characteristic that defines the fictional whore as she is imagined by those who write about her: she is available to everyone.

This quality is featured in one of Venier's sonnets in dialogue form featuring Helena, her *massera* (a female servant), and a prospective *moroso* (lover). As the sonnet opens, the lover arrives expecting to spend the night with Helena, only to be told by the maidservant that her mistress is already occupied upstairs with a nobleman named Moresini – probably the same man who later in the exchange is described by Venier as competing with Corner for Helena's attentions.[55] In the dialogue sonnet, the competition between Artusi's two lovers is dramatized; with the servant acting as go-between, the lover manages to talk Helen into a quickie in the storeroom before she goes back upstairs:

MA[SSERA]: Chi batte? MO[ROSO]: Avri, son mi! MA[SSERA]: An, vu sé vu?
MO[ROSO]: Sì, tira! MA[SSERA]. Mo. MO[ROSO]: Che mo? Tira, sti vuol.
MA[SSERA]: Mo missier per sta sera no se puol;

Chel Moresini ghe se vegnù lù
[...]
MA[SSERA]: Horsù ve tiro, aspettè la de zò.

Madonna se no so
Chi, che ve vuol mostrar un lavorier;
Andè, che starò mi quà con missier:
Vardè, sel podè hauer;
Madonna, aldì, no vel lassè scampar;
Andè da basso, chel ve sta a spettar.
HE[LENA]: Basta so zo, che far;

Horsù e uago. Mo[ROSO]: speranza morsù,
Daspuo chel Moresini se de sù,
E chel dorme con vù
Sta notte; andemo nu quà in sto mezzà,
Si cara fia, in t'un tratto se fà;
Massime mi, ti sà.
HE[LENA]: Oh dio. Mo[ROSO]: Mo presto. HE[LENA]: Andemo horssu, serrè.
Mo[ROSO]: Che feu? No perdè tempo, alzè. HE[LENA]: Mettè.

SERVANT GIRL: Who's there?
LOVER: Open up, it's me!
SERVANT GIRL: Ah, is it really you?
LOVER: Yes, let me in!
SERVANT GIRL: Now …
LOVER: What do you mean, now? Let me in, please!
SERVANT GIRL: But sir, this evening won't work. Signor Moresini is already
   here.
[…]
SERVANT GIRL [TO THE LOVER]: All right, I'll let you in. Wait down there.
[To HELENA]: My lady, there is a man here, I'm not sure who, who wants to
   show you something. Go, and I'll stay with his lordship. Look, my lady,
   if you can manage it, don't let him escape! Go downstairs, he's waiting
   for you.
HELENA: That's enough, I know what to do! I'm going.
LOVER: My love, since Moresini is upstairs, and he is sleeping with you
   tonight, let's go into the storeroom together. Come on, dearest, it will just
   take a minute! No longer than that, you know!
HELENA: Oh, God! Lover: Come on, hurry up!
HELENA: Let's go, now! Lock the door!
LOVER: What are you doing? Don't waste time, pull up your skirts!
HELENA: Put it in.[56]

In both form and plot scenario, Venier's poem recalls the *bulesca* comedies – also written in dialect – of the first few decades of the sixteenth century. Here Artusi is cast as a wily prostitute intent on bedding as many men as possible in one night. The presence of the female servant/procuress, a stock character in representations of prostitutes both literary and visual, reinforces the presentation of Artusi as a *bulesca*-style heroine. Artusi is figured as a whore more concretely in another sonnet: Venier suggests that Helena's husband, referred to here as "il dottor," was serving as her pimp:

Quel, che vù fe Madonna, el feu da vù?
O 'l feu, perche ve l'ordena el dottor?
Che se fa per la terra un gran remor,
Chi ghe n'habbia pi colpa o vù, o lù.
Chi dise, che l'è esso, c'ha vogiù,
Che divente puttana per amor,
che gh'avanzè d'i soldi, e del so honor,
che'l no s'incura esser becco fottù.
Chi dise, che lu se goffo, minchion;
E si no sa, che vù ve fè chiavar;
Mo che vù 'l fe da vù, che'l ve sa bon.
Talche de lu se sente a mormorar,
O'l non ha occhi in testa, l'è poltron,
Se'l non lo vede; o, che'l v'el fazza far.
De vù s'alde a zanzar,
ch'o se puttana de natura; o, che
Se troppo bona; el prima, se vù'l fè,
Perche vù ghe n'habbiè
Vogia; el segondo, se vù'l fe per lù,
che v'habbia fatto farlo, o messa su.
Aldine mi mo vù
Che ve dirò l'opinion, che ho;
Quel, che mi credo, e quasi quel, che so;
Se causa tutti do
No un solo de vù; lù, c'ha vesto
Per vadagnar a vù farve far questo;
E vù, che v'ha piasesto
Sempre ste cosse; e che senza sto mezo
Havessè fatto quel medemo, o pezo.

Do you do it of your own accord, my lady?
Or do you do it at the doctor's orders?
Because there is much gossip in the city
As to whether he, or you, is to blame.
Some say that he wanted you
To become a whore for love
and that you give him the money,
and he doesn't care about honour,
or being made a cuckold.
Others say that he is such a fool
that he doesn't know that you let yourself be screwed;
or else that he knows very well what you do when you are alone.
One hears whispers
that either he doesn't have eyes in his head, and he is stupid
if he doesn't see it, or, that he is forcing you.
As far as you are concerned, the gossip is
that either you are a whore by nature, or that
you are too good to him. In the first case, they say
that you do it because you want to,
and in the second, that you do it for him,
since he has made you do it, or put you up to it
You listen to me now,
and I'll tell you my own opinion:
what I believe, and what
I am almost certain of,
Is that both of you are to be blamed,
and not just one of you.
He, because in order to earn a profit
he makes you do this.
And you, because you have always liked
these sorts of things, and even without him as your go-between,
you would have done the same thing, or worse.[57]

Here Venier deploys the time-honoured trope of the inherent sex-ual appetite of the whore in his representation of Artusi as a "puttana di natura." His insinuations that Artusi's husband may have served as her pimp, whether or not they are based in reality, bring to mind a case featuring a married prostitute brought to light by Guido Rug-giero.[58] During the Carnival season of 1571, a woman named Letizia

Parisola was threatened at knifepoint by armed thugs in the service of a young patrician named Giacomo Zorzi. The proceedings of the trial reveal that Zorzi attacked Parisola in a fit of jealousy because she had refused to come out with him that night, choosing instead to spend the evening in the company of four other admirers. They also reveal that Parisola had been Zorzi's mistress and that her husband, a man of non-noble status, probably arranged her encounters with Zorzi and other rich noblemen. The power dynamic at work here – a lower-class woman who becomes a desired commodity of her patrician admirers – is echoed in the poems on Helena Artusi, in which both Venier and Corner continously lament the fact that Helena is pursued by so many other men.

Whatever the truth about Artusi's lived life, the poems penned by Corner and Venier target her through a paradox that recalls Venetian literary responses to identified courtesans, who were alternately idolized and denigrated. The manuscript collection weaves together encomiastic verse exalting Artusi's virtue and beauty with representations of her as a mercenary, sexually voracious whore willing to sell her body and soul for a new dress. Crucially, as we saw earlier, the poets themselves declare from the beginning that how they figure Artusi depends not on her behaviour, but on their own emotional states. In a *capitolo* chastising Helena for her promiscuity, Corner remarks sarcastically that of course she cannot restrain herself, since this characteristic runs in the family: "Se chi de gatta nasce sorze pia, / habbiando vostra mare, ch'è puttana, / che doveu mo far vù, che se so fia? / … Perché questi deffetti va per razza / a muo de le cavalle, e de le vacche, / e una puttana fa una puttanazza. " (If those born from female cats always catch mice, and you have a whore for a mother, what else would you, her daughter, do? … Because these vices are hereditary – just as with mares and cows, a whore begets a whore).[59]

The poem denouncing Helena as morally corrupt by nature is followed immediately by a pair of sonnets praising her beauty and her flowing golden hair. In form and rhyme scheme, both sonnets adhere to Petrarchan conventions, which is unusual in this exchange, in which most of the sonnets are of the *sonetto caudato* type more typical of burlesque verse. Here, the time-honoured commonplaces of female beauty drawn from the love poetry tradition (with a Venetian twist) are mixed in with earthy sexual innuendos. In the first sonnet, the poet compares Helena, who is drying her hair on her balcony as he passes by in his gondola, to the rising sun. As the poem continues, she morphs into a sensual siren whose come-hither expression lures the poet's gaze and incites his lust:

> Madonna quando che vu gieri fuora
> De la fenestra in mostra cussi brava,
> Mi alhora in barca de la via passava,
> E me parse de veder l'Aurora.
> Vù me vardassi cagna traditora,
> Quando che la massera ve chiamava;
> Con una certa ciera, che criava
> Da mille mia lontan, vien qua in malhora.
> Con quel saor e me n'anditti via,
> E co fu a casa, e fisi, che la man
> Dette un gran spasso a la mia fantasia.
> Sta purgason me tegnerà mo san,
> Fin, che me vegna un'altra malattia;
> Cussi la passarò d'ancuo in doman.

> My lady, when you leaned out the window,
> so beautifully on display,
> it seemed to me, passing by in my gondola,
> as if I were seeing the Dawn herself.
> You looked at me – you traitorous bitch! –
> until the maidservant called you inside,
> with a certain expression, that cried out,
> even from thousands of miles away, "Come here, damn it!"
> With that tasty thought, I went away,
> and when I got home, I used my hand
> to amuse myself with my fantasy.
> This purge will keep me healthy,
> at least until I get sick again,
> and so that's how I'll spend today and tomorrow.[60]

Corner figures his desire for Artusi, and the masturbation that follows, as sickness. In the low register of Venetian dialect the allusion to sexual desire as something unhealthy that the poet must eliminate through what he figures as "purging" reads as satire. Yet the persistence of this trope reveals a deeper preoccupation with the importance of maintaining control over the passions of the body, a principle that loomed large in the minds of early modern men. The trope of love-sickness continues into the next sonnet, where the poet casts Artusi as a *dolce stil novo*–inspired heroine whose golden hair makes him feel reborn. But the rebirth the poet alludes to comes from sexual climax. If Petrarch spoke of his sexual desire for Laura in veiled metaphors, here Corner transposes the conventional conceit of the lady who inspires her lover to commune with the divine down into the lower register of dialect, where the masturbatory fantasy is stripped of its blanket of poetic refinements:

Cappe mo che cavei mostravi al Sol?
Mo che testa se quella de velluo?
A dirve 'l vero mi son renassuo,
E squasio squasio deventà un storuol.
Mo v[u] ste megio cussi senza fazzuol;
E senza drezze, co v'ho vista ancuo,
col vostra cao d'oro cussi nuo;
Che quando v[u] vel conzè pi, che se puol
Mi n'ho vardà, che sia i zorni santi,
Che, co v'ho vista, m'ho cussi infiammao,
Che bia vù, co ve vegno dananti.
Ve priego, ch'ogni di ve lavè 'l cao.
Perche a sto muodo v[u] sugarè i mie pianti,
E 'l mio cuor restarà tutto immielao.

Damn, how about that beautiful hair you were showing off to the sun?
What about that gorgeous head of yours?
To tell you the truth, I was reborn,
and I almost turned into my own sickbed.
You look better without a kerchief,
and without braids, as I saw you today,
with your golden head nude and bare,
than you do when you get all gussied up.
I looked at you – God bless the day!
and when I saw you, I was so inflamed with lust
that I needed you, just seeing you there in front of me.
I beg of you to wash your hair every day,
because this way you will dry my tears
and my heart will remain covered in honey.[61]

Angelic Whores and Homoerotic Triangles

That Artusi is figured as both whore and angel – and sometimes as a hybrid creature with aspects of both – reveals the complexity of the ways in which Venier and his cohort deployed these tropes to negotiate issues of masculine identity both individual and collective. The literary "Helena" that Venier and Corner create on paper is literally passed back and forth between the two men (and later, among the other members of the Venier salon with whom they chose to share the poems) as they exchange their poems. In the manuscript, this phenomenon is accentuated by the fact that both men repeatedly represent her as a prostitute: a figure that brings to mind the imbrication of sex, desire, and commerce. A *capitolo* addressed to Helena by Venier highlights both Helena's dèsirability and the power of representation: "O ch'i ma ditto 'l vero, o ch'i s'insunnia, / basta, che m'è sta ditto, che se cento / zoveni e pi, Madonna, che ve dunnia" (Whether they have told me the truth, or whether they are dreaming, all that matters is that I have been told that there are a hundred men, or more, my lady, who are courting you).[62] As Venier himself points out, whether or not the rumours regarding Helena's moral integrity are based in reality is inconsequential. The poets appropriate and reduce the complexities of Artusi's lived life in the literary character they create: she is both a virtuous maiden and a corrupt whore, a pure inspirer of love poetry and a dangerous siren desired by countless men.

Crucially, the manuscript collection is as much about the relationship between the two poets as it is about their mutual attraction to Elena Artusi. For Domenico Venier, ill and housebound, the project must have provided a welcome diversion as well as assurance that his friend would visit him regularly. Not surprisingly, many of Venier's sonnets foreground his desire to see and talk to Corner. Here, Venier exhorts his friend to come for a visit:

Mo vù me fe morir
Mi a star tanto a no lassarve veder;
Oh v'ho un'amor, che nol possè mai creder.
E si no voio cieder
Nianca a l'amiga de volerve ben;
Ch'anca mi, quando no v'ho qua, me vien
No so che, che me tien

In desiderio sempre de parlarve;
Morsù mo, no fe pi desiderarve.

You are killing me
by making me wait so long to see you.
Oh, I have a love for you
that you cannot even imagine.
So much so that sometimes
I don't even want to share you with our lady friend.
Because I, too, when I don't have you here,
am overcome by something I can't
explain that keeps me always desiring to talk to you.
Come on, now, don't keep me in this state of desire for you![63]

Venier's eagerness to see his friend, and even his expressions of devoted love for him, are in many ways consonant with tropes of platonic friendship that were common during this time. But what Venier says next is ripe with erotic potential: "I love you so much that sometimes I don't even want to share you with our lady friend." Here Venier is imagining, just for a moment, the possibility of eliminating Artusi from the equation. Instead of a triangle in which the woman serves as mediator between the two men, Venier imagines a direct connection between himself and his friend, without the need for mediation. A similar technique is used later on by Corner, in a sonnet in which he casts himself as a wounded lover and Venier as a healer with the power to ease the burning pains of love:

Ogni volta, che mi parlo con vù,
E truovo un'acqua, che destua el mio fuogo,
Perche la fiamma no vaga pi in su.
E cussi de dolori e salto in zuogo
Per el dolce melazzo, ch'u mettè
Su le ferìe d'amor a tempo, e a luogo.
Mi son un'amalao, e vù si sè
El miedego, e 'l barbier, che me resana;
E ve rengratio del ben, che me fè.
Pregando Dio, che per ogni spanna
De piaser, che me fè, ve renda un brazzo;
E ve varda da donna, che sia lana.

Ascolteme, se volè haver solazzo;
Perche ve vogio dir ponto per ponto
Tutto quel che digo, e fazzo.

Every time I speak with you
it's like finding water that puts out my fire,
so that the flame doesn't burn any higher.
And just like that, my pains are transformed into a game,
because of the sweet balm that you put
on my wounds inflicted by love, in just the right time and place.
I am a sick man, and you are
the physician, the barber that makes me healthy again,
and I thank you for the good you do me,
praying to God, that for every measure
of pleasure that you give me, he gives you twice as much,
and that he protects you from wicked women.
Listen to me, if you want to enjoy yourself,
because I want to tell you point by point,
everything I say and do.[64]

Here, Corner's love for Artusi is represented through tropes that were already well established in Italian love lyrics: love as sickness and love as a burning fire. But, unexpectedly, the remedy for the lover's ailments is not the female beloved but instead his male confidante, Venier, who puts out the fire of love with cool water and eases Corner's pain by applying sweet balm to his wounds. With this unconventional role reversal, the poem foregrounds the relationship between the two men, who are bound together not only by the poetic project but also by their respective roles as sufferer and comforter. It also does something else, since in the love lyric tradition it is always and only the female love object that has the power to put out her lover's fire and soothe his pains. When Corner casts Venier as the remedy to his sickness, he is suggesting that his friend might take Artusi's place.

While of course there is homoerotic potential in this exchange, I am less interested in whether the two male poets desired one another than in why it is they use tropes of heterosexual desire to represent their relationship. Whatever their relationship is in life, the effect of this rhetorical strategy is to figuratively bring the two poets closer together. In the dialect exchange, then, the erotic triangle is not fixed but flexible in its configuration. The two poets mediate their relationship with each other through their mutual desire for and representation of the fictional female body; but at times, they transgress the structure of the triangle to contemplate the possibility of an unmediated relationship.

The dialect exchange is presented as an intimate dialogue between two friends, but in reality it circulated widely among Venier's literary collaborators – as will be discussed in detail in chapter 4. In that sense, the collection was also a display of poetic prowess intended to amuse, delight, and impress Venier's inner circle. Both of these levels of dialogue are apparent in a sonnet from Corner to Venier that appears about midway through the collection. Here, Corner confesses to Venier that he finds telling his friend about his trysts with Helena even more enjoyable than the encounters themselves.

> So che me bramè mi,
> come mi fazzo vù, mo vegnirò
> forsi doman, per dirve quel che so,
> che per dio mi ho
> maggior contento nel recitarne a vù
> i fatti miei, che d'averla fottù.
> Perché quel cazzar sù
> si è una certa dolcezza transitoria,
> mo el recitarla po si è bella historia.

> I know that you want me,
> as much as I want you, and I will come
> perhaps tomorrow, to tell you what I know.
> Because, by God, I find
> more happiness telling you
> about my deeds than in having fucked her.
> Because in getting it up
> there is a certain, transitory sweetness,
> but telling about it afterwards makes a good story.[65]

The alluring but threatening fictional "Helena" is the driving force behind the verse that unites the two poets. Corner's use of the phrase "bella istoria" – which we might translate as somewhere in between "lovely history" and "lovely tale" – to describe the exchange is telling. While sex is an ephemeral pleasure, writing about sex is something more significant, precisely because it is more permanent. The real fun, as Corner suggests, is in the telling of tales. The smuttier the better, since such racy material creates a sense of figurative intimacy between the teller and the confidante. But the smutty joke at Helena Artusi's expense, as we shall see in the next chapter, would also prove to be very appealing to both the circle of intimates who read the poems, and later readers who circulated, copied, and printed them.

Chapter Four

Dialect and Homosociality from Manuscript to Print

The culture of manuscript exchange in Venetian dialect continued and even intensified well after the arrival of the printing press. With those two overlapping technologies in mind, this chapter traces the circulation of erotic dialect poetry in the sixteenth and seventeenth centuries, and its eventual dissemination into print. The poems on Artusi seem to have been particularly popular; many of them were copied and recopied throughout the second half of the sixteenth century and well into the eighteenth. In 1565 – while Corner and Venier were still alive and well – a handful of the Artusi poems were printed in what is probably the first anthology of Venetian dialect poetry, a little book known as *La caravana*. When they appeared in the more public realm of print, the poems never bore the names of their patrician authors, and any identifying details were expunged. Despite this veil of anonymity, Venier's inner circle would have read the poems in manuscript, and thus recognized them as his. In that sense, the poems can be read as a titillating joke, for insiders only.

Given Domenico Venier's prominent position in Venetian politics and society, there are many reasons why he would have attempted to control the circulation of his risqué dialect poetry. Venier's public status as a figurehead for literary culture was at odds with such a low stylistic and thematic level; instead, it was closely connected to his carefully crafted reputation as a grave, decorous, and morally upright poet. Many of Venier's admirers coupled their praise of his poetic talent with hymns to his extraordinary virtue. Venier's health crisis seems to have only magnified the public myth that painted him as a model of aristocratic virtue and moral integrity. The printer Paolo Manuzio wrote to Venier in 1555, casting him as a saintly exemplar of virtuous suffering and appealing to him as a spiritual adviser:

I will leave behind my desires for ephemeral things, flee my passions, and I will attempt to imitate, as well as I am able, Your Magnificence, who, gifted with noble knowledge, and realizing the impossibility of obtaining complete salvation of the body, has dedicated himself to study and retreated from the dark haze of worldly cares, immersing himself in the light of heavenly thoughts.[1]

This idealized image of Venier persisted even after his death and well into the eighteenth century. In 1751, the clergyman and literary scholar Pierantonio Serassi presented Domenico as the embodiment of eighteenth-century modesty and morality in the biography he wrote as a preface to Venier's collected poems.[2] Serassi's portrait of Domenico contrasts his moral virtue – expressed through the virtuous content of his writings – against the licentiousness of his brother Lorenzo, who was corrupted by "that terrible man," the notorious Pietro Aretino:

In his youth, [Domenico] paid little attention to the imaginary doctrine and the wicked conversation of Pietro Aretino, behind whom his brother Lorenzo followed blindly. And for this reason, Domenico, in his speech and in his writing, always kept himself within the limits of the most virtuous modesty, whereas [Lorenzo], ruined and corrupted by the wicked school of that terrible man, published filthy writings.[3]

Serassi was evidently unaware of Domenico's bawdy dialect poems, or perhaps he thought better of acknowledging them in the context of his volume, which was intended as a gift to Domenico's eighteenth-century descendant Francesco Venier. Still, Serassi's attempt to distance Domenico from the corrupting influence of Aretino, tinged as it is with eighteenth-century moralism, provides an interesting window onto the complexities of the making of literary identity. Unlike his brother Lorenzo and his mentor Aretino, Domenico Venier crafted his reputation on two separate planes, artfully matching the style to the subject, as Bembo's principle of literary decorum dictated.

In the public arena of print, through their high-toned encomia of women and of one another, Venier and his circle fashioned an image of virtuous gravity, in matters both literary and civic. But the creation and circulation of dialect poetry was also an important vehicle, for self-fashioning as well as for negotiating relationships, as the collection of poems on Elena Artusi shows. Far from being opposites, these two strands of literary production energized and informed each other. And while the group's mainstream poetry was intended to publicize their elite status to a wide audience, the pornography of the dialect poems was publicity as well, albeit meant for a much more select group. In the British Library manuscript, the poems are presented as an intimate exchange between two friends. Yet they were far from private. In fact the poems were copied and recopied throughout the second half of the sixteenth century and well into the eighteenth. Many of them eventually ended up in print.[4] In the print editions, which date from the second half of the sixteenth century to the early decades of the seventeenth, the names of both patricians were omitted, as were any details that threatened to reveal their identities. Printing the poems anonymously offered a sort of liminal space between private and public, since the authors' identities would be clear only to those in the know.

There are physical as well as textual clues that suggest the British Library codex was intended for circulation. The most obvious hard evidence is that the codex was copied neatly in a sixteenth-century hand and later corrected by someone else (perhaps Venier himself). Furthermore, the manuscript was organized to mimic a printed book. This organization facilitated the readers' understanding of the collection as a whole, besides making it simpler to quickly find a favourite poem. The copyist compiled a complete index that lists *incipits* and folio numbers for each poem. The main body of poems, arranged in loosely chronological order, is prefaced by three sonnets addressed "a i Lettori" (to the readers) that introduce each of the three main protagonists (the two poets and the subject of their verse are all clearly identified by first and last names) as well as the subject matter. Each poem is clearly labelled with a rubric that identifies the author and the poem's addressee. The final poem in the collection, addressed to the readers by Venier, serves as a poetic conclusion: "Ben, che ve par de ste coionarie? / Haveu letto sto libro in fin in cao?" (Well, what do you think of this nonsense? Have you read this book all the way to the end?)[5] Venier's description of the exchange as a "book" with a beginning, middle, and end suggests that he did indeed conceive of it as a literary narrative; his address to the readers makes clear that the exchange is meant for an audience beyond his literary partner.

Another clue as to the manuscript's intended readership can be found in the penultimate poem in the collection, a lengthy *capitolo* from Corner to Venier. Here Corner claims to want to convince Venier to end their exchange on Artusi: "Finimo qua ste nostre poesie, / se non s'ha scritto assà, niente no vagia" (Let's stop our poems here – if we haven't written enough, then I don't know who has).[6] He alludes tantalizingly to the possibility of a public scandal, suggesting that they stop writing only "per qualche zorno" (for a few days) in order to preserve their reputations and "poder comparer in sti canei" (be able to appear in public).[7] He also claims to be concerned about provoking Elena's ire: "Per dio mi no farave pi una riga, / se fosse certo, e se fosse seguro / d'aver la mia morosa per nemiga" (As God is my witness, I wouldn't write another line if I were sure, if I were certain that my lover would become my enemy).[8] The air of secrecy and intrigue that Corner tries to convey in this poem may, of course, be simply a literary trope – here, too, the lines between the reality of his relationship with Artusi and the literary love triangle he and Venier have created are blurred. Yet it is this very drama, whatever the interplay between the real and the fictional, that animates the exchange from its beginning.

Two passages from the same *capitolo* offer another important clue as to what the two noblemen intended to do with their poems on Helena Artusi. Early in the poem, Corner begs Venier for his permission to end their exchange: "Donca serremo qua sto gran processo, / demme licentia adesso, *chel se liga*, / femmò, che sto favor me sia concesso" (So, let's close this case here. Give me permission now to *finish it / bind it*, concede to me this favour).[9] Corner's use of the Venetian verb *ligar* – literally translated as "to bind" – is ambiguous here, since it can be used to indicate the literal act of binding something together or, more loosely, "finishing" something. Later in the poem, Corner uses the same verb a second time: "El mio principo giera de operar / si fattamente che vù finesse / per poder dar sto libero a ligar" (my intention [in writing this poem] was to proceed in such a way that you would stop [writing poems about Artusi] so we could take this book to be bound).[10] Here we are confronted with another ambiguity, since at mid-century it was still common practice to bind manuscripts.[11] Was Corner planning to have the poems published or did he mean instead to have them bound in manuscript form?

I am inclined to believe the latter. Given Domenico Venier's wealth, prestige, and many connections to the printing industry in Venice, if he had wanted to have the dialect exchange published, he would have had the means to do so. Thus the fact that no printed copy of the codex exists today suggests that Venier preferred to keep his dialect poetry out of the hands of the wider public. Scribal publication would have allowed Venier more control over who had access to his poetry, even as it facilitated the circulation of dialect poetry among a select group of literary intimates.

"Rime in lingua veneziana di diversi"

The most important extant collection of poems in Venetian dialect by sixteenth-century authors is a manuscript of 445 folios at the Biblioteca Nazionale Marciana in Venice, "Rime in lingua veneziana di diversi ... " (Poems in the Venetian language by various authors).[12] Giovanni Querini (1567–1610), a poet from the nearby mainland city of Vicenza, compiled and copied the poems from a multitude of sources.[13] The collection includes a large number of poems attributed to Maffìo Venier (although many of these are in fact by Domenico). Other authors include Querini himself, Benetto Corner, Antonio Da Molin (also known as "Burchiella"), and a handful of patrician poets identified only by their family names, including a Morosini, a Tron, and a Mocenigo.[14]

This codex offers important evidence of the poetic practices employed by sixteenth-century Venetian poets. While it contains some occasional and politically themed poems, a predominating theme is the prostitutes and courtesans of Venice, portrayed here in various guises both positive and negative. Most of the poems in the collection are either Petrarchan sonnets, *sonetti caudati*, or *capitoli in terza rima*, the metrical form popularized by Francesco Berni and other burlesque poets during the late fifteenth and early sixteenth centuries as a vehicle for irreverent humour and ridicule.[15] As I mentioned briefly in the previous chapter, these two forms were also favourites of Aretino, whose erotic and satiric writings would have been well-known to Venier and his group (and to other literarily inclined Venetians). It is difficult to establish authorship for the vast majority of the poems in the codex; that said, there is much evidence that many were addressed to members of the Venier circle.

One example can be found in an unattributed sonnet addressed to "Corso mio caro" (my dear Corso), who is probably Anton Giacomo Corso, the poet from Ancona who inserted a few lines of Venetian dialect in his *capitolo* to Domenico Venier. The author of the sonnet claims that he has written it to accompany some "stantie" (literally, "stanzas," but here most likely used in the more generic sense, "poems") that he has sent along to Corso:

Corso mio caro el se quatro o sie dì
che mi ho fatto le stantie che vedè,
e si le fisi mo co' vu savè
per passatempo e no sapiando a chi.

L'è vero ben, che subito pensè
che ghe sarave certo purassè
che no mettando qua, che donna l'è
se penseria de chi no digo mi.

My dear Corso, it's been a few days
since I wrote the poems that you see here.
And I wrote them, as you know,
just to pass the time, not knowing to whom.
Although it's true that right away you'll think
that it is very certain
that if I don't say here which woman it is,
people will think of the one of whom I don't speak.[16]

The gossipy tone and the poet's coy refusal to divulge the name of the lady in question suggest that the poems accompanying this one are defamatory, or at least unseemly in tone. What's more, immediately following the sonnet are a group of poems targeting Helena Artusi for her promiscuity. All of the poems on Artusi in the Marciana codex are also present in the British Library collection (which, as we recall, was composed before 1550 and thus well before Querini began his collection). It seems likely, then, that "Corso mio caro" was written by either Benetto Corner or Domenico Venier to accompany the series of poems on Artusi that Querini transcribed in the pages immediately following. This is further proof that Corner and Venier were circulating the Artusi poems among their circle.

The group of Artusi poems in the Marciana codex includes a sequence of eight sonnets exchanged between Corner and Venier (all eight are also present in the British Library manuscript).[17] All eight sonnets use the Ciceronian rhetorical strategy of *comparatio*, or comparison, to foreground Helena Artusi's promiscuity. In the sonnet that Querini transcribed first, Venier uses a string of course, earthy similes to emphasize the number of men competing for Helena's attention: "Non ha tanti peocchi un galeotto / nè tante mosche a torno un can levroso [...] / quanti morosi ha l'Artusetta bella" (There are not so many lice on a galley slave, nor flies buzzing round a leprous dog ... as the beautiful Artusetta has lovers).[18] Corner's sonnets are variations on the same theme. The two poets make use of such diverse elements as the abundance of ripe melons in the summertime, the amount of firewood needed in the winter, and even the number of "buzeroni" (literally, buggerers) in Venice to illustrate their point.

The basic conceit the poets are experimenting with here has its roots in Petrarch's famous sestina, "Non a tanti animali il mar fra l'onde" (There are not so many creatures in the waves of the sea) (*RVF* 237). One of Corner's sonnets begins with two comparative elements drawn directly from the first stanza of Petrarch's sestina (the fish in the sea and the birds in the air): "No ghe se tanti pesci in tutto el mar; / ne svola per el cielo tanti osei [...] / quanti morosi dunnia Helena Artusi" (There are not as many fish in the entire sea, nor as many birds flying in the sky ... as there are lovers courting Helena Artusi). This self-conscious reference to the Italian lyric tradition, transposed to the low register of the obscene dialect poems between Corner and Venier, was most likely amusing to sixteenth-century readers, who would have immediately recognized the reference to Petrarch. The recasting of Petrarchan tropes for comic effect was a strategy often used by disciples of Pietro Aretino – such as, we recall, Lorenzo Venier.

Venier had experimented with Petrarch's model in his poems in literary Italian – for example, in a sonnet that appeared in *Il sesto libro delle rime* (1553):

Non ha tante, quant'io pene e tormenti,
stelle il ciel, l'aere augelli, e pesci l'onde,
fere i boschi, erbe i prati, e i rami fronde,
giorni gli anni, ore i dì, l'ore momenti.

There are not as many stars in the sky,
birds in the air, fish in the sea,
beasts in the woods, blades of grass in the fields, leaves on the branches,
days in the year, hours in the day, moments in the hour
as I have pains and torments.[19]

In his dialect poems, Venier had transposed Petrarch's elegant comparisons into a low register to illustrate Helena's loose morals; here, he uses the same technique to foreground the poet's amorous distress resulting from his lady's resistance to his advances. Ironically, the chaste lady represented here may well be Helena Artusi; this sonnet heads the *micro-canzoniere* that includes the sonnet likening his lady to Helen of Troy.

La caravana: An Anthology of Pleasure

Six of the poems present in the British Library manuscript were printed without attribution in 1565 in the first print anthology of Venetian dialect poetry, *Delle rime piasevoli di diversi auttori nuovamente raccolte da m. Modesto Pino et intitolate la Caravana* (Some pleasant verse by various authors, newly gathered by Mr Modesto Pino and entitled *La caravan*, hereafter *La caravana*). Four different Venetian publishers printed at least six editions of the book during the second half of the sixteenth century, and another six editions were printed during the seventeenth century.[20] Surprisingly, *La caravana* has been mentioned only in passing by previous scholars of Venetian culture and literature.

The title proclaims that a certain "Modesto Pino" (literally, "modest pine tree" – probably a witty pseudonym) gathered the poems together. The identity of this man is still a mystery, but in the early twentieth century, Manlio Dazzi argued that he was Alessandro Caravia (1503–1568), a Venetian jeweller and dialect poet who was a friend of Aretino.[21] Given Caravia's connection to Aretino, Dazzi's hypothesis is intriguing, but there is no hard evidence to back it up. Whoever he was, our Modest Pino accompanied his volume with an extended justification of his decision to publish poems in the low register of Venetian dialect. The unsigned preface to the volume, written not in Venetian but in literary Italian, presents the poems as both pleasurable and pedagogical. The anonymous author makes a nod to Horace's prescription that poetry should both delight and instruct: "Having laboured for a few years to collect, from various authors, different forms of poems written in their native Venetian language, I decided, having been persuaded by friends, to gather them together and to publish them for your delight and benefit."[22] The "various authors" alluded to in the preface are never identified; in fact, the entire volume is anonymous. Later in the preface, the editor continues his emphasis on the instructional value of the poems, pointing out that the "very pleasurable expressions" found in the book also have "many allegorical meanings."[23] The preface ends with a promise to publish further collections of similar poems, a project that was never realized.

La caravana begins with "Il primo canto di Urlando furioso, nuovamente trasmutao" (The first canto of *Orlando furioso*, newly translated), a Venetian version of the first canto of Ariosto's *Orlando furioso*. As we recall, Ariosto's poem, first published in 1516, had become especially popular after the revised third edition came out in 1531. In 1554 a certain

Benedetto Clario had published *Il primo canto de Orlando furioso in lingua* the first Venetian "translation" of the first canto of Ariosto's epic to go to print.[24] In short order, Clario's book was reprinted twice by the Venetian printer Mattio Pagan. So we might hypothesize that Modesto Pino opened his collection with a Venetian version of the celebrated epic in the hope that the vogue for translations of Ariosto would sell more copies of his book. By placing the translation of Ariosto in a collection of very Venetian poems, Pino is appropriating Ariosto into the Venetian literary canon. This move also validates his collection, since the presence of Ariosto (even in translation) would have conferred a certain literary lustre on the rest of the poems in the volume in the minds of contemporary readers.

Yet the Venetian translator took some telling liberties with both the plot and the lexicon of Ariosto's poem. Ariosto's initial description of Orlando's lovesickness, for example, had stated simply that "per amor venne in furor e matto" (for love he became furious and mad).[25] The Venetian poet writes instead that "per puttane el devantà insensao" ([Orlando] went mad because of whores), a revision that self-consciously lowers the register of Ariosto's original text.[26] It also introduces the familiar theme of the wiliness of whores, which dominates the entire volume. The shadowy presence of Ariosto in Pino's collection calls to mind the mock epic poems on whores by Lorenzo Venier, which were also written in the poetic meter of *ottava rima*. From the *puttana errante* to the Venetian *puttane* who drive Orlando to madness, the genre of epic parody was a particularly congenial frame for stories of fictional whores.

The Ariosto parody is followed by another Venetian poem in octaves, "Le berte, le truffe, i arlassi, e le magnarie, che usa le puttane a i so bertoni recitae da Nico Calafao da l'Arsenale" (The jokes, tricks, offences, and illicit profits that whores use in dealing with their johns, recited by Nico Calafao from the Arsenale). The fictional narrator, "Nico Calafao," is a lowly ship's caulker employed at the Arsenale, Venice's renowned shipyard and naval depot. Addressing an audience of Venetian men ("fradelli"), Nico laments the loss of his property and status at the hands of the whores of Venice. Before he began consorting with prostitutes, he was one of the richest men in the Arsenale. Now, he has lost everything, even the clothes off his back: "Adesso paro un becco cornuo, / non ho pì drappi, i se tutti impegnai / e in pe del paonazzo a pena adesso / ho sta povera strazza de comesso" (Now I look like a stupid cuckold, I don't have any clothes – they have all been hocked – and instead of a purple gown, all I've got now is this poor, raggedy doublet).[27]

The poem's function as a cautionary tale is reinforced by the presence of an illuminated initial letter enclosing an image of Cupid astride a man crouched down on all fours. This "lettera parlante" (speaking letter) recalls the legend of Aristotle and Phyllis, a moralizing example of female wiliness and the perils of lust that was told and retold from the thirteenth century onward.[28] In one of the earliest versions of the story, Aristotle is seduced by the beautiful Phyllis, who insists that he let her ride on his back as if he were a horse before giving into his desires. In *La caravana*, the illuminated letter evoking the downfall of Aristotle at the hands of the seductive courtesan is a visual reminder of the perils of love and the trickery of women, themes that are prominent throughout the volume.

The final section of Pino's volume contains thirty-four poems arranged according to form: *mattinate, capitoli, canzoni, sonetti,* and one *desperata*. It is here that we find the six poems also present in the British Library manuscript. Two of these, "Sel dissi mai che in te la mia scuella" and "Sel dissi mai, che quando vago a donne," are attributed to Benetto Corner in the British Library codex, where they are part of a sequence of eight *canzoni* initiated by Venier.[29] All eight poems are virtuosic parodies of Petrarch's *canzone* "S'i' 'l dissi mai, ch'i' vegna in odio a quella" (RVF 206).[30] In the manuscript, all of the poems except the final one ("Sel dissi mai, che quando vago a donne") reproduce precisely the intricate rhyme scheme and rhyme sounds of Petrarch's poem: like the Petrarchan model, each Venetian *canzone* is constructed using only three rhyme sounds (-ella/-ei/-ia).[31]

Known as *coblas unissonans* (literally, "unison stanzas") in the Provencal poetic system, this technique was particularly popular among troubadours. Provencal poets considered it a demonstration of virtuosity since the use of limited, predetermined rhyme sounds taxed the author's ingenuity. In Petrarch's *canzone*, the poet-lover protests his innocence in the face of accusations that he has betrayed his lady by declaring his love for another. Corner transposes Petrarch's original conceit to a lower register: "Sel dissi mai che habbia i dragoncei, / e le buganze da poltronaria. / Sel dissi che mi sia per Marzaria / menà a quell muodo che se mena i rei." (If I said it, let me be stricken with mumps and chilblains. If I said it, let me be dragged through the *Merceria* like a criminal).[32] The version of "Sel dissi mai che in te la mia scuella" in *La caravana* is a motley mixture of stanzas taken from two of Corner's poems in the British Library manuscript, assembled without regard for the original rhyme scheme.[33] This editorial choice under-scores the comic, low register of the poem while de-emphasizing the technical skill displayed in the more structured rhyme scheme of the original.

La caravana also features, among an eight-sonnet sequence of comic invectives against Cupid, three poems from the British Library manu-script: one sonnet by Corner, "Cagozzo fantolin, frasca cornua" (Little shitty-pants, silly little cuckold) and two by Venier, "Maliazo la mare che t'ha fatto" (That wretched mother who made you) and "Chi dirave che 'l mosto imbriagasse" (Who would have said that [freshly pressed grape juice] could get you drunk).[34] Corner's sonnet depicts the god of love as a snivelling little boy: "Corri, va da to mare che ti mua, / e te metta davanti el bavarol / E te coverza el corpo con l'albuol / Che le verole [sic] no te faza bua" (Run, go to your mother so she can change you, put your bib on, and cover up with a breadboard, that way the witch won't hurt you).[35] The editor of *La caravana* made several changes to Corner's sonnet, probably for the purpose of making it less unseemly in its more public form in print. First, he chose the milder adjective "cornua" (cuckolded) where the British Library manuscript version of the poem has "fotua" (fucked), a move that tones down the poem's obscenity. In addition, only the first fourteen lines of the poem were printed in *La caravana*, omitting the coda found in the British Library manuscript, where the poem appears as a *sonetto caudato* of twenty-three lines. Tellingly, the omitted lines refer indirectly to Helena Artusi, transforming the sonnet from a generic invective against Cupid into a comment on the multitudes of admirers who pursue Artusi:

Ve priego nol lassè
pratticar in contrà de San Marcuola,
che la ghe stà una gran mariola,
che ve 'l desvia da scuola,
E 'l tien in casa tutto el di al balcon
trazanao a quanti passa un veretton.

I beg you not to let him frequent
the parish of San Marcuola,
since a very cunning woman lives there,
who will lead him astray
and keep him at her house all day long on the balcony,
shooting arrows at everyone who passes by.

When Corner wrote this sonnet (sometime before 1550), Artusi was still living with her husband in the Venetian parish of San Marcuola – a biographical detail that is mentioned several times in the British Library collection.[36] In context, it would have been clear to those readers who knew Corner that the "gran mariola" who lived in San Marcuola was Artusi. That the editor of *La caravana* did not print these lines suggests either that the version of the poem he had access to was incomplete or that he intentionally omitted the allusion to Helena Artusi in an attempt to further disguise the identity of the poem's author. Artusi had been dead for fifteen years when *La caravana* was first published in 1565, but it is likely that Corner and Venier, both alive and well at the time, would have preferred that any identifying information be removed from the printed version of their poems.

The satiric transformation of the Cupid myth in Corner's "Cagozzo fantolin, frasca fotua" recalls a similar scene in the *Zanitonella*, a rustic pastoral parody in macheronic Latin by the Mantuan poet Teofilo Folengo published in 1521. The theme seems to have been especially popular among authors in the Veneto; indeed, the well-known Venetian poet Andrea Calmo wrote a sonnet with a very similar *incipit*, "Cagozzo fanduglin da sculazzuni" (Little shitty-pants worthy of being spanked), found in the 1559 edition of his *Rime pescatorie*. Five years later, Marc'Antonio da Pordenone set to music a text on the same theme, "Ah fandulin cagozzo, ti è turnao" (Ah, little shitty-pants, you are back) in his *Primo libro de madrigali* (1564). Although the popularity of this theme among sixteenth-century dialect authors has been attributed to Andrea Calmo,[37] it is likely that Corner's "Cagozzo fantolino" predates Calmo's "Cagozzo fanduglin." Corner's version was almost certainly composed in the late 1540s, at least nine years before Calmo published his variation. In any case, the similarities in theme and lexicon between the two poems are striking and certainly suggest some sort of contact between the two authors.

Another poem in the British Library manuscript, Domenico Venier's "E vorave saver, colonna mia" (I would like to know, my beloved), was also abridged in *La caravana*. Here the poet apologizes to his lady after a quarrel, assuring her that he is no longer angry with her and recounting the grief he has suffered during their separation. Only the first six stanzas of Venier's poem (which is eleven stanzas long in the British Library manuscript version) were printed in *La caravana*. Perhaps not coincidentally, *La caravana*'s version of "E vorave saver" was cut off just before the lines in which Venier mentions Helena Artusi

by name: "E me destruzo per ti Helenetta, / co fa la neve al sol" (And
I'm destroying myself for you, Helenetta, like snow that melts in the
sun).[38] This editorial choice, especially when considered along with the
similar abridgement of Corner's poem, suggests that someone (either
the editor, who was perhaps a member of Venier's circle, or the poets
themselves) was making at least a token effort to disguise the identities
of the patrician authors.

The British Library poems are not the only connections to Venier's
circle to be found among the pages of *La caravana*. The volume contains a series of three *capitoli in terza rima* (one in the masculine voice
and two *risposte* in the voice of the first poet's courtesan lover) that
can be attributed to Benetto Corner. In the first poem in the sequence,
the poet recounts his grief on having to leave his lover for a long voy-
age at sea: "Morosetta mia cara, quel affanno / c'ho habuo sta notte in
sta mia parenzana / Me ha consumà pì che le tarme un panno" (My
dear little lover, the torment that I endured last night as we prepared
to shove off has consumed me more than a cloth eaten by worms). The
poet-narrator, in the guise of a humble sailor from the Arsenale (this
detail recalls "Nico Calafao," the ship caulker who is the narrator of the
second poem in the volume denouncing the vices of whores), recounts
that he was so aflame with love that when he placed a piece of bread
over his heart, "in meza horetta el venne un biscotello" (in a half-hour
it became a piece of toast).[39] When he sighed in despair, his fiery breath
caused the beard of a nearby policeman to burst into flames.[40]

This bizarre anecdote, along with the comic tone and low register of
the poem, recalls the fanciful tales told by Corner's *arcibravo veneziano*
discussed earlier. The similarity is more than coincidental; a manuscript
source suggests that the "Morosetta mia cara, quel affanno" sequence
in *La caravana* was in fact penned by Benetto Corner. The manuscript,
titled "Rime di Dom[eni]co Veniero, e d'altri" by an early bibliogra-
pher, preserves poems by Venier and his circle, including variants of
"Morosetta mia cara" and its *risposta* (response) in the feminine voice.[41]
While in *La caravana* the opening line of the *risposta* has been printed as
"Se te soio, ben mio se mi t'inganno," in the Marciana codex, the *incipit*
of the same poem bears Corner's name instead: "Se te soio, Corner, se
mi t'inganno". What's more, in the manuscript version of the *risposta*
the female speaker addresses Corner by his given name – "No te voi
miga dir caro Benetto"[42] – clearly identifying the addressee as Benetto
Corner. This, too, was expurgated in the print version, where the name
"Benetto" was replaced with the pseudonym "Ninetto."[43]

What are we to make of the disguised identities of the patrician authors who contributed to Pino's volume? Given the wide circulation these poems had in manuscript form among a select circle of Venetian literati, it is likely that those who had been reading and copying the poems for years would have recognized them as part of the exchange between Corner and Venier despite these minor alterations. Venetian poets like Venier may well have encouraged the circulation of their work among select circles even as they attempted to keep it out of the hands of a wider public. In sending the Venetian poems to press, Venier was displaying the more active, aggressive sexual persona that the register of Venetian dialect allowed. But by withholding his name, he could maintain the standards of patrician decorum to which he and his aristocratic colleagues were held when in the public eye.

Versi alla venitiana

Still more of Domenico Venier's poems appeared in *Versi alla venitiana*, an anthology of Venetian poetry first published in 1613 by Girolamo Brescia, a printer from Vicenza.[44] As indicated in the complete title, the volume contains poems by the poet and dramatist Angelo Ingegneri (1550–1613?) as well as "altri bellissimi spiriti" (other very clever chaps) who are never identified by name.[45] Ingegneri was a Venetian by birth who spent most of his time travelling from court to court at the service of various princes. A prolific writer of drama, poetry, and prose, he is known above all for being the editor of the first complete edition of Torquato Tasso's *Gerusalemme liberata* in 1581. Along with Tasso, Ingegneri was a friend of Domenico's nephew, Maffio Venier, which may explain why the *Versi* devotes such a large section to Maffio's poetry, even though he had died in 1586, almost thirty years before the volume was printed.

Versi alla venitiana was dedicated to the Venetian nobleman Alvise Foscari by a writer using the comic pseudonym "Brustolao dalla Zueca" (Roasted-one from the Giudecca), possibly Angelo Ingegneri. In the dedication, Brustolao dramatizes the tale of how he was inspired to compile the volume of dialect poetry as a gift for his patrician patron. Highlighting Foscari's strength and skill as a hunter, he recalls that he once witnessed Foscari's expert killing of a wild boar. To celebrate the kill, Brustolao recounts, he burst out in song ("m'è insuniao de cantar").[46] It is the memory of his patron's pleasure upon hearing his singing, he claims, that moved him to compile the volume. As for the poems themselves, Brustolao recounts that some of them are

> those verses that pleased you so much, the ones that I sometimes used to sing when we went bird-hunting. And so, leaving aside nets, eel spears, barges, and fish, I set myself up on the deck and wrote up these few little things – composed, in part, by the most illustrious citizens of our city, and in part by your poor servant – and I send them to you as they are, so that you can sing them with your beautiful new bride.[47]

This passage is important for several reasons. First, it implies that the compiler of the volume – again, possibly Angelo Ingegneri – contributed poems to the collection. It also describes the authors of the volume as "the most illustrious citizens" (i primi cittadini) of Venice, without identifying them by name. But when we open the book, we find more clues to who these "illustrious citizens" may have been. The book is divided into two parts. The first section purports to contain "Versi alla venetiana del signor Anzolo Inzegneri" (Poems in the Venetian style by signor Angelo Ingegneri).[48] The second section is identified more cryptically as "Rime venetiane del Clarissimo M.V." (Venetian poems by the Most Illustrious M.V.), which is a feigned attempt to disguise the identity of the patrician writer responsible for the poems by providing only his initials. Since the adjective "Clarissimo" was normally used only for men of patrician status, contemporary readers would have suspected that the writer was a nobleman.

The initials "M.V." were likely intended to suggest to those in the know that the poems were authored by Maffio Venier. Yet at least two of the poems printed in this section were penned not by Maffio but by Domenico himself. The first of these is "Quel che par senza cassa un orinal" (Like a urinal without a case [to put it in]), a comic sonnet on male friendship that in the British Library manuscript is attributed to Domenico Venier and addressed to Benetto Corner.[49] In both versions of the poem, the poet addresses Corner by name in the last tercet: "Quel che par senza scarpe un calegher / ... / son parso mi Corner, sti dì che se sta fuora senza vù, / mo sia ringrazià Dio, ch'u se vegnù" (I have been ... like a cobbler without shoes, Corner, while you have been away. Thanks be to God that you have come back now).[50] But where the British Library manuscript presents the sonnet as part of a sequence of poems in which Venier laments that Corner has not come to visit him for several days, in the print version it is taken out of context and sandwiched between two sonnets on the beauty of women.

Another poem attributed to Maffìo Venier in *Versi alla venitiana*, the *sonetto caudato* "Sta note forsi un'hora inanzi dì" (This morning, perhaps an hour before daybreak), was probably penned instead by Domenico. Although the poem was not included in the British Library manuscript, it is likely that Domenico Venier wrote it as part of the exchange with Corner on Helena Artusi. The poem is addressed to a "Corner" and mentions a woman the poet calls "Artusa," who is almost certainly Artusi. In comic tones, the poet recounts that she appeared to him in a dream, in which she scolded him for writing poetry about her and then smacked him on the head. In the final lines of the sonnet, the poet vows to stop writing poetry in praise of Artusa and to make her, instead, the subject of defamatory verse:

> Mo se l'hò laudà
> co i miei versi fin quà sta mariola,
> no ghe ne voio far mai pì parola.
>   E pur che no ghe zola,
> con dir tuto el contrario, un do da drio,
> pur che no 'l fazza, el voio far per Lio.
>   Forsi che a sto partìo,
> con dir mal d'essa, e ghe farò piaser,
> za che a dir ben ghe fazzo dispiaser.
>   Spetè donca, Corner,
> e canzon, e capitoli, e sonetti,
> che parlerà de tuti i so defetti.
>
> While I've praised this trickster
> with my verse until now,
> I don't want to write another word about that.
> And even if, by saying the exact opposite,
> I don't give her a kick in the behind,
> even so, I want to do it, by God.
> Maybe, in this way,
> by speaking ill of her, I will please her,
> since I displeased her by speaking well of her.
> You can expect, then, Corner,
> *canzoni*, *capitoli*, and sonnets
> that will speak of all her flaws.[51]

A second edition of *Versi alla venitiana* was published in 1617, this time by Angelo Salvadori, a printer and bookseller who specialized in music printing.[52] The 1617 edition of the *Versi* is essentially a reprint of the first edition, with the exception of the dedication, addressed in the later edition to Massimo Muleri and signed by the printer Salvadori. However, a quick glance at the text of the 1617 dedication reveals that even that is essentially a shortened and adapted version of the letter printed in the first edition. Two years later, Salvadori printed a short pamphlet titled *Aggionta ai versi alla venetiana*. As its title indicates, it seems to have been intended as a sort of addendum to the *Versi*.[53] This little volume was compiled by Remigio Romano, an anthologist and editor who is known mainly for compiling two important anthologies of poetry for music in the early seventeenth century, the *Scielta di bellissime canzoni* and the *Raccolta di bellissime canzonette*, both also printed by Angelo Salvadori.[54] The involvement of both Romano and Salvadori in the second edition of *Versi alla venitiana* and its *Aggionta* suggests that some of the dialect poems in the collection were probably written as song texts. This connection is noteworthy, especially when considered along with the references to singing in the original dedication of the *Versi* (and given that at least one of Domenico Venier's dialect poems, "E vorave saver," was set to music during his lifetime). Finally, the full title of the *Versi* specifies that the poems it contains are "in aieri moderni" – a phrase that may mean either "in modern styles" or "[to be set to] modern tunes."

Like the *Versi*, the *Aggionta* contains poems that are also found in the British Library manuscript. The first of these is "No m'agreva el morir" (It doesn't pain me to die), labelled as a "madregal del Ven.[ier] a mad[onna] Helena" ([poetic] madrigal by Venier to madonna Helena) in the manuscript:

Non m'agreva el morir zà che 'l ve piase,
cagnazza traditora,
man a morir za che volè che muora.
Xe ben la veritae, che me despiase
che no posso daspuo
veder pi quel visetto de velùo.
E se ben spiero andar co muoro in [cielo]
no ghe ne dago un pelo:
che a tegnirve ficcà i occhi in tel viso
e son ni pi ni manco in [paradiso].

It doesn't pain me to die because it pleases you,
you traitorous bitch,
but rather to die because you want me to.
The truth is that what displeases me is
that, from that moment [on], I'll no longer
see your gorgeous face.
And although I hope to go to heaven when I die,
I don't care one bit about that,
since by keeping my eyes fixed on your face,
I am no more and no less in paradise.[55]

In the printed version, the words "cielo" (heaven) and "paradiso" (paradise) were replaced with ellipses, probably because religious references in the secular, risqué context of the book would have raised objections on the part of censors. The basic conceit of the poem – the lover who blasphemously equates looking at his lady's face with paradise – recalls "Io m'agio posto in core a Dio servire," a sonnet by the thirteenth-century Sicilian poet Giacomo da Lentini that would have been well known to Venier's group of vernacular poets. Venier's madrigal is a witty transposition of da Lentini's theme, right down to the lower stylistic register of Venetian dialect poetry.

Another poem, a *sonetto caudato*, "Tocca pi la camiza che 'l zipon" (literally, "The shirt touches us more than the jacket"), attributed to Venier in the British Library manuscript, is given a prominent place as the final poem in the *Aggionta*.[56] The first line is a reference to a traditional Venetian proverb that can be loosely translated as "We think first of ourselves before thinking of others." The proverb sets the theme for the poem, in which Venier laments that his friend and interlocutor Benetto Corner has not been to visit him for four days. Congratulating Corner on his success in bedding Helena Artusi, Venier comments ironically that he shouldn't complain about his friend's lack of concern, since it is only natural that Corner prefers to spend time with his lover (and thus put his own pleasure before his friend's desire for his company). In the *Aggionta*, the name of a noble rival for Helena's affections (a certain Malipiero)[57] has been substituted with an ellipsis, in yet another attempt to disguise the identity of both the author and the man mentioned in the poem. This poem foregrounds the tension inherent in the erotic triangle. While the exchange between the two men is energized and enabled by their mutual attraction to Artusi, when Corner lets his desire for her interfere in his relationship to his friend, Venier is quick to correct him.

Poetry in Venetian dialect was an integral part of the Venier salon's literary experimentation and a particularly apt vehicle for relationships between poets in Venier's circle. Writing and reading in Venetian dialect was a way to assert membership in the "gentlemen's club" that met regularly at Venier's house. The use of the Venetian vernacular implied, of course, a restricted readership and thus conferred a sense of exclusivity and sometimes even secrecy. In addition, poems written in dialect were imbued with the familiarity and immediacy of the spoken vernacular, rather than the stylized formality of Tuscanized Italian. This effect was heightened by the fact that most dialect poems circulated in manuscript form, making possible a more limited readership (or at least the illusion of such). The earthy, erotic themes of dialect poetry offered a ludic space in which men could display their sexual maturity even as they reinforced their bonds to one another.

Chapter Five

Women Writers between Men: Gaspara Stampa and Veronica Franco

Alone, my burning desire to follow your footsteps
Does not suffice – please, give me your hand so I may follow you,
Temple and vessel of all gentility, so, just as one nest gave birth to us both,
May one flight exalt us two with your grace,
And let me share (in part) in your acclaim.

Gaspara Stampa, Rime, 1554[1]

And it's with great delight that I talk with those who know, so as to have further chances to learn, for if my fate allowed, I would happily spend my entire life and pass all my time in the academies of talented men.

Veronica Franco, Lettere familiari, 1580[2]

If, as I have been arguing throughout this book, the exchange of fictional women was a means for consolidating homosocial bonds between men, what space was there in sixteenth-century Venice for women who wrote? This final chapter shifts gears to focus on the literary careers of two women writers with ties to the Venier circle, Gaspara Stampa (c. 1523–1554) and Veronica Franco (1546–1591). Stampa, born in Padua to a wealthy mercantile family, moved to Venice as a child with her mother and siblings.[3] She first made a name for herself there as a *virtuosa*, a solo singer who performed in private salons.[4] It was probably in 1548 that Stampa met the nobleman Collaltino di Collalto, to whom she addressed many of her love poems.[5] Three of these were published in 1553 in *Il sesto libro delle rime di diversi eccellenti autori*, the same anthology that hosted the Venier circle's first appearance in print as a group.

After Stampa's death in 1554, her sister Cassandra had 310 poems published by Plinio Pietrasanta in Venice in a volume titled *Rime di Madonna Gaspara Stampa*.[6] The majority of the collection is made up of love poems dedicated to Collalto, but it also includes a sizeable sequence of encomiastic sonnets addressed mainly to male poets. Among these are a sonnet to Domenico Venier and several others to prominent members of his circle, including Girolamo Molino and Sperone Speroni. While there is no direct evidence that Stampa was a regular at the Venier salon, her sonnets to the group suggest that she hoped to engage them in a collaborative project, perhaps a collection in honour of Collalto.

Almost two decades after Stampa's death, the *cortigiana onesta* Veronica Franco began to frequent the gatherings at Domenico Venier's house. Although Franco never names him directly, Venier is probably the supportive literary mentor to whom she alludes in many of her letters and poems. Franco's father Francesco was a *cittadino originario*, a member of the native-born citizen class of Venice who ranked just below patricians in the city's strict social and political hierarchy.[7] Her mother Paola Fracassa was also a courtesan, if we are to believe the *Catalogo di tutte le principali et più honorate cortigiane di Venezia* (c. 1565), where Paola's name appears twice, once as courtesan herself and once as *pieza*, or go-between, for her daughter.[8] Veronica was at the height of her fame in the 1570s, when she began to cultivate Venier's support for her literary projects. In 1574, she entertained in her own home the future Henri III of Valois, an event she would later commemorate in print. In 1575 she published her *Terze rime*, a collection of *capitoli in terza rima* that includes eighteen of her own poems and seven written by men.[9] In her poems, as well as in her *Lettere familiari* (1580),[10] Franco dramatized her connections to her elite male interlocutors, fashioning a literary persona that was both sensual and erudite. But the dubious morality associated with her profession meant that her relationships with patrician patrons had to be displayed with discretion.

By way of conclusion, the following pages focus on the ways in which Stampa and Franco appropriated and transformed the discursive terrain of sixteenth-century Venetian culture. In a network that was supported by the trafficking of the fictional female body, both women resisted tropes that cast them as objects of exchange by presenting themselves as literary organizers and collaborators. Reading both poets alongside and against their male contemporaries brings into sharp relief the sexual politics of literary exchange both within the confines of the Venier circle and in the wider context of sixteenth-century Venice.

Because Stampa and Franco operated in similar social contexts, it is useful to think about the parallels between them in terms of how they negotiated literary subjectivity. Both were admired for their beauty, and both found support – however limited – for their literary endeavours. But both were also targets of satiric attacks on the part of their male colleagues. Stampa was denounced as a "puttana Venitiana" by one detractor, and accused of plagiarism by another. Franco was the target of satiric attacks that demoted her from honoured courtesan to whore. As hypersexualized caricatures, then, the fictional Stampa and Franco could support masculine interests. But as writing women who represented themselves, they were an unsettling presence, and their efforts to participate fully in the Venetian literary sphere were often met with resistance.

Stampa, Franco, and the Sexual Politics of Venetian Literary Culture

Because Venier's group did not keep official minutes or lists of members, we must rely on allusions in literary sources to illuminate the role women played in their gatherings. These tend to represent women either as objects of men's discourse or as impediments to homosocial bonding. Think, for instance, of the literary portraits of the salon produced by the insiders Parabosco and Marcellino, discussed in chapter 3. Parabosco's fictional fishing expedition in *I diporti* self-consciously excluded women from discussions of poetry, music, and love in its idealized portrait of the salon. And Marcellino's *Il diamerone* cast Venier's salon as a gentlemen's club with nary a woman in sight. Yet, even as both texts create a virtual salon that excludes women from the conversation, they make the woman question a main topic of discussion. *I diporti* begins with a debate on the worth of women and ends with a discussion of the beauty and virtue of a catalogue of noble ladies. And *Il diamerone*, which presents itself as a philosophical discussion on the meaning of death, features a long excursus by Sperone Speroni on the dangers of the beauty of women, with a rebuttal by Girolamo Molino.

Despite such representations of the salon as an exclusively male space, there is much evidence to the contrary. Veronica Franco alludes in her letters and poems to her own participation in the Venier group's literary activities, but her presence there was never acknowledged in any of the detailed, encomiastic reports of male insiders. That said, the presence of other courtesans and high-status prostitutes at noble gatherings had been routine in Venice at least since the time of the Compagnie della Calza, when such women often acted, danced, or sang as part of the evening's entertainment.[11] In addition, although there is no direct evidence to support the presence of female solo singers (some of whom may or may not have been courtesans) at Venier's gatherings, allusions to their solo performances in encomiastic literature make their presence very likely. Suggestive in that regard is a sonnet by Domenico Venier praising the musical talents of Franceschina Bellamano, a famous singer and lutenist who had entertained him with her sweet harmony.[12] As for Gaspara Stampa, it is possible, although not certain, that she participated in musical evenings at Venier's salon, especially given her connections to Molino and Parabosco, both musicians themselves.[13]

Another woman whose presence at Venier's gatherings is documented through literary allusions is his dialect muse Elena Artusi, perhaps a prostitute of some sort, perhaps not, but similarly marginal in terms of social status. A poem written after Artusi's death by Domenico Venier and addressed to the grieving Benetto Corner casts Elena as dialect muse to the entire "brigà" (the Venetianized form of the Italian *brigata* – a company of friends) of men who met at Venier's palace in the late 1540s. Venier begins by praising Corner's poetic talent but soon moves on to exhort his friend to get over the loss of Artusi and find a new lover: "Desmentegheve quella ch'e passà, / Che s'e la giera ben miracolosa / Tanto, che l'incantava la brigà, / Se la giera ben bella, e' gratiosa, / Che credeu, che tra tant' altre ch'e restae / Non ghe sia qualc'un'altra gloriosa?" (Forget about her, she is in the past. After all, though she was truly a wonder, so much so that she enchanted our group, and she was very beautiful and charming, do you really think that among all of the other women who are left there isn't another just as glorious?).[14] Corner's response, using the same rhyme scheme, assures his friend that he will follow his advice and find a new lover to take Artusi's place as whorish muse: "Subito po che trovo la signora / Ve ne scrivero un'altra, pi de vena" (As soon as I find myself a lady, I will write you another, more lively [poem]).[15]

Artusi's position in the fraternity of discourse was paradoxical. On the one hand, as inspirer of the poet's verse, she was at the centre of their literary production. Yet as literary construct, Artusi is figured as whore – the ultimate exchange object, and a replaceable one, at that. This is not to say the poets represent her in this way unproblematically; in fact there are many moments in the dialect exchange in which the fictional Artusi threatens to escape the boundaries of the text. One strategy the poets use to mediate these tensions is to appropriate Artusi's voice, whether by casting her as interlocutor in dialogic sonnets or by writing rejoinders to their own verse in her name. In one of these dialogue sonnets, "Helena" is portrayed as a wily prostitute willing to sleep with two men in one night in order to make a profit.[16] In another, she coyly resists the advances of an unnamed "moroso" (lover) until he promises to keep their encounter a secret. What follows is a graphic sex scene that takes place on Helena's husband's bed, recounted by the two characters themselves.

The appropriation of the female voice was a common rhetorical strategy among male writers of this period and can traced back to earlier texts such as Ovid's *Heroides*.[17] But Venier's theatrical sex scene recalls the structure and content of Aretino's *Sonetti lussuriosi*, a text much closer to home. Like the protagonists of Aretino's scandalous sonnets, Venier's two lovers narrate the details of their encounter in the first person. But what is remarkable about Venier's poem is that he has cast the woman he claims was his ex-lover as the star of his sexual fantasy. In doing so, the poet is able to manipulate – in a figurative sense – both the actions and the words of a woman who may not have been as responsive to his demands as he would have liked. He even creates a scene in which an awestruck Helena admires the body of her lover: "Uh parè bon, / Che bel homo, che gamba, che ventrin. / Vù no sete so dir un fantolin" (My, you look good! What a handsome man you are, what nice legs, what a nice chest. You are no little boy, I tell you!).[18] Venier's narcissistic, sexualized ventriloquism is especially striking in light of the fact that at this point in his life he was bedridden, and presumably impotent; or at least that is the way he represents himself: in an earlier poem, he suggests that his disability and his inability to perform sexually are the reason Helena broke off their relationship.

Immediately following the dialogic sonnet are two "risposte del Venier per le rime a nome di madonna Helena" (responses by Venier following the rhyme scheme [of the previous poems] in the name of Lady Helena).[19] Once again, the poet appropriates Helena's voice, this time in the form of two long *capitoli in terza rima*, both of which respond to accusations of promiscuous conduct levied by Venier himself in previous poems. Instead of denying his accusations, Venier's Helena confirms them, boasting that "Con dar speranza a tutti a tutti vegno / a satisfar de tal sorte, ch'i crede / condurme tutti un zorno al so dessegno. / Vu 'l disè vù medemo, e tutti 'l vede" (In getting every man's hopes up,

I satisfy all of them in such a way that all think they will be able to convince me to go along with their plans one day. You yourself said it, and everyone can see it).[20] These strategies of appropriation are especially telling when we consider that the poems in Helena's voice are part of the extended poetic exchange between Venier and Corner, which was read not only by the two men who authored it but also by other poets who were part of Venier's circle. Through the creation and exchange of the fictional Helena, the two writers consolidate the bonds between them even as they display their poetic and sexual prowess to their circle of male readers.

In contrast to such strategies of appropriation of the female voice, Gaspara Stampa and Veronica Franco transformed tropes of literary and sexual exchange in their own writing. Today Stampa and Franco have become two of the most studied and appreciated writers in the Italian Renaissance female canon. Yet neither woman was particularly celebrated for her literary talents during her lifetime. In the 1540s, Stampa's fame as a singer earned her several dedications. But her poetic skill went unremarked by her contemporaries, with the exception of Ortensio Lando, who described her as a "gran poeta e musica eccellente" (a great poet and excellent musician).[21] After Stampa's death, when she could be transformed into a suitably remote inspirer of verse, a few encomiastic sonnets by literary luminaries such as Benedetto Varchi and Torquato Tasso appeared at the beginning of her *Rime*. The volume ends with a sonnet addressed to Stampa by Leonardo Emo, an otherwise obscure Venetian patrician poet with whom she apparently exchanged verse in manuscript. Her two responses to him using the same rhyme scheme are also included, highlighting her poetic skill. The volume begins and ends with poetry by men, framing Stampa's poetry with male praise. Whoever arranged the poems (probably her sister Cassandra, with help from the poet Giorgio Benzone) took care to display Stampa's connections with her male contemporaries. Despite such pains, a complete edition of Stampa's *Rime* would not be reprinted until the eighteenth century, although a few poems appeared in 1559 in Lodovico Domenichi's anthology of Italian women poets.[22]

Franco's work garnered even less attention, and her death appears to have gone unnoticed, at least in print. Only two men praised her poetic talent in print during her lifetime, both in response to her own initiative. In 1575 a poet writing under the name of Giovanni Scrittore described her as "Veronica celeste, unica, e vera / Dea tra noi di beltà, di cortesia" (Divine Veronica, unique and true goddess of beauty and courtliness) in a volume of commemorative verse she herself had compiled.[23] And in 1591 the courtier Muzio Manfredi wrote to Franco from his post in France to thank her for a sonnet she had written in praise of his tragedy *La semiramis*, not knowing she had died three months before the date of his letter, which did not appear in print until 1596.[24]

Neither Stampa nor Franco was praised in print by a Venetian patrician poet during her lifetime, although both addressed encomiastic sonnets to their aristocratic contacts. In that regard, the poet and courtesan Tullia d'Aragona, who lived during the first half of the sixteenth century, makes an interesting point of comparison. D'Aragona was Roman by birth, but her career kept her moving. Her presence is documented in Siena, Venice, Ferrara, and Florence, among other places. *Rime della Signora Tullia di Aragona e di diversi a lei*, a collection of poems by her and to her, was published in 1547 by the prestigious Giolito press in Venice.[25] D'Aragona's poetic interlocutors included the duke of Florence Cosimo I de' Medici and the duchess Eleonora di Toledo, to whom she dedicated the book, as well as other members of the Florentine ruling class. Over two-thirds of the collection consists of poems signed by important political figures such as Cardinal Ippolito de' Medici and Filippo Strozzi, as well as literary luminaries like Girolamo Muzio, Benedetto Varchi, and Francesco Maria Molza. These men praised d'Aragona openly in print for her beauty and her literary talent. Also in 1547, d'Aragona published her Neoplatonic *Dialogo della infinità d'Amore*, which she set in her home in Florence, casting herself as a participant alongside Benedetto Varchi and Lattanzio Bennucci. Like Stampa and Franco, d'Aragona was the target of criticism from various male authors, including Pietro Aretino and his erstwhile disciple Niccolò Franco.[26] And yet d'Aragona successfully engaged the public support and collaboration of a wide circle of men of letters, politicians, and rulers. As a consequence, her work was much more widely published (and presumably, read) than that of either Stampa or Franco.[27]

Unlike her Venetian colleagues, d'Aragona saw both of her major works reprinted during her lifetime. The prestigious Giolito press of Venice, which had published the first edition of her *Rime* in 1547, reprinted the book twice in short order. Giolito would also publish and reprint her dialogue on love. Only four years after her death, the Venetian brothers Sessa published the posthumous first edition of her final work, *Il Meschino,* an epic poem in octaves that recounts the adventures of a nobleman kidnapped by pirates who travels the world searching for his parents. This text, which d'Aragona based on a popular fourteenth-century prose text by Andrea Barberino, has the distinction of being the first epic poem published by a woman.[28]

There are several factors that may explain d'Aragona's literary success in comparison to that of her fellow Veronica Franco. The most obvious relates to chronology: by the time Franco entered the literary sphere in the 1570s, the Counter-Reformation was in full swing and it had become increasingly difficult for courtesans and other marginal figures to participate in literary culture.[29] But I suspect that the underlying reason d'Aragona was able to recruit the public support of her patrons had more to do with geography than anything else. Florence, where d'Aragona cultivated the support of the powerful Medici clan and where she was living when she published her *Rime* and *Dialogo,* seems to have been relatively open to such alliances.[30] When in 1547 d'Aragona was denounced for having disobeyed the sumptuary laws that required courtesans to wear a yellow veil, it was Duke Cosimo I himself who exempted her on the grounds that she was a poet.[31] To gain the duke's support, d'Aragona had prepared, with the help of Benedetto Varchi, a petition to the Duchess Eleonora di Toledo, complete with sonnets from various admirers.[32]

Venice was a much less hospitable environment for women writers. This applied even – and especially – to women of the highest social classes. During the sixteenth century, while aristocratic women poets flourished and were celebrated elsewhere in Italy, in Venice very few women of the patrician class published at all – and not one of them ever published a single-authored volume.[33] In a city that expected aristocratic women to keep a low profile, Stampa and Franco were in some ways better equipped to craft literary careers in the public arena of print than their patrician sisters. But their access to male literati was a double-edged sword, since it was precisely their freewheeling lifestyles that made them suspect. In Florence, a duke could defend a courtesan; in Venice, social and cultural norms did not allow patrician men to openly align themselves with women of lower status and questionable morality, especially in a public endeavour such as writing. Stampa and Franco, then, were in a bind, since the very men who could not, or would not, offer them public support were at the centre of political and literary influence in Venice.

Gaspara Stampa

Many of Stampa's friends and literary interlocutors had both social and literary connections to the Venier circle. One of these was her fellow musician Girolamo Parabosco, who in 1545 praised Stampa for her "angelic voice" in one of his *Lettere amorose*.[34] Another intriguing connection is Pietro Aretino, who made no mention of Stampa herself but addressed several fawning letters to her poetic beloved, Count Collaltino di Collalto.[35] Stampa's immediate circle in Venice consisted mainly of middling-status composers, musicians, and writers. In addition to Parabosco, these included the well-connected *poligrafi* (printers and writers for the press) Francesco Sansovino and Girolamo Ruscelli.[36] It was Ruscelli who edited the three poems Stampa published in the anthology *Il sesto libro delle rime* (1553), shortly before her death.[37] Stampa's connections to Ruscelli and other *poligrafi* were certainly important in terms of getting her published. Yet she also seems to have been well aware of the influence that patricians like Domenico Venier wielded over the Venetian literary scene, as the sonnet she wrote to him attests.[38] Perhaps because she died just as her writing was starting to gain traction, Stampa seems to have remained on the outskirts of the Venier group's literary activity. Nonetheless, for reasons I will discuss in more detail below, I believe that Stampa may well have been planning to engage the Venier circle in some sort of poetic collaboration.

In the early twentieth century, Stampa was the subject of a firestorm of controversy sparked by the Italian literary critic Abdelkader Salza. "Gaspara Stampa," wrote Salza in 1913, "must step down from the pedestal upon which our admiration has placed her. Indeed she should be placed in the group – if not with those *sciaguratelle* [miserable wretches] and cheap *sgualdrinette* [little tramps], as they called them – with those other wretched women, of whom the best known were, until now, Tullia d'Aragona and Veronica Franco."[39] The same year, Salza published the first modern edition of Stampa's poems, along with those of Veronica Franco, specifying that his decision to edit them together was based on their shared "condizione della vita" (life condition[s]).[40] In response, a host of literary scholars rose to Stampa's defence, crafting carefully researched rebuttals to what they saw as Salza's condemnation of Stampa's moral virtue. These included Giovanni Cesareo, who titled his response "Gaspara Stampa, signora non cortigiana" (Gaspara Stampa, lady not courtesan), and Elisa Innocenzi Greggio, who wrote "In difesa di Gaspara Stampa" (In defence of Gaspara Stampa).[41]

Others defended Salza's conclusions, most notably Benedetto Croce, who added that Stampa "was a woman, and usually women, when they aren't aping men, make use of poetry by subjugating it to their feelings, loving their lovers or children more than they love poetry."[42]

I bring up this controversy not to demonize old misogynist critics but instead to emphasize that Stampa's ambiguous social position has proved profoundly unsettling for her readers. As an unmarried woman who wrote amorous poetry to at least two men, Stampa did not fit neatly into any of the three conditions of early modern womanhood as defined by moralists (virgin, wife, or nun) or even as redefined by Aretino and his followers (nun, wife, or prostitute). And then there was the problem of her fame as a *virtuosa*. While Stampa was probably not a courtesan by profession, as a singing woman without the shelter of marriage or nobility to protect her reputation she would have inspired similar doubts in regard to her morality and chastity. While not all female singers were courtesans, many courtesans were singers. Tullia d'Aragona owned music books and was admired for her sight-singing abilities, and Veronica Franco entertained friends in her home by playing and singing.[43]

The figure of the siren, which had both heavenly and earthly connotations, is emblematic of associations between courtesans and female singers.[44] On the one hand, a singing woman could evoke the heavenly music of Plato's celestial sirens in harmony with the spheres. On the other, her song could evoke the beautiful but deadly mythological creatures, half bird and half woman, whose song had the power to lure men to their deaths. Tellingly, both Gaspara Stampa and Veronica Franco were represented by their sixteenth-century observers as sirens at once dangerous and divine. In 1545, Parabosco cast Stampa as a siren capable of driving her enthralled male listeners out of their minds in his *Lettere amorose*.[45] Two years later, the composer Perissone Cambio dedicated his first book of madrigals to Stampa, noting that "thousands and thousands of courteous and noble spirits ... having heard your sweet harmonies, have given you the name of divine siren."[46] And Veronica Franco was lauded as a "sirena gentil" (courteous siren) who made use of her talents to lure male poets "per la dritta via" (down the right path) in a collection she organized to commemorate the death of a slain war hero.[47]

It was not only women's singing that was problematic, but also their writing. In 1537, Aretino had portrayed music and literature as the gateways to female promiscuity: "i suoni, i canti, e le lettere che sanno le femmine, sono le chiavi che aprono le porte della pudicizia loro" (the sounds, songs, and literature that women know are the keys that open the doors to their chastity).[48] In that sense both Stampa and Franco were doubly suspect. But even women writers with spotless reputations were not immune to satiric attacks upon their virtue. A notable example is the noblewoman and poet Veronica Gambara, denounced by Pietro Aretino in 1534 as a "meretrice laureata" (prostitute laureate) in a printed pamphlet containing mock astrological prognostications for the year ahead.[49] Aretino's barb does not seem to have hindered Gambara's literary success. By the middle of the sixteenth century, she was second only to Vittoria Colonna as the most celebrated and published woman poet of her time. But women like Stampa and Franco, because of their precarious social positions, were easier targets for such insults.

It may have been Stampa's entrance into print that provoked hostility from a man named Girolamo Ferlito, a priest and amateur poet hailing from Palermo. Very little is known about Ferlito's life and literary activities, but he is thought to have spent some time in Venice, where he was a member of the Accademia dei Dubbiosi, a group that Stampa also may have frequented.[50] Like Stampa, Ferlito contributed to Ruscelli's lyric anthology *Il sesto libro delle rime* (1553).[51] Ferlito glossed his copy of the *Sesto libro* with a host of gossipy little notes on many of the other authors in the book, most likely for the benefit of his friend and fellow southerner Fabrizio Valguernara, to whom the book was eventually sent as a gift.[52] Domenico Venier is described as "a Venetian nobleman, always sick in bed, wasted from his waist down, an incredibly precise and famous poet in our language."[53] While Ferlito's glosses of Venier and others are generally respectful, his description of Stampa degrades her as a "puttana venetiana" (Venetian whore).[54]

This insult to Stampa's morality can also be seen as an attempt to undercut her poetic talent. Ferlito's catty epithet, intended for the amusement of his friend, demotes Stampa from talented poet to base whore, an object of degradation and ridicule to be exchanged between men. Tellingly, Ferlito did not write anything at all under the name of Tullia d'Aragona, who has a *canzone* and a sonnet in the volume, nor under that of Ippolita Mirtilla, another female contributor. That he singled out Stampa as the target of his defamation suggests he may have had personal and professional reasons for such an insult, especially if he and Stampa were indeed moving in the same circles.

There is also concrete evidence that Stampa's attempts to carve out a niche for herself in the Venetian literary sphere were not always appreciated. A sixteenth-century codex in the Vatican library preserves a sonnet attributed to an "incerto autore" (unknown author) that figures Stampa as both whore and plagiarist:

> Fermati, viator, se saper vuoi
> L'essitio de la mia vita meschina:
> Gaspara Stampa fui, donna e reina
> Di quante unqua puttane fur tra voi.
> M'ebbe vergine il Gritti, ed ho da poi
> Fatto di mille e più cazzi ruina;
> Vissi sempre di furto e di rapina,
> M'uccise un cazzo con gli empiti suoi.
> Vergai carte d'amor con l'altrui stile
> Che per quel fatto i versi mi facea
> Il Fortunio, mio compare gentile.
> Va' in pace, e, per temprar mia pena ria,
> Innestami con membro tuo virile,
> Chè sol quel, mentre vissi, mi piacea.

> Halt, traveller, if you want to know
> the end of my miserable life.
> I was Gaspara Stampa, a lady and the queen
> of all the whores there have ever been among you.
> Gritti had me when I was still a virgin, and since then
> I have ravaged more than a thousand dicks.
> I lived by stealth and stealing,
> I was killed by the thrusting of a dick.
> I wrote pages of love poems, in the style of another,
> since Fortunio, my kind friend,
> wrote the verses for me in exchange for that deed.
> Go in peace, and to ease my wicked suffering,
> pierce me with your virile member,
> since that, while I lived, was the only thing that pleased me.[55]

The sonnet is in the voice of the departed Stampa, who exhorts passers-by to stop for a moment and listen to the sad tale of her miserable end. The exact date of composition is unknown, but it may well have been written shortly after Stampa's death and the appearance of her *Rime* in print. The invocation to the reader echoes the inscriptions found on Roman roadside tombs, which often begin with the exhortation "Siste, viator" (Halt, traveller). In the sixteenth century, poets wrote satiric epitaphs in both Venetian dialect and literary Tuscan as vehicles for ridicule of politicians and prostitutes alike.[56] One example can be found in the same manuscript collection of Venetian dialect poems that contains some of the poems on Helena Artusi.[57] This time, the dirty joke is on a woman described as "Diana ladra sporca sodomita" (Diana, the dirty thief and sodomite). When she is dead, it will be impossible to tell how her soul has left her body, because she will be found "co la bocca la potta il cul aperto" (with her mouth, her cunt, and her ass wide open).[58]

The sonnet on Stampa brings to mind themes that would have been familiar to sixteenth-century readers from popular texts that satirized the lives and deaths of courtesans, circulated as short pamphlets or sometimes as illustrated broadsheets. Most of these followed a moralizing, formulaic plot that began with the courtesan's initiation into prostitution, told the story of her short-lived success and subsequent downfall, and culminated in her miserable death by venereal disease.[59] One of the best-known texts of this type is *Il lamento della cortigiana ferrarese* (The lament of the Ferrarese courtesan), a verse *capitolo* that has been attributed variously to Maestro Andrea Veneziano, Giambattista Verini, and even Pietro Aretino.[60] Probably first printed in 1520, and then reprinted at least six times throughout the century in various incarnations, the *Lamento* is in the voice of a courtesan who recounts her downfall after having been infected with syphilis. She begins by crying out in pain and entreating onlookers to recognize her as "the famous courtesan from Ferrara." She had once worn pearls; now her body is adorned instead with the telltale sores of disease. Sick and desperately poor, she begs for alms to buy a flask of poison so that she can put herself out of her misery.

In a similar vein, the author of "Fermati, viator" appropriates Gaspara Stampa's voice, transforming her from celebrated *virtuosa* and poet to syphilitic whore. Following the typical trajectory that satirists projected for courtesans, the anonymous poet has Stampa tell the tale of her initiation into prostitution at the hands of a man named Gritti.[61] The next step for the ventriloquized Stampa is her descent into the dark underworld of prostitution, which involves both sexual transgression and "stealth and stealing" – all vices commonly attributed to prostitutes of all levels. The satirist's fantasy of Stampa's death "by the thrusting of a dick" insinuates that she too was infected with the venereal disease that had killed the *cortigiana ferrarese* and so many others. The image also brings to mind the unsettling literary violence of Lorenzo Venier's tale of the gang rape of Angela Zaffetta.

Yet the sonnet on Stampa deploys the whore trope not simply to dishonour her but also to deny her literary talent. In the first tercet of the sonnet, the ventriloquized Stampa confesses that she did not write the love poems for which she was so famous. Instead, she convinced a man named Fortunio to write them "in exchange for that deed" and then passed them off as her own.[62] Here the satirist is probably playing off of one of Stampa's own sonnets, in which she had thanked the poet Fortunio Spira for his advice regarding poetic style: "Io dirò ben che, qualunque io mi sia / per via di stile, io son vostra mercede, che mi mostraste sì spesso la via" (I will say this: that whatever's mine by way of style I owe to you, since you so often showed the way to me)."[63] The satirist distorts Stampa's public acknowledgment of her literary mentor to suggest that she exchanged sexual favours for poetry, demoting her from accomplished poet to whorish plagiarist.

Stampa as Literary Organizer

In the 1554 edition of Stampa's *Rime*, there is a sequence of occasional poems that begins with an ambitious pair of sonnets addressed to Henri II and his queen, Caterina de' Medici. Following these, we find a series of over fifty sonnets addressed to contemporary male poets, many of whom were Venetian or moving in Venetian literary circles. Virginia Cox has argued that this sequence of occasional poems, which also includes some poems on religious themes, may represent the beginning of an attempt by Stampa to revise her image and reinvent herself as a more "unobjectionable" sort of poet.[64] If Stampa was indeed trying to revamp her literary persona, one of her strategies for doing so was to engage the famous and well-connected poets of Ca' Venier in literary collaboration. In fact the sequence includes a sonnet addressed to Venier himself, followed closely by poems to two of his closest adherents, Sperone Speroni and Girolamo Molino. Stampa's sonnet to Venier, "Se voi non foste a maggior cose volto" (If you were not occupied with greater things), is positioned before the others addressed to his circle, as if to acknowledge his position as group leader and literary adviser. She opens by declaring that it is her esteem for Venier that keeps her from asking him to write poems in praise of her beloved, Collaltino di Collalto:

Se voi non foste a maggior cose volto,
Onde 'l vostro splendor VENIER sormonte,
Havendo sì gran stil, rime sì pronte,
E de' lacci d'amor essendo sciolto.
Vi pregherei, che 'l valor, e 'l bel volto
E l'altre gratie del mio chiaro Conte,
A la future età faceste conte,
Poi che 'l poterlo fare a me è tolto.
E faceste ancor conto il foco mio,
E la fede oltra ogni fede ardente
Degna d'eterna vita, e non d'oblio.
Ma poi degno rispetto nol consente,
Vedrò tal qual'io sono adombrarn'io
Una minima parte solamente.

If you weren't turned to greater things
to elevate your own splendor, Venier,
I'd ask you – since you've rhymes at the ready
and such fine style, and are freed from the noose of love –
to ensure that the valor and gorgeous face
and other graces of my worthy count
were to a future age of some account,
since the means to do so myself are denied me.
And you could make sure that my fire counts,
and my faith that all others' outshines – worthy
not of oblivion, but eternal life.
But respect for you doesn't let me ask,
and I'll see if I can venture such as I am
to adumbrate the smallest part of my passion.[65]

Here Stampa couches her request for literary collaboration in hypothesis. Were Venier not so occupied with other more important things, she would ask him to write poems in praise of Collalto. She ingratiates herself to Venier through hyperbolic praise of his "gran stil" (great style) and "rime sì pronte" (ready verse), acknowledging his talent, his fame, and his influence as literary patron. This pose of humility and ingratiation mirrors the same strategies used by male poets in Venier's circle who also sought his approval and collaboration. In a *capitolo* addressed to Venier, Parabosco praises the patrician by comparing him to Orpheus, whose song moved even the stones: "voi, con l'armonia, con la dolcezza / Del vostr'unico stil, fate cantando / romper le pietre, e pianger di dolcezza" (You, with the harmony and sweetness of your unique style, make the stones break down and weep with your singing).[66] These compliments are immediately followed by Parabosco's humble plea to be readmitted into Venier's good graces: "E se vi par che il vostro Parabosco / Sia per l'amor, ch'egli vi porta, degno … se vi par, torno a dir, ch'egli sia degno / di vostra grazia ancora, fatel palese" (And if you decide that your Parabosco, is – for the love he bears you – worthy … if you decide, I say again, that he is worthy once again of your mercy, let me know).

Like Parabosco, Stampa emphasizes her ties (whether real or desired) with her interlocutors. In her sonnet to Speroni, she asks not for poems but instead for support and mentorship. The pun on the etymological origin of Speroni's name (*spronare*, to spur) in the second line displays her erudition and her poetic wit even as it flatters her addressee:

Speron, ch'à l'opre chiare, et honorate
Spronate ogn'un col vostro vivo essempio,
Mentre d'ogni atto vile illustre scempio,
Con l'arme del valor vincendo fate,
Poi che di seguir' io vostre pedate,
Per me l'ardente mio desir non empio;
Voi, d'ogni cortesia ricetto, e tempio,
A' venir dopo voi la man mi date.
Sì che, come ambe due produsse un nido,
Ambe due alzi un vol, vostra mercede,
E venga in parte anch'io del vostro grido.
Così d'Antenor quell'antica sede,
E questo d'Adria fortunato lido,
Faccian de' vostri honor mai sempre fede.

Speroni, with your living example
you spur us on to bright and honorable deeds,
while with your arms of valor you make all
other illustrious acts foolish and lowly.
Alone, my burning desire to follow
your footsteps does not suffice – please,
give me your hand so I may come after you,
temple and vessel of all gentility,

so just as one nest gave birth to us both,
may one flight exalt us two with your grace,
and let me share (in part) in your acclaim.
Thus may that ancient site of Antenor
and Adria's fortunate shores
forever keep faith with your honorable name.[67]

Here Stampa creates a poetic portrait of Speroni as her attentive mentor, willing to stretch out his hand and lead her down the path to literary fame. While their partnership may not yet exist, her poem functions as a public declaration of the ties that she hopes will someday bind the two of them together. To that end, she foregrounds an important link between them: their shared city of birth, Padua. Stampa has chosen her metaphors carefully to simultaneously praise Speroni's literary talent and highlight her own poetic aspirations, which mirror his. Both of them were born in the same "nest," and if he helps her, both of them will reach the same poetic heights. The final lines of the poem reinforce yet again their shared provenance and goals of poetic glory. Both of them hail from the same city that produced Antenor, the wise hero famous for his counsel to Priam during the Trojan War. With Speroni's support and counsel, Stampa will write poetry from Venice that will ensure lasting fame both for her mentor and herself.

The two sonnets Stampa addressed to Girolamo Molino, "Io vorrei ben, Molin, ma non ho l'ale" (Molin, I would like to, but I don't have the wings) and "Tu, ch'agli antichi spirti vai di paro" (You, equal to the ancient spirits), are invitations to Molino to write in honour of Collaltino. In her sonnet to Molino, Stampa couches her praise of the older, patrician poet in the rhetoric of submission, just as she did in her sonnet to Venier: "A me dié solo amarlo, e l'amo quanto / si puote amar; ma 'l celebrarlo poi / è d'altro stil incarco, che di donna" (I was meant only to love him, and I love him as much as one can love. Celebrating him is the duty of quite another style, not that of a woman).[68]

The posthumous edition of Girolamo Molino's *Rime*, published in 1573, does include a sonnet "Alto colle famoso al ciel gradito" (Lofty, famous hill, favoured by the heavens), which is a transparent play on the count's name.[69] Could Molino have written the sonnet on Collaltino in response to Stampa's request? There are several clues in the sonnet itself that suggest he may have done so, although of course this is impossible to prove. Molino's sonnet begins as an encomium to Collaltino, but only the first quatrain is actually dedicated to praising its addressee. The remaining lines are devoted instead to an unnamed woman poet, who is clearly still alive and who is invoked as a "nova sirena" (new siren), a metaphor used also by Parabosco for Stampa.

Ed ella ancor fra l'altre illustre e prima
Teco n'andrà, che con più chiara vena
Scrisser mai le lor fiammer in prosa e in rima.
Talché il mondo dirà: Nova Sirena
Poggiò cantando un colle alto ed in cima
Fe' 'l verde eterno e l'aria ognor serena.'

And she, first and illustrious among all other women,
will accompany you, since nobody has ever written of her own flames [of love] with such a worthy style, in prose or in verse.
So that the world will say "A new siren,
alighted singing on a high hill, and on its peak
she created eternal spring, and serene air."[70]

If, in fact, Molino's sonnet was meant for Stampa, one wonders why Cassandra chose not to publish it with the handful of dedicatory poems in praise of her sister that she included in the 1554 edition. Of course, the reason for this could be simply that Cassandra did not have a copy of it. But since Molino was still alive at the time Cassandra was preparing the edition, the sonnet's absence could also be related to the same constraints of patrician propriety that would keep Domenico Venier from acknowledging his own mentorship of Veronica Franco decades later. What is clear from Stampa's own poems is that she was cultivating the support of Venier and other elite male poets as literary mentors, as well as collaborators. Stampa's cluster of sonnets to Venier and other members of his circle, like the sonnets written by male poets in lyric anthologies, can also be seen as attempts to write herself into the most prestigious literary circle in the city.

In contrast to her attempts to engage the august figures of Venier, Molino, and Speroni, Stampa does not seem to have addressed poems to lower-status men associated with the group such as Girolamo Parabosco – or, if she did, her sister decided not to publish them. Parabosco, however, had addressed a long letter "Alla virtuosa Madonna Gasparina Stampa" (To the *virtuosa*, Lady Gasparina Stampa) in the first volume of his *Lettere amorose* (1545):

Would you believe, my sweet Lady, that never in the past did I want to accept that a man can burn and freeze in a single spot? Do you think that

I ever thought I would meet a woman perfect in all the virtues? Do you think that I ever thought that the song of the Sirens had the power to drive its listeners out of their minds? Of course not, but from now on, I will not be able to deny it, since your ladyship has made it all clear to me ... What shall I say of that angelic voice, that, when it strikes the air with its divine accents, makes such sweet harmony that in the guise of a Siren ... infuses life into the coldest stones, making them weep with its excessive sweetness? You can be certain, most beautiful and gracious Lady Gasparina, that every man who sees you is bound to be your perpetual servant. Of these, although I may be perhaps the most unworthy in regards to talent, I shall not be unworthy in love, and from now on, I will make this very clear to you in everything that I think will please you.[71]

Parabosco casts himself as Petrarchan lover and Stampa as the poetic beloved. But in the guise of Siren (i.e., when she sings), she is both enchanting and dangerous.

This letter also suggests that Parabosco heard Stampa sing – a very real possibility, given her well-established reputation as a singer and lutenist by the mid-1540s. The famous madrigalist Perissone Cambio dedicated his *Primo libro di madrigali a quattro voci* to Stampa in 1547.[72] In his dedication letter to her, Cambio emphasizes her fame and talent as a musician, affirming that "it is well known by now that no woman in the world loves music more than you, nor possesses it more uniquely."[73] Cambio provides yet another link to Domenico Venier's circle – Venier had lamented the composer's death in a sonnet answered by the poet Girolamo Fenaruolo and first published in Fenaruolo's collected poems in 1574.[74]

Parabosco praised Stampa again in his first book of poetry, *La prima parte delle rime*, published in 1546.[75] His sonnet "Se mira il ciel questa divina Stampa" portrays Gaspara as a sort of *donna angelicata* whose beauty is powerful enough to raise the dead. Roses and violets spring from the ground she walks on, and Nature herself is jealous of the beauty of Stampa's features. In the last tercet of the poem, she is surrounded by little cupids who sing her praises, an image that aligns her with Venus, the goddess of love: "Venere questa, a noi diletta madre" (This is Venus, our adored mother). The identification of Stampa with Venus adds a sensual twist to Parabosco's portrait of his poetic beloved.

Another way in which Stampa may have sought to engage in the Venier circle's literary activities can be found in her experiments with poetic forms and conceits that were of particular interest to the group. Domenico Venier was renowned above all for his complex reworkings of the Petrarchan sonnet. In this vein he is considered to have invented what the modern Spanish poets and critics Dámaso Alonso and Carlos Bousoño have called the "correlative" sonnet.[76] Perhaps the best-known example is Venier's "Non punse, arse, o legò, stral, fiamma o laccio," first published in Andrea Arrivabene's *Libro terzo delle rime* in 1550 and subsequently reprinted many times throughout the 1550s and 1560s.[77] A "correlative" sonnet is characterized by the initial presentation of multiple elements (in this case, three verbs: punse/arse/legò), which are subsequently linked together with equal numbers of corresponding elements (here, the nouns stral/fiamma/laccio). In Parabosco's *I diporti*, Fortunio Spira uses this sonnet, along with another, as an example of Venier's poetic fame: "Your two unique and gorgeous sonnets, wonderful among all others ... are all that is needed to make you known to the world as the unique and noble spirit that you are."[78]

Parabosco's reference to these two sonnets as a source of fame for Venier suggests that they were probably circulating in manuscript form well before Parabosco mentioned them in 1550. There are at least two sonnets in Stampa's *canzoniere* that seem to have been inspired by Venier's experiments with the correlative sonnet technique. In the first of these, Stampa reworks the Petrarchan paradox of the lover who weeps and burns with passion in the same moment. She presents a triad of verbs and then rearranges them using different verb tenses: "Arsi, piansi, cantai; piango, ardo e canto; / piangerò, arderò, canterò sempre (I burned, I wept, I sang; I weep, I burn, and I sing; I will weep, burn, and sing forever). The sonnet that follows, "Altri mai foco, stral, prigione o nodo," is even more elaborate and closer in complexity to Venier's original. Venier's sonnet is based on a triad of elements; Stampa presents four elements in the first line (*foco, stral, prigione,* and *nodo*), with each successive line containing a correlative adjective or verb for the initial four nouns:

> Altri mai foco, stral, prigione o nodo
> sì vivo e acuto, e sì aspra e sì stretto
> non arse, impiagò, tenne e strinse il petto,
> quanto 'l mi' ardente, acuto, acerba e sodo.

> Never did fire, arrows, prison, or chains –
> so blazing and sharp, and so harsh and so tight –
> burn, wound, confine, and bind another heart
> as they do mine; burning, sharp, bitter, and hard.[79]

Veronica Franco

Both Stampa and Franco experimented with the *capitolo in terza rima*, a form that was also popular among male poets of the Venier group. The form makes use of the intricate rhyme scheme of interlocking tercets (*terza rima*) most famously employed by Dante in the *Divina commedia* (ABA BCB CDC ...) but also has its roots in the Provencal *tenso*, or *tenzone*. The name *tenso*, roughly translated as "contest" or "dispute," reflects the inherent dialogic nature of this form, which entered the Italian poetic tradition in the thirteenth century as a means for personal exchange and debate between two or more poets. The first author proposed the subject of the debate (often love, religion, or politics) and set the rhyme scheme, and the second author responded in like rhyme. While earlier *tenzoni* were most often conducted using the sonnet form, by the sixteenth century, poets were beginning to use the *capitolo in terza rima* instead, following the lead of the Tuscan burlesque poet Francesco Berni. In the hands of Berni and his followers, the *capitolo in terza rima*, considered a highly sophisticated form because of the difficulties posed by its complicated rhyme scheme, was used as a vehicle for irreverent humour and erotic jokes.[80]

Venier's group seems to have been particularly interested in this form, although they were not, of course, the only sixteenth-century poets to use it. The *capitolo*, along with the *sonetto caudato*, was often used in the Venetian dialect exchanges penned by Venier, Corner, and other members of the salon. And the sharp-tongued Aretino, who delighted in the Venetian exchanges penned by his friends, used the *capitolo* form often, both to flatter and attack powerful men. There is also evidence that Venier was writing *capitoli* in Tuscan, although he never published them. Girolamo Ruscelli recorded in 1559 that Venier's "other very noble talents" were in the habit of writing "versi sciolti, e di terze rime ... principalmente volendo contrafar la pedanteria" (blank verse, and poems in *terza rima* ... with the intent of making fun of pedantry).[81] As Margaret Rosenthal has argued, Franco's *capitoli*, which are presented in the form of *proposte* and *risposte* between the courtesan and her male interlocutors, link her to the poetic exchange in Venier's salon.[82]

Franco's *Terze rime* was dedicated not to any of her Venetian patrician contacts but to Guglielmo Gonzaga, the duke of Mantua and Monferrato and the son of Federico II, whom we encountered earlier as the recipient of Lorenzo Venier's *La puttana errante*.[83] Franco's book contains eighteen of her own *capitoli* along with seven poems by male interlocutors who are anonymous, with one short-lived exception. A few copies of the book attributed the first *capitolo* to a "Magnifico Marco Veniero," probably the same Marco Venier who was a distant relative of Domenico and an important figure in Venetian politics.[84] At some point thereafter, for reasons unknown, Marco's name was removed and the poem was ascribed instead to a male "incerto autore" (unknown author).[85] Marco's poem is openly erotic, begging the courtesan to satisfy his physical desire. She responds in kind, promising him sexual fulfilment, but under the condition that he engage with her in literary collaboration.

Given such explicit eroticism, the removal of Marco Venier's name from Franco's book is not surprising. Among friends, it was perfectly acceptable, and even desirable, for a nobleman to boast of his intimate relationship with a woman of lesser or marginal status – as in the poems circulated by Domenico Venier and Benetto Corner on Elena Artusi. But Venetian patricians, especially those who held high-profile political offices, were expected to display ideals of decorum and moral restraint in public. The appearance of Marco Venier's name in print alongside that of a courtesan, even one of Franco's level, would have besmirched not only Marco himself but also the idealized image of Venice's purity and social order.

Franco followed similar rules of propriety and discretion in her volume of familiar letters, which she dedicated to not one but two powerful foreigners. The first was Cardinal Luigi d'Este of Ferrara, patron to another writer associated at least tangentially with Venier's group, the brilliant poet Torquato Tasso.[86] Despite her attention to local decorum, Franco's dedication of her book of letters to a man of Luigi d'Este's status and religious affiliation did not go without harsh criticism. In 1590, the Veronese gentleman Giovanni Fratta pointed to Franco as a negative example in his *Della dedicatione de' libri, con la correcion dell'abuso, in questa materia introdotto* (On the dedication of books with correction of the abuse introduced in this matter), a dialogue that is concerned in a general with the increasingly mercenary motivations underlying book dedications.[87] Here Fratta argues that it was inappropriate for a courtesan to dedicate her book to a cardinal, on the grounds that authors should offer works to monarchs only if the work is concordant with the "interests" of the dedicatee.[88] That Fratta should single Franco out for criticism of this sort is particularly interesting given that the two writers had collaborated about fifteen years earlier. In 1575, Fratta solicited a sonnet from Franco for a collection he was compiling in honour of the "felice dottorato" of Gioseppe Spinelli, where Franco is described as "la virtuosissima Signora Veronica Franco" (the most virtuous Signora Veronica Franco).[89] Women like Franco, then, were encouraged to participate in literary projects, but only within the circumscribed literary space deemed appropriate by their male collaborators.

The second dedicatee Franco chose for her *Lettere* was Henri III of Valois, whom she had hosted in 1574.[90] Franco's dedication to Henri III makes no secret of their encounter and foregrounds the night they spent together in her home: "To the immensely high favor that Your Majesty deigned to show me, coming to my humble house, by taking my portrait away with you ... I am unable to reciprocate."[91] The two sonnets she includes with the dedicatory letter continue this theme, making public her status as the king's preferred lover.[92] Fratta does not seem to have been as offended by Franco's dedication to Henri III, which he does not even mention as problematic, as he was by the dedication to the cardinal d'Este.

It may seem paradoxical that Franco named such illustrious figures – a duke, a cardinal, and a king – while omitting the names of her patrician supporters in Venice. But Franco's foreign dedicatees were powerful enough that they had little to lose from being publicly acknowledged as the patrons of a Venetian courtesan, especially from a safe distance. The only Venetian whose name appears in Franco's printed work is the painter Jacopo Tintoretto, whom she thanks for having painted her portrait in one of her letters. By making her connection to Tintoretto public, Franco could broadcast her status as someone who was important enough to have her portrait made by the same painter who had immortalized noblemen, cardinals, and doges. And while Tintoretto was neither royal nor foreign, as an artisan his public image was less bound up in idealized principles of civic morality and virtue than that of Franco's patrician contacts.

Even Domenico Venier, who mentored Franco behind the scenes, is never mentioned by name in her published work, nor did he ever acknowledge her as his protégée in print. This is not to say that readers familiar with the Venetian literary scene would not have known of Franco's connections to Marco, Domenico, and other patrician interlocutors. But the public display of these relationships had to be negotiated carefully by both Franco and Venetian patrons. In *capitolo* 15, for instance, Franco describes her addressee as an invalid confined to his bed and surrounded by a circle of learned men, which she praises as a "celebre concorso" (famous assembly).[93] The bedridden man surrounded by his academicians could only have been Domenico Venier, as anyone in Franco's circle would have known. This was a strategic move on Franco's part. By invoking Venier without naming him directly, she could represent herself as a member of his elite coterie to other insiders while still hewing to ideals of Venetian morality.

Franco negotiated both Venetian social mores and the discursive dynamics of her circle in a verse collection she edited to commemorate the death of the Brescian war hero Estore Martinengo.[94] She dedicated the volume, published probably in 1575, to Francesco Martinengo, the brother of the dead hero.[95] In the dedication, Franco writes that she has included herself among the poets making up the "pretiosa corona di così divini intelletti" (precious crown of divine intellects) who have contributed sonnets to the volume – eleven male poets plus Franco herself.[96] The first sonnet is attributed to a "Clarissimo Signor D.V." – presumably the illustrious Domenico Venier, who even in this thoroughly respectable context is invoked only by his initials. Following Venier are several men who can be tied to his circle: the Venetian nobles Marco Venier and Orsatto Giustinian, the Paduan Bartolomeo Zacco (Franco's interlocutor in manuscript), and the Venetian *cittadino* Celio Magno.[97] While each of the male poets is represented by no more than two sonnets, Franco chose to publish nine of her own, which she placed last in the line-up. Her contributions lament Estore's death, but she is also careful to pay homage to Francesco, whom she figures as "vivo … invitto, e forte" (alive, undefeated, and strong).[98]

The Martinengo volume – the only commemorative verse collection of its kind from this period edited by a woman – is proof of Franco's extraordinary ability to fashion her persona as literary organizer and collaborator in a culture that usually reserved these activities for men.[99] Unlike Franco's single-authored *Terze rime* and *Lettere*, the book includes the full names of her male colleagues – with the exception, as we saw, of Domenico Venier, whom those in the know would have easily identified as the man behind the initials "D.V." The presence of the full names of the other men is likely due to the subject matter. Despite their presumed support in private, in print Marco and Domenico Venier could only acknowledge their connections to Franco in the most irreproachable circumstances. A volume in honour of a slain military hero fit the bill, while Franco's *Terze rime* and *Lettere* did not. Franco's collection allowed the Venier poets to preserve patrician respectability, but it also reinforced the familiar discursive dynamic of a literary exchange between men like that of Venier and Corner on Helena Artusi. As the compiler of her male colleagues' poems, Franco, like Artusi, becomes a mediator of men's relationships with one another. At the same time, by "inserting and interweaving" her own poems in the anthology, Franco is negotiating a position as writing subject and literary collaborator.

While she seems to have enjoyed considerable support behind the scenes from Domenico and Marco Venier, Franco's entrance onto the Venetian literary scene, like that of Gaspara Stampa, was met with open hostility by other poets in her circle. Just as Franco was preparing to publish her first two books, she was the target of a series of poems in Venetian dialect penned by Maffio Venier (1550–1586), Lorenzo's son and Domenico's nephew.[100] Maffio's poems, which he circulated in manuscript, demote Franco from *cortigiana onesta* to "ver unica puttana" (truly unique whore), figuring her body as wasted, wrinkled, and infected with syphilis. Maffio's attacks on Franco may have been motivated, in part, by the fact that she was directly in competition with him for the attention, support, and resources of his powerful uncle. But Franco was not, by any means, the only courtesan that Maffio targeted. Others included Livia Azzalina, to whom the *Catalogo di tutte le principal et più honorate cortigiane di Venetia* was dedicated, and Andriana Savorgnan, the courtesan we encountered earlier who was accused of using love magic to ensnare her noble Venetian lover.[101] In that sense, Maffio's dialect poems on Franco and other courtesans can be read as literary descendants of his father Lorenzo's satiric caricatures of Elena Ballarina and Angela Zaffetta, published in the 1530s and written in literary Tuscan under the guidance of Aretino. Also important, of course, is the dialect exchange between Maffio's uncle Domenico and his friend Benetto Corner on Elena Artusi, which had cast its female protagonist as alternately alluring and venal. But like the anonymous author of the satiric sonnet on Gaspara Stampa, Maffio accuses Franco not only of venality but also of social and literary pretensions.

Maffio's *capitolo* "Franca, credeme che per San Maffio" (Franco, believe me, I swear by Saint Maffio) expresses a dialectical relationship of tension and opposition with its female protagonist. The poet figures his target as whore, but he does so through a Petrarchan posture that casts him as the abject lover and her as the unresponsive, cruel lady.

To that end, he uses the more formal "voi" of love poetry to address Franco, as opposed to the usual "tu" of satiric invective:

Franca, credeme che per San Maffio,
L'è quattro mesi che fazzo custion
Se me diebbo ingrisar o star indrio:
Da una banda me piase, me sa bon
El vederve, el sentirve a rasonar.
Dall'altra sé un carigolo boccon.
Intendo che, quan'un ve vuol basar,
Volé cinque o sie scudi, e con fadiga
Con i cinquanta ve lassé chiava.
Pècca, alla fe', i parenti che no liga
Quei che ve fa ste paghe, co' avesse
El balsamo o la mana su la figa.
Quando ve vardo, sì che me infrisé;
Ma quando penso ai scudi, cazzo Amor
Co tutti i so seguazzi sotto pé.
Per darve el corpo, per donarve el cuor,
Veggiar le notte e passizar el dì
El faro da valente servidor.
...
Perché el fotter no ha gusto né savor,
I basi no xe basi, e spente spente,
Senza quel certo che se chiama Amor.
    ...
Ma un vero amor fondà su santa fede,
Un servir sviserao con tutto el cuor,
Xé d'ogni gran chiavar degna mercede.
Quest'è in conclusion tutto el mio Amor.

Franca, believe me, I swear on Saint Maffio
that I've been debating for four months
whether I should let myself fall in love with you, or hold back.
On the one hand I like it, it pleases me
to see you and to hear you talk.
On the other, you are an expensive little morsel!
What I mean is, when someone wants to kiss you,
you want five or six *scudi*, and you barely

let yourself be screwed for fifty.
It's truly a shame that families
don't tie the guys up who pay you such sums.
As if you had balsam or manna on your cunt!
When I look at you, I can't help but fall in love,
but when I think about those *scudi*, I stomp on Love
and all his followers.
To give you my body, to give you my heart,
stay up with you all night long, and walk with you all day,
I would serve [Love] valiantly.

...

Because fucking is neither pleasant nor tasty,
kisses are not kisses, nor thrusts, thrusts,
without that certain something that we call love.

...

But true love based on sacred fidelity,
and service with one's whole heart
are the just rewards for every great fuck.
This, in conclusion, is the extent of my love.[102]

On one level, Maffio's poem is a parody of the desperate Petrarchan lover who offers anything to win his lady's love. In that sense, we might read it as an attack aimed not only at Franco but also at the powerful men who wrote love poems in her honour.[103] Yet this poem also reveals a preoccupation with the relationship between courtesans and their lovers. In the opening verses, the poet sets up the tension between desire for the courtesan and repulsion for the cash transaction required to spend the night with her, a conceit that drives the entire poem. Like a proper poetic beloved, the courtesan in the poem enchants the lover with her beauty and clever conversation at the beginning of the poem. The problem, at least in this poem, is the exchange of money for sex. If the courtesan is figured as a venal whore, what does that make the man who patronizes her? Is he a courtly lover offering devoted service, or is he a sex-starved fiend willing to pay for a fix?

Four of Maffio's poems directed to Franco were edited by the Venetian scholar Manlio Dazzi in 1956, in a little book he titled "Il libro chiuso" (The closed, or secret book), a moralizing allusion to their obscene content.[104] Since then, it has been assumed that the poems edited by Dazzi represent the extent of the attack on Franco's reputation. However, given Franco's visibility in Venetian literary circles, it seems likely that there are many more that have yet to be identified. One of these is a *sonetto caudato*, "Passarà pur anche sti quatro dì" (These four days, too, will pass), found in the printed dialect anthology *Versi alla venitiana*, where it is attributed to Maffio Venier.[105] Here the poet mentions what appears to be a poetic contest between himself and the courtesan – a reference that brings to mind the challenge issued by Veronica Franco to her anonymous satirist in her *capitolo* 13, "Non più parole: ai fatti, in campo, a l'armi" (No more words! To deeds, to the battlefield, to arms!).[106] The dialect poet seems to respond to this challenge in the opening lines of his sonnet:

Passarà pur anche sti quatro dì
De st'infelice termine prescrito,
Se sarà vero quel che m'havè ditto,
e vederò, che ve burlè de mi,
se trovo, che la cossa sia cussi
voio farve un soneto el pì polito
c'habbiè mai visto, e laudar fina el sito
dove la prima volta ve scontrì.[107]

Let these four days pass
of our unhappy agreement,
and if what you've told me is true,
and I see that you are making fun of me,
if I find that that's how it is,
I want to write you the most refined sonnet
that you have ever seen, and praise you highly
where I criticized you the first time.

This sonnet reworks and expands on many of the specific conceits and metaphors Maffio had made use of in previous invectives targeting the courtesan to poke fun at her physical appearance (her extreme thinness, her long nose, and her missing teeth, for example).

Also directed to Franco, I believe, is the *capitolo* "Adesso che le zanze xe compiè" (Now that the chatter has died down), found in a manuscript in the Biblioteca Nazionale Marciana of Venice.[108] This codex, copied in an unidentified seventeenth-century hand, contains a collection of poems attributed to Maffio Venier. In the opening lines of the poem, the author declares that since gossip about the courtesan has begun to die down, he hopes with his poem to remind the city of Venice of her misdeeds.[109] He also implies that he has circulated invectives about her before, making it possible that the courtesan in question is Veronica Franco: "Mo no saràvio una bestià scannà, / se mi e te lasserò andar de sora, / e che no fosse quel che ho scomenzà (Now, wouldn't I be a crazy beast if I were to let you come out on top and not finish what I started)?"[110] Whether or not the poem is addressed to Franco, it does target a courtesan who is also a writer, linking her immorality and sexual voracity with her inferior poetic talent:

> Adesso, che le zanze xe compiè,
> E che qualche un se l'ha desementegà;
> Vogio da valent'homo far le mie.
> Mo non saravio una bestia scannà,
> Se mi e ti lasciarè de sora
> E che no fosse quel, che ho scomenzà.
> Ti è sta sempre una cagna traditora,
> Che ancora ti ha d'andar al hospedal
> Con le braze distese su una stuora.
>   …
> El zorno della ferta, e dei perdoni
> ti haverà in cao una mezza vesiga
> impegolà con verza dai cantoni.
> Pranzando te dirà voleu, che diga,
> bone persone, qualche horation?
> E loro te dirà, mostra la figa.
> Ti te sentarà zoso in t'un canton
> con l'haver sempre intorno cento putti,
> e strazze, e mosche, e scorze de melon.
> Meschina, ti sarà sogià da tutti.

> Now that the gossip has died down,
> and some people have forgotten,
> I want to make my own gossip, as a gentleman should.
> Wouldn't I be a crazy beast,
> if I let you come out on top,
> as if I weren't the one who started it.
> You have always been a traitorous bitch;
> soon you will end up in the hospital
> with your arms spread on a straw pallet.
>   …

The day of the offering, and of the pardons,
you'll have a gourd cut in half on your head,
decorated with discarded cabbage leaves.
During the banquet, you'll say, "Good people,
would you like me to recite something for you?"
And they'll say to you, "Show us your cunt!"
You'll crouch down in a corner,
with hundreds of beggar children,
rags, flies, and melon peels all around you.
You miserable wretch, you'll be ridiculed by everyone.[111]

Here it is clear that the poet is targeting the courtesan's literary pretensions. He begins by reminding her that she will end up "with her arms spread out on a pallet" – an allusion to the hospitals where prostitutes infected with syphilis ended their days. To ensure that the courtesan does not "come out on top" in their literary battle of wits, he fantasizes a scene of complete humiliation, to take place at a banquet held on a religious feast day in the presence of a crowd. Instead of the laurel wreath of an honoured poet, she wears a gourd adorned with cabbage leaves – a common trope in courtesan invective, and one used by his father Lorenzo in La puttana errante. When the courtesan offers to amuse the assembled guests with "qualche oration" – a speech or recitation of poetry – they respond only with the vulgar line, "Mostra la figa" (Show us your cunt)! Here, as in the satiric sonnet on Gaspara Stampa, the fictional courtesan is simultaneously stripped of her poetic talent and reduced to the status of sex object: her offer of poetry is rejected, and she becomes instead the object of the male gaze, synecdochically transformed into a detached, degraded vagina. The poem ends with an image of the silenced courtesan as a marginalized, ridiculed figure relegated to the alleys with beggars, street urchins, and scraps of rotting food. In the fantasy world created by the poet she is transformed from a cortigiana onesta acclaimed for her literary talent into one of the many sex workers who walked the streets of the city.

Poetry, Prostitution, and the Currency of Collaboration

Critics have been both scandalized and delighted by Veronica Franco's forthright acknowledgment of her profession as courtesan.[112] And not without good reason, since the explicit depictions of physical love and sexuality in Franco's Terze rime are quite unusual. While Gaspara

Stampa famously alluded to her physical union with Collaltino in her sonnet to the night, Franco wrote and published several passages that represent her sexual experiences quite openly.[113] The paired set of *capitoli* that open the *Terze rime* highlight Franco's erotic expertise even as they foreground her literary talent, dramatizing the tension between these two aspects of her career. Marco's *capitolo* 1, with which Franco chose to open her collection, begins with the conventional Petrarchan lament regarding the lady's resistance to his pleas. But the poet soon reveals that what he wants from Franco is sexual satisfaction, imagining that he will first admire her "membra ignude" (naked limbs) and then ravish her in her bed: "Quando giacete ne le piume stesa, / che soave assalirvi! E in quella guisa / levarvi ogni riparo, ogni difesa!" (When you lie stretched out upon the pillows, how sweet to fall upon you! And in that way to strip you of any retreat or defence!).[114] The male poet does acknowledge Franco's literary talent, but in the end, he urges her not to let her aspirations of literary fame prevent her from fulfilling her duties as courtesan. The proper use of the gifts she has received from Venus, he reminds her, is the way to fame: "Le tante da lei grazie a voi donate / spender devete in buon uso, sì come / di quelle, che vi diede Apollo, fate: / con questo eternerete il vostro nome, / non men che con gli inchiostri; e lento e infermo / farete il tempo, e le sue forse dome" (You must put to good use all the gifts that Venus made you, as you do those granted you by Apollo; you'll make your name immortal through Venus's gifts no less than you will do with your ink: And you'll slow down time, and weaken its force).[115]

At first glance, Franco's response seems to acquiesce to her lover's demands and to highlight her sexual skills rather than her literary ones. In her response, she takes up Marco's opposition between Apollo and Venus, assuring him that any man who spends time with her in bed will forget all about her singing and writing:

> Febo, che serve a l'amorosa dea,
> e in dolce guiderdon da lei ottiene
> quel che via più che l'esser dio il bea,
> a rivelar nel mio pensier ne viene
> quei modi che con lui Venere adopra,
> mentre in in soave abbracciamenti il tiene;
> ond'io istrutta a questi so dar opra
> sì bene nel letto, che d'Apollo a l'arte
> questa ne va d'assai spazio di sopra,

e 'l mio cantar e 'l mio scriver in carte
s'oblìa da chi mi prova in quella guise,
ch'a' suoi seguaci Venere comparte.

Phoebus, who serves the goddess of love,
and obtains from her as sweet reward
what blesses him far more than being a god,
comes from her to reveal to my mind
the positions that Venus assumes with him
when she holds him in sweet embraces;
so that I, well taught in such matters,
know how to perform so well in bed
that this art exceeds Apollo's by far,
and my singing and writing are both forgotten
by the man who experiences me in this way,
which Venus reveals to people who serve her.[116]

Yet Franco's emphasis on her erotic expertise over her literary talent should not be taken at face value. Her ultimate goal in *capitolo* 2 is
to convince Marco to collaborate with her by contributing poems to a
collection she is compiling – perhaps the volume commemorating the
death of Estore Martinengo.[117] This is made clear in the final lines of the
poem, where she insists on seeing the poems he has promised her as a
prerequisite for mutual love and sexual satisfaction for both of them:
"Fate che sian da me di lei vedute / quell'opre che io desìo, ché poi
saranno / le mie dolcezze a pien da voi godute; / e le vostre da me si
goderanno / per quello ch'un amor mutuo comporte" (Let me see the
works I desire from you, for then you'll enjoy my sweetness to the full,
and I will also enjoy yours, in the way that mutual love allows).[118]

Given Franco's profession and the environment in which she was
writing, the sexually explicit imagery in her *Terze rime* was a necessary
tool in her arsenal. As Jones and Rosenthal have pointed out, Franco's
insistence on literary collaboration as a prerequisite to erotic fulfilment
is unprecedented in women's writing of this period.[119] I would add that
what makes this rhetorical strategy particularly bold is how Franco
reverses conventional dynamics of gender and power in her representation of literary exchange itself. To Marco's request that she satisfy him
sexually, Franco responds by insisting that he satisfy her first by writing
poetry on her terms, a move that allows her to assume the role of literary organizer. She is careful to specify that the payment she requires is

not monetary, since "di mia professïon non è tal atto" (such an act does not suit my profession).[120] At the same time, by offering sexual satisfaction in exchange for poetry, Franco has appropriated and transformed the denigrating whore trope to assume control of the exchange of both poetry and sex, at least in the fictional world she creates in her poem.

A madrigal by Girolamo Parabosco, first published in his *Rime* of 1547, provides an interesting context for Franco's self-fashioning as a courtesan with literary aspirations. Parabosco's madrigal is in the voice of a poet who is offended by a courtesan's demands for payments – a precursor, perhaps, to Maffio Venier's dialect poem accusing Franco of similar venality. But Parabosco's poet goes one step further, proposing an exchange of her art (sex) for his (poetry):

Madonna, i' vi vo' dire
Et è questo il Vangelo,
Voi non m'amate un pelo:
Ché d'amor non fu mai segno né atto
Chiedere a un suo quattro o sei scudi a un tratto.
A non dirvi bugia,
Con la vostra vorrei far de la mia
Arte cambio e baratto:
Sì che, se voi volete,
Haver da me potrete
Canzoni e madrigali,
E a me poscia darete
Di quel che non vi costa e car vendete:
Così saremo uguali.
E quando non vi piaccia
Tal mercato, dirò: buon pro vi faccia;
Ch'anzi per spender quattro scudi o sei
In voi, di castità voto farei.

Lady, I want to tell you something,
and this is the Gospel truth:
you don't love me one bit.
Because asking one's lover for four or six *scudi* at a time
was never a sign or an act of love.
I won't lie to you,
with your art I would make of mine
an exchange, a barter:

so that, if you wish,
you'll have *canzoni* and *madrigali* from me,
and then you'll give me some of that which,
although it costs you nothing,
you sell at such a high price.
This way we will be equals.
And if that deal doesn't suit you,
I'll say, "Much good may it do you!"
Because rather than spending four or six *scudi* on you,
I would prefer to take a vow of chastity.[121]

Parabosco's peculiar position in Venetian society – at once inside and outside the privileged world of Venetian nobility – may help explain why this and many of his other literary works play heavily on themes of class and status. On one level, Parabosco's poem is a parody of the courtly lover who offers poems to win his lady's love. That said, it also reveals some of the same anxieties we saw earlier in the dialect poem by Maffio Venier. For the lover in Parabosco's madrigal, gift exchange is superior to cash payment: he wants to forget that his *Madonna* is a courtesan and thus earns her living through the exchange of physical love for material compensation. The other side of the coin, of course, is that the poet is not really the courtly lover he'd like to be, since he is the one who has presumably initiated the transaction. While he desires the courtesan, he is uncomfortable with the ramifications of exchanging money for sexual fulfilment.

Franco's *capitolo* 2 responds to and reverses the discursive dynamics of literary exchange as Parabosco had troped them in his madrigal. Parabosco's poet had offered his courtesan poetry in exchange for sexual gratification, declaring that with the exchange of his art for hers, they would be "equals." In her response to Marco Venier, Franco's literary persona proposes the reverse, turning the gender dynamic on its head. She wants poems first. Only after he has provided the literary collaboration she seeks will she fulfil his physical desires. Franco also mirrors but then reverses the claims that Parabosco had made regarding the relative value of sex and poetry. Parabosco's poet had admonished his courtesan that she should not charge so much for "something that cost her nothing." For her part, Franco assures her lover that while his poems are worth quite a lot, writing them will cost him nothing: "Dal merto la mercé non fia discosta, / se mi darete quel che, benché vaglia / al mio giudicio assai, nulla a voi costa" (There'll be no gap between merit and reward if you'll give me what, though in my opinion has great value, costs you not a thing).[122]

Through the literary persona that Franco fashions in the *Terze rime*, she challenges the sexual politics of literary exchange by appropriating the discursive terrain of the Venier salon, a homosocial network created by and for men. Stampa, too, had sought to engage powerful patrician interlocutors in literary collaboration, albeit with more conventional rhetorical strategies. Both women used the trope of literary collaboration in their poetry to negotiate a subject position as writers, resisting tropes that cast them as objects of exchange between men. Reversing and transforming tropes of currency, sex, power, and literary exchange, both Stampa and Franco reveal an extraordinary knowledge of the workings of textual masculinity.

Notes

Introduction

1 Pietro Aretino, "Capitolo di Messer Pietro Aretino al Duca di Mantova," in Aretino, *Edizione nazionale delle opere di Pietro Aretino*, vol. 6, *Operette politiche e satiriche*, pt. 2, 165. For the dating of the poem to 1530, see Marco Faini, "Nota ai testi," ibid., 324. I cite Aretino's works from the *Edizione nazionale delle opere di Pietro Aretino* (Rome: Salerno editrice, [1992]–), hereafter AEN, whenever possible. All translations are mine except where otherwise indicated.

2 "Venuta è l'ora, che pe' miei peccati / ho di freddo e di sete a morirmi io. / Che dirò? Che faro?" Pietro Aretino, "Capitolo di Messer Pietro Aretino al Duca di Mantova," 164.

3 "Una valigia inzeppata d'orpello; / con quello ancor, che poco fa gl'i ho chiesto." Pietro Aretino, "Capitolo di Messer Pietro Aretino al Duca di Mantova," 165.

4 Venier, *La puttana errante*, ed. Nicola Catelli, 42. All citations hereafter are from this edition.

5 Venier, *La puttana errante*, 90.

6 On Aretino's use of print to elicit compensation from patrons, see Richardson, *Printing, Writers, and Readers*, 91–5.

7 Before going to Mantua, Aretino had been in Florence under the protection of Cardinal Giulio de' Medici after he angered the new Pope, Adrian VI, with his unflattering pasquinades on the conclave that resulted in the Pope's election. By February 1523, Aretino was in Mantua, but he returned to Florence in April of the same year. For transcriptions of letters exchanged between Aretino and Gonzaga from this period, see Baschet, "Documents," 107–30.

8 Gonzaga to Giulio de' Medici, 24 February 2013: "la elegantia del comporre, et de' varii ragionamenti, la dolceza che copiosamente se ritrova nel prefato M. Pietro." Cited in Baschet, "Documents," 111.

9 Gonzaga to Pietro Aretino, 13 November 1524: "Piacene anche ve pregamo farne qualche volta gustar delli vostre compositioni, quando fati qualche cosa che ne possi delettar." In Baschet, "Documents," 117.

10 On Giulio Romano, Federico II Gonzaga, and the decoration of Palazzo del Te, see Hickson, "More than Meets the Eye," 41–60.

11 None of the original drawings have come to light, and we have only a few extant fragments of Raimondi's series of engravings. See Talvacchia, *Taking Positions*, 21–48.

12 "in luoghi dove meno si sarebbe pensato." Vasari, *Le vite de' più eccellenti pittori*, vol. 5, 418.

13 Aretino to Battista Zatti, 11 December 1537, in AEN, vol. 4, pt. 1, 424–6.

14 Ibid., 424–6.

15 Talvacchia argues that after he arrived in Venice in 1527, Aretino was responsible for publishing a printed book that combined Raimondi's images and his own sonnets. *Taking Positions*, 81–3. See Turner, however, for the argument that such a book may never have existed. "I modi and Aretino," I, 561.

16 Aretino to Cesare Fregoso, 9 November 1527, in AEN, vol. 4, pt. 1, 66.

17 See Talvacchia, *Taking Positions*, 45.

18 See Ergon Verheyen, *Palazzo del Te in Mantua*, 40–1 and 63.

19 Aretino and Gonzaga parted on difficult terms. While still in Mantua in 1527, Aretino wrote a bitter and satirical prognostication targeting Pope Clement VII and his court, which he dedicated to Gonzaga, who had just been appointed Captain General of the Church. After receiving a letter of protest from the Pope, Gonzaga informed Aretino that he was no longer welcome in Mantua. For more on this conflict, see Talvacchia, *Taking Positions*, 18–19.

20 "una Venere sì vera e sì viva che empie di libidine il pensiero di ciascuno che la mira." Aretino to Gonzaga, 6 August 1527, in AEN, vol. 4, pt. 1, 65. On the statue, see Boucher, who argues that Sansovino never finished it. *The Sculpture of Jacopo Sansovino*, 2: 375–6.

21 "Aspettava con devotione la Venere, hora che intendo che l'è tanto laudata lì quanto voi scriveti [sic] l'aspetto con maggior desiderio" (I had been awaiting the Venus with devotion, but now that I hear she is as praised there as you have written to me, I am waiting for her with even greater desire). Gonzaga to Aretino, 26 February 1528, in Luzio, *Pietro Aretino*, 79.

22 Gonzaga to Aretino, 21 May 1530, in AEN, vol. 9, pt. 1, 48–9.

23 On the location of Venier's palazzo, see Feldman, *City Culture*, 85n6. Feldman points out that Venier's tax report from 1566 confirms that the family palace was in the parish of Santa Maria Formosa but does not specify its exact location. For the tax report, see ASV, Dieci Savi alle Decime (166–7), b. 130, fol. 653.

24 Aretino to Domenico Venier, 18 November 1537: "I fiori del vostro aprile matureranno nel suo autunno i più soave frutti che si gustasser mai." AEN, vol. 4, pt. 1, 332.

25 Aretino to Domenico Venier and Federico Badoer, 9 June 1538. AEN, vol. 4, pt. 2, 37.

26 For more evidence that Aretino was a frequent visitor to Venier's house, see his letter to Luigi Morosini of October 1549, in which he remarks that he enjoys spending time with Morosini "tutte le volte che vi trovo dove per mala fortuna istassi il nostro Veniero innocente giovane, e come voi dotto, e come voi cortese" (all the times that I find you [in that place where] due to bad fortune, our Venier – innocent youth, erudite and courteous as you are – resides). AEN, vol. 4, pt. 5, 273.

27 The earliest description of the tomb (which was later dismantled) is in Francesco Sansovino's edition of Lodovico Dolce, *Le transformazioni tratte da Ovidio* (Venice: Francesco Sansovino, 1568), f. 4r. On Domenico Venier's epitaph for Aretino, see Monica Bianco (who was the first to attribute the epitaph to Venier), "Domenico Venier e l'epitaffio di Pietro Aretino," *Quaderni veneti* 41 (2005): 129–36.

28 For a description of the *Rime di diversi* series, see Robin, *Publishing Women*, 219–42. On the complex history of the series, see Clubb and Clubb, "Building a Lyric Canon," 332–44; and *Biblioteca del libro italiano antico*, 243–4. As Clubb and Clubb point out, although the series is decidedly a set, it has a "dubious unity," since it includes volumes by different printers and editors.

29 The concept of fragmentation of the beloved was brilliantly analysed by Vickers in "Diana Described."

30 "La casa adunque di un sì gran letterato, e quella di Bernardo Capello gravissimo poeta altresì frequentando egli nella età sia giovinetta poco curando la immaginaria dottrina, e la rea conversazione di Pietro Aretino, dietro a cui andava follemente perduto Lorenzo il fratello. E per questo Domenico e nel parlare e nello scrivere si tenne sempre entro i limiti della più castigata modestia, laddove l'altro dalla rea scuola di quel pessimo uomo guasto e corrotto, e pubblicò scritture laide" (Thus, Domenico frequented the house of such a great literary man [i.e. Pietro Bembo], as well as that of Bernardo Capello, an equally serious poet, in his tender

youth, paying little attention to the imaginary doctrine and the evil conversation of Pietro Aretino, whom his brother Lorenzo madly followed. And for this reason, Domenico always remained, in speech and in writing, within the limits of the most virtuous modesty, while the other one, ruined and corrupt by the evil school of that most terrible of men, published filthy writings). Pierantonio Serassi, "La vita del Veniero," in Domenico Venier, *Rime*, 5.

31 "Sonetti e poema in italiano di Benedetto Corner e di Domenico Venier di Venezia – corretti da altra mano più tardi," MS Add. 12.197, BL. See Feldman, *City Culture*, 101–2. I am indebted to Martha Feldman for bringing the British Library codex to my attention and encouraging me to work on it, as well as for her generosity in sharing with me her microfilm copy.

32 MS Add. 12.197, BL, fol. 1r.

33 Ibid., fol. 1r.

34 See Claude Lévi-Strauss, *The Elementary Structures of Kinship*; Rubin, "The Traffic in Women," 157–210; and Sedgwick, *Between Men*.

35 Sedgwick, *Between Men*.

36 Sedgwick, *Epistemology of the Closet*, 15.

37 Girard, *Mensonge romantique*.

38 Sedgwick, *Between Men*, 26.

39 On courtesans as a cultural trope in the imagination of Classical and Hellenistic Greece, See McClure, *Courtesans at Table*.

40 Catullus, Gaius Valerius, poems 41 and 42, in *The Poems of Catullus*, translated by Charles Martin (Baltimore: Johns Hopkins University Press, 1990), 41–2.

41 Catullus, poem 11, in *The Poems of Catullus*, 11.

42 See Ruggiero, "Prostitution: Looking For Love," for a perceptive analysis of sixteenth-century responses to prostitution: "Paradoxically, across the long sixteenth century the perception of prostitution appeared to be moving in two virtually opposite directions at once. On the one hand, it was viewed with increasing insistence as reprehensible morally, socially, and economically. But at the same time it flourished and was celebrated as never before, provided a wide range of services that were perceived as needed, fit relatively comfortably into the social and marital order of society, and even played a role in widely shared desires to more strictly define social distinctions" (158). For a discussion of the vexed questions of terminology for prostitutes, both in early modern Rome and in modern scholarship, see Cohen, "Back Talk." Throughout this book, I use the term "prostitute" as a general term for women who made their living

through the exchange of sex for material compensation (whether in cash or goods). I mean for the term to resonate as neutrally and technically as possible, despite the negative connotations inherent in its etymology. The verb form derives from the "classical Latin *prōstitūt-*, past participial stem of *prostituere* to offer for sale, to prostitute, to put to an unworthy use, to expose to public shame, dishonor" (*The Oxford English Dictionary*, s.v. "prostitute, v.," accessed 18 November 2013, http://www.oed.com).

43 This observation comes from Benjamin's notes on the French poet Charles Baudelaire (1821–1865). Benjamin, *The Arcades Project*, 361.

44 Sanudo, *I diarii*, 8: 414. More precisely, Sanudo records that Venice is home to 11,564 "femene da partido" (literally, women to be shared).

45 L. Venier, *La Zaffetta*, 11.

46 "Di Venezia non parlo, dove per magnanimità e liberalità della illustrissima repubblica … le puttane sono esempte da ogni aggravio; e son manco soggette a leggi che gli altri, quantunque ve ne siino tante." Giordano Bruno, *Il candelaio*, Biblioteca rara, vol. 18 (1863 [First ed. 1583]), 128–9.

47 Sanudo, *I diarii*, 35: 140.

48 Sanudo, *I diarii*, 35: 140.

49 Sanudo, *I diarii*, 35: 140.

50 "Polo Zigogna, di cui si fa gran stima, fu a cha' de Eugenia putana ch'el fè la cusina" (Polo Zigogna, greatly esteemed by all, was at the house of Eugenia the whore, where he ate her up). Sanudo, *I diarii*, 35: 140.

51 Sanudo, *Diarii*, 35: 155. The Signori di Notte, or "Lords of the Night" (the name derives from the fact that initially they were responsible for patrolling the city during the night), were a magistracy of the Venetian government responsible for public order and involved in policing and judging crimes such as theft, murder, and slander. For a general definition, see Andrea Da Mosto, *L'Archivio di Stato di Venezia, indice generale, storico, descrittivo ed analitico* (Rome: Biblioteca d'Arte, 1937), 1: 97. On the policing of slander or other forms of verbal injury by the Venetian government, see Horodowich, *Language and Statecraft*, 98.

52 Sanudo, *I diarii*, 35: 155.

53 "In questo zorno, se intese *publice* di uno paro di noze fatte di sier Andrea Michiel di sier Francesco da san Canziano vedovo, in una Cornelia Grifo vedoa meretrice somptuosa et bellissima, qual è stata *publice* a posta di sier Ziprian Malipiero, et hora era di sier Piero da Molin *dal Banco*, e stata di altri, rica, qual li ha in dota dà ducati … milia. Et fu fatte le noze nel monasterio di S. Zuan di Torcello; che è stata gran vergogna a la nobiltà veneta." Sanudo, *Diarii*, 41: 166. Cited and translated in Labalme, White,

and Carroll, "How to […] Get Married," 64. Sanudo's description of
Cornelia as a "meretrice somptuosa" (sumptuous or luxury prostitute)
echoes his description of Julia Lombardo in 1522 (*I diarii*, 33: 233). This
phrase may have been used for particularly wealthy prostitutes in Venice
before the term *cortigiana* became fashionable. On this, see Franco, *Poems
and Selected Letters*, 3.

54 Stanley Chojnacki, "Marriage Regulation in Venice, 1420-1535," in *Women
and Men in Renaissance Venice*, 65. See 53–75 of same for a discussion of
marriage laws in Venice during this period.

55 The *Libri d'Oro* were instituted in 1506 by the Council of Ten. On this
mandate, see Chojnacki, *Women and Men*, 63.

56 "Tener al tuto emaculato et neto el grado et ordine de la Nobilita … et in
cio consister et l'honor et la quiete et la conservacion del stato nostro" (To
keep entirely immaculate and pure the rank and order of the nobility … in
this is constituted the honor, peace, and conservation of our State). Cited in
Chojnacki, *Women and Men in Renaissance Venice*, 142n63.

57 I am thinking here of Louis Althusser's notion of ideological interpellation,
filtered through Judith Butler's subsequent work on interpellation, gender,
and performativity. See Althusser, "Idéologie et appreils idéologiques,"
67–125; and Butler, *Bodies That Matter*, 7–8.

58 The complete title of this text, which gives a better idea of its content,
is *La tariffa delle puttane di Vinegia overo Ragionamento del Forestiere e del
Gentilhuomo: nel quale si dinota il prezzo e la qualità di tutte le cortigiane di
Venegia col nome delle ruffiane. Et alcune novelle piacevoli da ridere fatte da
alcune di queste famose signore a gli suoi amorosi* (The price list of the whores
of Venice, or the discourse of the foreigner and the gentleman, in which
is indicated the price and the quality of all the courtesans of Venice, with
the names of the procuresses. And a few short, laughable tricks that some
of these famous ladies played on their lovers). All citations here are from
*La tariffa delle puttane di Venegia, accompagné d'un catalogue des principales
courtisanes de Venise, tiré des archives vénitiennes (XVIe siècle) et traduit
pour la première fois en français*, edited by Guillaume Apollinaire (Paris:
Bibliothèque des curieux, 1911), based on a manuscript copy of a sixteenth-
century edition printed in 1535. For a discussion of *La tariffa* in the context
of sixteenth-century satires targeting courtesans, including some passages
from the texts mentioning Aretino and Venier, see Rosenthal, *The Honest
Courtesan*, 39–40, 247n89. For a reading of the whore trope in *La tariffa* and
other texts of this period as a reflection of the changes in the socio-political
structure of Venice (and in particular, the identity of the patrician class),
see Pucci, "Decostruzione disgustosa."

59 Paul Larivaille has suggested that the author of *La tariffa* was Antonio
Cavallino, a correspondent of Aretino. On this, see his *Pietro Aretino*,
98–100, 442. See also Pucci, "Decostruzione disgustosa," 31n2. Larivaille's
suggestion is based on a 1536 letter from Cavallino to Aretino regarding a
text with a similar title: "Per ora non mando la Tariffa delle puttane, perché
non l'ho potuta riavere; per la prima mia la manderò" (For now I am not
sending the *Tariffa delle puttane*, because I haven't been able to get it back;
I will send it as soon as I am able), in AEN, vol. 9, pt. 1, 48–9, 234. I am
more inclined to interpret this letter as proof that Aretino was involved in
the circulation of the text (and perhaps collaborated in writing it). Further
evidence of Aretino's knowledge of the text is found in his *Dialogo, nel
quale la Nanna il primo giorno insegna a la Pippa sua figliola a esser puttana*
(Turin, 1536), in which Nanna mentions "[il] Furioso e la Tariffa de le
cortigiane di Vinegia" as appropriate topics of conversation with which to
distract lovers.

60 *La tariffa*, 28.

61 See the last line of the poem, in which the *forestiere* exclaims: "Hor fermo
son d'odiarle tutte quante" (Now I am resolved to hate them all). *La tariffa*,
130.

62 See, for example, the sonnet by Aretino that was included in Lorenzo
Venier's *La puttana errante*, which explains that the poem is meant to warn
young Venetian noblemen of the risks of frequenting whores. In Venier,
La puttana errante, 35.

63 *La tariffa*, 130.

64 *La tariffa*, 30.

65 *La tariffa*, 34.

66 *La tariffa*, 34–6.

67 For a discussion of Maffio Venier's criticisms of Veronica Franco along
these lines, see Rosenthal, *The Honest Courtesan*, 51–2, 156, 317n58.

68 For a transcription of Lotto's account books, see "Libro dei Conti di
Lorenzo Lotto," in *Le gallerie nazioni italiane: notizie e documenti*, 1: 141.

69 See MS It. Cl. IX 453 (6498), fasc. 5 (untitled), BNM. The dedication to
Cornelia is followed by a satiric *capitolo in terza rima* attacking a prostitute
named Jacomina, which also includes a mock-Roman, obscene epitaph
purporting to commemorate Jacomina's death. It is possible that Jacomina
is the "Iacoma" mentioned in a long list of "cortigianuzze o puttanelle"
(silly little courtesans or whores) in the *Dialogo dello Zoppino*, 71.

70 Turner, *Libertines and Radicals*, 1.

71 Turner, *Libertines and Radicals*, 2.

72 For a discussion of the importance of love in Renaissance prostitution, see
Guido Ruggiero, "Prostitution: Looking for Love," 157–74.

73 All three terms appeared in many different forms: *meretrice = meretrize*,
puttana = putana, cortigiana = cortesana, cortegiana, cortiggiana, etc. Here I use
the standard modern spelling for the sake of clarity.

74 For a discussion of the control of prostitution by Venetian authorities, see
Ruggiero, *Binding Passions*, 48–56.

75 *Provveditori sopra la Sanità*, Capitolare, I. c. 33r, ASV. Cited in Pavan, "Police
des moeurs," 263. Another decree, also dated 1524, uses similar language
to define courtesans as a type of whore: "le cortesane e altra sorte de
puttane et femmine de tal sorte" (courtesans and other kinds of whores
and women of that sort). *Sette Savii*, Giustizia nuova, c. 109, ASV.

76 Cohen, "'Courtesans' and 'Whores,'" 204.

77 Cohen argues that "the problem with Renaissance prostitutes was an
irreducible ambiguity or doubleness in what they represented to others.
Courtesans and whores, alike, were at once desirable and despicable,
appealing and appalling." "'Courtesans' and 'Whores,'" 201.

78 Burchard, *Diarium sive rerum urbanarum*, 2: 442.

79 Burchard, *Diarium sive rerum urbanarum*, 3: 187.

80 For an illuminating discussion of the terms *onesto* and *disonesto*, see Bette
Talvacchia, "Terms of Renaissance Discourse about the Erotic," in *Taking
Positions*, 101–24.

81 On the meaning of *cortigiana onesta*, see Jones and Rosenthal's introduction
to Veronica Franco, *Poems and Selected Letters*, 3.

82 For a modern edition of the census, see Mariano Armellini, "Un
censimento della città di Roma sotto il pontificato di Leone X," offprint
from *Gli studi in Italia* IV–V (Rome: A. Befani, 1882). Armellini dates
the census between 1511 and 1518. I have not been able to consult the
original document (which, according to Armellini, is held in the Biblioteca
Apostolica Vaticana).

83 See Arturo Graf, "Una cortigiana fra mille: Veronica Franco," *Attraverso il
cinquecento* (Turin: E. Loescher, 1888), 226.

84 The oft-cited phrase "cortesana da lume" occurs only once in Armellini's
transcription of the Roman census, and Armellini himself was uncertain
that he had transcribed it correctly. "Un censimento," 74.

85 See Horodowich, *Language and Statecraft in Early Modern Venice*, 125.

86 The *Vocabolario degli Accademici della Crusca* (Venice: Giovanni Alberti,
1612) defined the word *meretrice* as "femmina, che fa copia del suo corpo
altrui per mercede" (a woman who allows another to benefit from her
body for compensation) (523). The definition for *puttana* is identical except
that it adds the adverb "disonestamente" (dishonestly): "femmina, che,
per mercede, fa copia *disonestamente* altrui del suo corpo [italics mine]" (a

woman who, for compensation, *dishonestly* allows another to benefit from her body) (668). The crucial difference between the two, then, was the "dishonest" way in which they sold their bodies, not the act of selling sex itself. Talvacchia and others have focused on *onesto* and *disonesto*, when applied to prostitutes, as qualifiers that indicate social and economic status of both the women themselves and their partners. I would add another layer to the significance of that binary: *onesto* could also mean "dicevole" (literally, "sayable"), or seemly.

87 See the entry for "puttana" in the *Dizionario etimologico della lingua italiana* (Bologna: Zanichelli, 1985).

88 *Ragionamento del Zoppino fatto frate, e Lodovico puttaniere, dove contiensi la vita et geneologia di tutte le cortigiane di Roma* (Venice: Francesco Marcolini, 1539).

89 *La prima parte de Ragionamenti di M. Pietro Aretino cognominato il Flagello de prencipi, il Veritiero, el Divino, divisa in tre giornate, la contenenza de le quali si porra ne la facciata seguente* (Bentigodi [London]: [John Wolfe], 1584), 355–401.

90 See Lanfranchi's introduction to *Dialogo dello Zoppino: de la vita e genealogia di tutte le cortigiane di Roma* (Milan: L'Editrice del libro raro, 1922), 7. For a more recent discussion of the authorship of the Zoppino dialogue, as well as an English translation, see Salked, "History, Genre and Sexuality," who discounts the attribution to Delicado.

91 "[P]uttana è un nome composto di vulgare e di Latino. Perchè ano in latino si dice quel che in nostra lingua si chiama culo, dove che si compon di potta et ano: et in vulgar nostro, puttana vuol dire, che li pute la tana, e cortigiana, cortese dell'ano." *Dialogo dello Zoppino*, 55.

92 "Le puttane dunque, o cortigiane, che tu dire le vogli, Ludovico mio caro, son mala cosa." *Dialogo dello Zoppino*, 42. This line is probably an homage to the so-called "novella delle papere" (the novella "of the ducks") in the introduction to the fourth day of Boccaccio's *Decameron*, wherein a father teaches his son the same lesson: "Figliuol mio, bassa gli occhi in terra, non le guatare, ch'elle son mala cosa" (My son, look down at the ground, don't look at them, for they are an evil thing). Boccaccio, *Decameron*, 465.

93 Pasquino, *Consigli vtilissimi*, cited in Vittorio Cian, *Galanterie italiane del secolo XVI*, 60.

94 Speroni, "Orazione contra le cortegiane," in *Opere*, vol. 3, 220.

95 Ruggiero, *Binding Passions*, 33.

96 For a discussion of the status, wealth, and possessions of Julia Lombardo, one of the courtesans satirized in *La tariffa delle puttane*, see Cathy Santore, "Julia Lombardo."

97 Ruggiero, *Binding Passions*, 38.

98 Documents related to Savorgnan's trial are found in Sant'Uffizio, busta 47, ASV. On Andriana Savorgnan, see Ruggiero, *Binding Passions*, 24–56. See also Milani, *Streghe e diavoli*.

99 Ruggiero, *Binding Passions*, 55.

100 Sant'Uffizio, busta 47 (Andriana Savorgnan, testimony of Laura Savorgnan), fol. 76v, ASV. The transcription of the original text is mine. The translation is Ruggiero's in *Binding Passions*, 32.

101 On the *Provveditori alle Pompe*, a council of the Venetian government that regulated dress and display of wealth in general, focused on prostitutes, see Ruggiero, *Binding Passions*, 49. On Andriana's arrest and confinement, see same, 37.

102 Ruggiero, *Binding Passions*, 37. A case involving the Florentine courtesan Giuliana Napolitana, also uncovered by Ruggiero, makes an interesting complement to this one and underscores the power that some courtesans had to choose their lovers. In 1562 the Venetian patrician Luigi Dolfin sought legal action against Giuliana after she refused to spend the night with him, despite having taken money from him earlier in the day to guarantee her presence. The court ordered Giuliana to fulfil her promise but gave her the option of refusing to do so, on the condition that she repay Dolfin his deposit. See Ruggiero, "Who's Afraid of Giuliana Napolitana?"

103 Sant'Uffizio, busta 47 (Andriana Savorgnan, testimony of Aloisio Soranzo), fol. 11r. ASV. Cited in Ruggiero, *Binding Passions*, 28. I have slightly adapted Ruggiero's translation.

104 Sant'Uffizio, busta 47 (Andriana Savorgnan, testimony of a male witness [Angelo?], and of Catherina Bereta), fol. 3r, ASV. Transcription and translation mine.

105 See Giovanni Battista Lorenzi, ed., *Leggi e memorie venete sulla prostituzione fino alla caduta della Repubblica* (Venice: [Published privately for Lord Orford], 1870–2).

106 For a contemporary example of this belief, see Sanudo: "Nota che, per influxi celesti, da anni doi in qua, zoè da poi la venuta de' francesi in Italia, si ha scoperto una nova egritudine in li corpi humani dicto mal franzoso, lo qual ma sì in Italia come in Grecia, Spagna et quasi per tutto il mondo è dilatado" (A note that, because of celestial influences, for two years now – that is, since the arrival of the French in Italy, we have discovered a new disease of the human body, called the French disease, which has spread in Italy, as in Greece, Spain, and almost the entire rest of the world). *I diarii*, vol. 1, pt. 1, 233–4.

107 See Shemek, "Mi mostrano a ditto tutti quanti."

108 Venier, *La puttana errante*, 134.

109 Shemek, "Mi mostrano a dito tutti quanti," 58.

110 Although the majority of texts considered "alla bulesca" are in Venetian, some are partly or entirely in other regional dialects, mainly *pavano* (a rustic form of Paduan dialect used most famously by the playwright Angelo Beolco, also known as Ruzante) or *bergamasco* (the dialect associated with the city of Bergamo).

111 I will use the Venetian spelling here (*bulo/i*, as opposed to the Italian *bullo/o*). The first documented use of the adjective "bulesco" to describe this literature is found in a letter written by Aretino in 1549 to Domenico Venier. Aretino describes an outing in a gondola with several Venetian noblemen during which he was enraptured by "non so che bulesco in canzone" (an unknown *canzone* about *buli*). Aretino to Venier, AEN, vol. 4, pt. 5, 312.

112 Cesare Vecellio describes *bravi* as armed thugs who were paid to serve various masters: "erano chiamati anticamente gladiatori et hoggidì bravi, overo sbrichi, i quali per danari servono hor questo hor quello, biastemando et bravando senza proposito, et commettendo varii scandali et homicidii" (in the old days they were called gladiators, and today *bravi*, or sbrichi, who for money serve various masters by turns, blaspheming and causing trouble without instigation, and committing various scandalous acts and murders). Vecellio, *Habiti antichi e moderni*, 128r.

113 See Walker, "*Bravi* and Venetian Nobles." Walker points out that modern historians of Venice often use *bandito* (bandit, or exile) as a synonym for *bravo*, although the two terms were not synonyms in legislation: "*bravi* were often *banditi*, but *banditi* were not necessarily *bravi*" (85).

114 The most influential example of this type is probably *La canzona de Averzi Marcolina con la risposta insieme di Marcolina, et una bella bravata et uno bello sonetto, stampata novamente* (The *canzone* 'Ah, open up, Marcolina,' together with Marcolina's response, a lovely *bravata*, and a lovely sonnet, newly printed, (s.l.: s.d., Giovanpiero Stampadore), which circulated in pamphlet form in the 1520s and was mentioned by Aretino in his comedy *Il Marescalco*, printed in 1533 but composed a few years earlier. AEN, vol. 5, pt. 1, 38–9.

115 *La bulesca* is found in a codex in the Biblioteca Nazionale Marciana of Venice ("Commedie varie del secolo XVI," MS It. Cl. IX 288 [6072]), which also contains Ruzante's *La Pastoral* and two anonymous Venetian

comedies, *La Venexiana* and *Ardelia*. On this codex, the only known copy for all four of the comedies it contains, see Da Rif, *La letteratura "alla bulesca,"* esp. 39–43.

116 "Sbrichi," yet another word for Venetian *bravi*, can be literally translated as "raggedy" – a reference to how these characters must have dressed.

117 "In questa sera, in una casa a San Zane Polo, per li compagni chiamati Zardinieri, fo, poi cena, recità una comedia tra loro piacevole de sbrichi venitiani, che fu bel veder, et molti vi andano a vederla." Sanudo, *I diarii*, 19: 122. For more information about the possible date of *La bulesca*, see Da Rif, *La letteratura "alla bulesca,"* 20–8.

118 See Da Rif, *La letteratura "alla bulesca,"* 3.

119 Sanudo, *I diarii*, 18: 265.

120 Sanudo, *I diarii*, 52: 553.

121 Cited in Da Rif, *La letteratura alla "bulesca,"* 53.

122 "[M]a la ne ha dao perfina a un sarasin" (But she's even given it up to a Turk). In Da Rif, *La letteratura alla "bulesca,"* 55.

123 Molmenti, *La storia di Venezia*, 2: 468–9.

124 Da Rif, *La letteratura alla "bulesca,"* 55–6.

125 My translation is influenced by Da Rif's gloss in *La letteratura "alla bulesca,"* where she suggests that "Te par che 'l sona?" (literally, "Do you think he jingles?") is an allusion to the clinking of coins.

126 Da Rif, *La letteratura "alla bulesca,"* 58.

127 Ibid., 56–7.

128 Examples of these are the *Bravata che fa un giovane innamorato di una cortigiana, e lei dandogli la baglia mai gli volse aprir la porta* (*Bravata* of a young man in love with a courtesan who, tricking him, never wanted to open the door for him, s.l., s.d.) and the *Bulata alla veneziana ridicolosa, esempio a quelli che leggeranno* (Ridiculous *bulata* in the Venetian style, an example to those who will read it). For a modern edition of this last, see Da Rif, ed., *La letteratura "alla bulesca."*

129 "Il diletto mi si converse in doglia … mostrandomi che la infermità vi aliena da i negozii della republica … Onde il letto dove giacete vi è diventato istudio e palazzo. Palazzo con ciò sia ne i maneggi de lo stato, i di voi consigli non gli sono di minore importanza che l'essercizio de la vostra persona; studio imperocché l'intelletto di che soprabbondate, non prefersice attimo, punto, o momento, che si appartenga a i debiti de la imaginazione, del comporre, e de lo scrivere … E perché nulla manchi, la frequenza de lo erudito comerzio vi allegerisce in modo il peso de l'afflizione, con la grazia dei nobili ragionamenti, che i rimedii de le medicine confessano di non essere così bene atti a giovarvi. Perché

invero più conforto di convaliscenza recano due visite de l'amico, che mille ricette di Galeno; il fruire con la vista la sembianza salutifera de l'amorevole sozietade, è una valitudine incomprensibile." Aretino to Domenico Venier, Venice, March 1546, in AEN, vol. 4, pt. 4, 26. I have translated "sozietade" as "sodality," given the context of male discourse and friendship.

130 Foucault, "The Discourse on Language." Foucault's original reads "société de discours" (society of discourse), which the English translator has rendered as "fellowship of discourse." In this context I prefer "fraternity" in order to emphasize the discourse society's potential to cement bonds between men and the ways in which, during this period, it could exclude women. I am grateful to Karen-edis Barzman for generously pointing me towards this text and sharing with me her thoughts on the usefulness of this concept for early modern groups. See her *The Florentine Academy and the Early Modern State*, especially chap. 6, "Fellowships of Discourse: The Academy's Confraternity and Guild," which has animated my discussion here.

131 Foucault, "The Discourse on Language," 225.

132 The poem is "Adesso, che le zanze xe compìe, e che qualche un se l'ha desmentegà, / vogio da valent'huomo far le mie" (Now that the chatter has finished, and some people have forgotten, I want to make my own [chatter], as a gentleman would). MS It. Cl. IX 217 (7061), 63r., BNM.

133 Ruggiero, *Machiavelli in Love*, 8.

134 Ruggiero, *Machiavelli in Love*, 8. As Ruggiero points out, his argument regarding the ways in which men could negotiate their societal identity is a reworking of Stephen Greenblatt's concept in *Renaissance Self-Fashioning*.

135 See Ruggiero, "Marriage, Love, Sex," 10–30; and *Machiavelli in Love*, 24–8. For a discussion of masculinity in Renaissance comedy, see Giannetti, "Men in Women's Clothing," ch. 3 in *Lelia's Kiss*, 113–52.

136 See Wiegman, "Unmaking."

137 Breitenberg, *Anxious Masculinity*.

138 Breitenberg, *Anxious Masculinity*, 1.

139 See Butler, *Gender Trouble*.

140 Finucci, *The Manly Masquerade*, 7.

141 Milligan and Tylus, *The Poetics of Masculinity*, 21. See also Milligan's insightful readings of the spectre of effeminacy in Castiglione and Machiavelli: "The Politics of Effeminacy in 'Il cortegiano" and "Masculinity and Machiavelli."

142 Simons, *The Sex of Men in Premodern Europe*, 17.

1. Gang Rape and Literary Fame

1 On Aretino's residence in Venice and his relationship with his landlord Domenico Bollani, see Cairns, "Domenico Bollani," 193–205.
2 The letter, which is addressed "Al divino signor Pietro Aretino il suo Lorenzo Veniero" (To the divine Signor Pietro Aretino from his Lorenzo Veniero), can be found in Aretino, *Al gran marchese*.
3 Lorenzo Venier, "Al divino signor Pietro Aretino il suo Lorenzo Veniero," in Aretino, *Al gran marchese del Vasto*, n.p.
4 For Aretino's letters to Lorenzo Venier and about him, see AEN, vol. 4, pt. 1, letters 203 and 280; vol. 2, letters 131, 409, and 457; vol. 3, letters 357 and 652; vol. 4, letters 12, 113, 516, 578, 580, 584–5, 620, and 638; vol. 5, letters 355–356.
5 Pietro Aretino, *De le lettere di m. Pietro Aretino. Libro primo* (Venice: Marcolini, 1538).
6 See Amedeo Quondam, *Le carte messaggiere* (Rome: Bulzoni, 1981), 30.
7 Aretino to Lorenzo Venier, Venice, 24 September 1537, in AEN, vol. 4, pt. 1, 290.
8 Aretino to Lorenzo Venier, Venice, October 1546. "Io, che per la consanguinità dell'amore ardisco di cognominarmivi padre, non credeva ch'a si fatta sorte di affettione potesse intervenire altra conditione di benevolenza; e non è percio' il vero, perochè si unisce con le sue caritatevoli intrinsichezze di amistade la tenace copula della sacra affinità del comparatico. Onde sentomi ricercare lo intrinseco fervor delle viscere con tacita dolcezza di affettione: che più non se ne può sentire, quanto a le tenerezze carnali." AEN, vol. 4, pt. 3, 312–13.
9 For a discussion of the social dynamics of godfathering and friendship in early modern Florence, see Christiane Klapisch-Zuber, *Women, Family, and Ritual in Renaissance Italy* (Chicago: University of Chicago Press, 1985), 85–93.
10 Aretino to Lorenzo Venier, Venice, October 1549. AEN, vol. 4, pt. 5, 278.
11 For Franco's biography and literary career, see Paul F. Grendler, *Critics of the Italian World, 1530–1560: Anton Francesco Doni, Nicolò Franco & Ortensio Lando* (Madison: University of Wisconsin Press, 1969). On Franco and Aretino, see Raymond B. Waddington, "A Satirist's Impresa: The Medals of Pietro Aretino," in *Renaissance Quarterly* (1989): 655–81.
12 Aretino to Francesco Zeno, Venice, January 1546: "Io cominciai con l'obligo con che sempre voglio che mi teniate legato, allora che vi parse (per aver autorità di amicizia seco) commettere il Veniero Lorenzo, garzone di nobile ingegno, a la cura dei miei andari. Onde e dal di voi pensar ciò e dal di lui

ciò sperare e dal di me ciò credermi, è riuscita sua Magnficenza della stima che ognun vede. Talche la vostra opinione, la sua fidanza e la mia credenza merita lode, commendazione e onore." AEN, vol. 4, pt. 3, 487.

13 For a list of modern editions of Lorenzo Venier's poems and letters, see Catelli, ed., *La puttana errante*, 29–30.

14 Pietro Aretino, "Capitolo di Messer Pietro Aretino al Duca di Mantova," in AEN, vol. 6, pt. 2, 165.

15 Aretino addressed Lorenzo as "magnifico figliuolo in a letter of 1537 (Aretino to Lorenzo Venier, Venice, 23 September 1537, in AEN, vol. 4, pt. 1, 290). See note 7 above.

16 Pietro Aretino, *Opera noua zoe strambotti sonetti capitoli epistole barzellette & una desperate* (Venice: Zoppino, 1512).

17 Aretino to Vittoria Colonna, 9 January 1538. AEN, vol. 4, pt. 1, 312.

18 "La monica tradisce il suo consagramento, e la maritata assassina il santo matrimonio; ma la puttana non la attacca né al monistero né al marito: anzi fa come un soldato che è pagato per far male, e facendolo non si tiene che lo faccia, perché la sua bottega vende quello che ella ha a vendere." Aretino, *Ragionamento- Dialogo*, 275. Translation by Raymond Rosenthal, in *Aretino's Dialogues*, 150.

19 The phrase comes from the rubric preceding the first day's discussion, which reads as follows: "In questa prima giornata del Dialogo di Messer Pietro Aretino la Nanna insegna a la sua figliola Pippa l'arte puttanesca" (In this the first day of Messer Pietro Aretino's Dialogue, Nanna teaches her daughter Pippa the art of being a whore). See the first edition of *Aretino's Dialogues*.

20 "Se ci è alcun vertuoso, accostategli con faccia allegra, mostrando di apprezzar più loro che (mi farai tutto si bandisse di quelle ladre cose che sanno dir de le donne: e ti staria bene che fosse stampata la tua vita come non so chi scioperato ha stampata la mia, come ci mancassero puttane di peggior sorte di me." Aretino, *Ragionamento-Dialogo*, ed. Carla Forno (Milan: Rizzoli, 1998), 324. Translation mine.

21 For the phrase "dialoghi puttaneschi" (whorish dialogues), see Aretino's letter to Gianiacopo Lionardi, 9 December 1537, in AEN, vol. 4, pt. 1, 389. On Aretino's cultural impact in sixteenth- and seventeenth-century England, see Moulton, *Before Pornography*.

22 For a discussion of the composition and dating of Aretino's dialogues, see Paolo Procaccioli, "*Ragionamento e Dialogo* di Pietro Aretino," in *Letteratura Italiana Einaudi*, vol. II, ed. Alberto Asor Rosa (Turin: Einaudi, 1993).

23 In 1555, Medoro Nucci wrote to Aretino accusing him of having written both the *Trentuno della Zaffetta* and the *Puttana errante*. Cited in Catelli, *Puttana errante*, 23n9.

24 Venier, *La puttana errante* ([Venice]: n.p., n.d.) and *La Zaffetta* ([Venice]: n.p., n.d.), in the BNF (Enfer 559 and 559bis). The BNF also holds two other undated octavo pamphlets containing *La puttana errante* (Enfer 560) and *La Zaffetta* (Enfer 561). These, too, have been dated to the sixteenth century; tellingly, each has a frontispiece incorrectly indicating its author as "Maf. Ven." (Maffio Venier [1550–1586], Lorenzo's son and the author of erotic dialect poems). Finally, there is a third sixteenth-century edition of both poems bound together with fourteen woodcuts of Giulio Romano's "I modi," along with Aretino's accompanying sonnets. This volume (known as the "Toscanini" volume because it was once in the possession of Walter Toscanini, the son of the famous conductor) is now in a private collection, but a microfilm copy can be found at the British Library (P.C.16.h.3). For a description of these early editions, along with a discussion of printing dates, see Venier, *La puttana errante*, 94–6.

25 The lost edition is described in Giovanni Maria Mazzuchelli, *La vita di Pietro Aretino, scritta dal conte Giammaria Mazzucchelli* (Brescia: Pietro Pianta, 1763), 237; and in Salvatore Bongi, *Annali di Gabriel Giolito de' Ferrari da Trino di Monferrato, stampatore in Venezia*. 2 vols. (Rome: Ministero della Pubblica Istruzione, 1890), vol. 2, 30. Both sources mention only *La puttana errante*, but since in the 1531 pamphlet *La puttana errante* appears first and each poem has its own title page, it is possible that the 1538 edition also included *La Zaffetta*.

26 On Ippolito Ferrarese and Aretino's poem, see Giancarlo Petrella, '"Ad instantia d'Hippolito Ferrarese". Un cantimbanco editore nell'Italia del Cinquecento,' in *Paratesto*, 8 (2011), 23–79. On Ferrarese and the culture of cheap print, see Rosa Salzberg, "In the mouths of charlatans: street performers and the dissemination of pamphlets in Renaissance Italy," in *Renaissance Studies* 24, no. 5 (2010): 638–53, and idem, *Ephemeral City: Cheap Print and Urban Culture in Renaissance Venice* (Manchester: Manchester University Press, 2014). I am grateful to Rosa Salzberg for sharing with me the proofs of her book just before it went to press.

27 On Aretino's identification with Pasquino, the famous talking statue of Rome, see Waddington, *Aretino's Satyr*, 18–27.

28 Venier, *La puttana errante*, 35.

29 "Il Divino Pietro Aretino all'autore," in Venier, *La puttana errante*, 36.

30 For the sonnet, see Ms. It. Cl. XI 66, BNM, 324r. where it is titled "Pietro Aretino pel suo ritratto che zetta la laurea ghirlanda" (Pietro Aretino, on

his portrait in which he rejects the laurel wreath). On the portrait, see Freedman, *Titian's Portraits*, 37.

31 See Waddington, *Aretino's Satyr*, esp. 93–107.

32 See Marsand, *I manoscritti italiani*, 753.

33 Venier, *La puttana errante*, 37.

34 This motif has a rich literary history before Petrarch. See Petrarca, *Trionfi*, 240.

35 Cf. Francis Petrarch, *Triumphi*, II, vv. 79–87; and Venier, *La puttana errante*, canto II, octave 43.

36 "Beati coloro che aprono le orecchie del cuore alla gran tromba del quinto Evangelista, San Giovanni Boccaccio, e guai a quelli che agli incazziti fernetichi di Messar Petrarcha si lasciano menar la fava, perché l'uno è accesa candela de la buona strada, e l'altro è tenebre di chi coglionescamente crede che la sua Monna Laura pisciasse acqua d'Angioli, e cacasse ambracane." Venier, *La puttana errante*, 2. Ambergris (*ambracane*) is a very valuable substance found in the intestinal tract of the sperm whale, still in use today as an ingredient in perfume.

37 Venier, *La puttana errante*, 34.

38 The origin of the term is uncertain. Giuseppe Boerio's *Dizionario del dialetto veneziano* (Venice: A. Santini, 1829) defines the expression "aver un trentauno" as "aver gran paura" (to be very scared). See also Raya's introduction to Venier, *La Zaffetta*, xxviii. Raya notes (without citing his source) that Apostolo Zeno believed Angela's misfortune was the reason this expression came to refer to a particularly traumatic event experienced by the speaker. An Italian (rather than Venetian) phrase, "fare trentuno per forza" (to be forced to do something against one's will), is mentioned in the *Nuovo vocabolario illustrato della lingua italiana*, edited by Giacomo Devoto and Gian Carlo Oli (Milan: Le Monnier, 1987), 2: 3297. The same source notes that the expression probably derives from a card game called *trentuno*, a variation on the better-known game of *ventuno* (twenty-one).

39 See Ruggiero, "Marriage, Love, Sex," 17–18. On the prosecution of rape, see Ruggiero, "Violence and Sexuality: Rape," ch. 5 in his *The Boundaries of Eros*, 89–108.

40 See Jacques Rossiaud, "Fraternités de jeunesse et niveau de culture dans les villes du Sud-est à la fin du moyen âge," *Cahiers d'Histoir* 1–2 (1976): 67–102.

41 I am grateful to Guido Ruggiero for this insight, which he offered in a private communication.

42 On the *charivari*, see Edward Muir, *Ritual in Early Modern Europe* (Cambridge: Cambridge University Press, 2005), 106–12, 120–3. On the *mattinata*, see Christiane Klapisch-Zuber, "The 'Mattinata' in Medieval

Italy," in *Women, Family, and Ritual in Renaissance Italy*, trans. Lydia
G. Cochrane (Chicago: University of Chicago Press. 1985), 261–82.

43 Klapisch-Zuber, "The 'Mattinata' in Medieval Italy," 270.

44 Venier, *La Zaffetta*, 63

45 Venier, *La Zaffetta*, 31.

46 Venier, *La Zaffetta*, 39.

47 Venier, *La Zaffetta*, 39.

48 "E tu savia ... Pater noster ... verrai vestita da uomo, perché
questi palafrenieri ... qui es in celis ... fanno di matti scherzi la
notte ... santificetur nomen tuum ... e non vorrei che tu scappassi in
un trentuno ... adveniat regnum tuum ... come incappò Angela del
Moro ... in cielo et in terra." AEN, vol. 5, pt. 1, 306.

49 Pietro Aretino, *Ragionamento-Dialogo*, 242.

50 Aretino, *Ragionamento-Dialogo*, 295.

51 Aretino, *Ragionamento-Dialogo*, 298.

52 Aretino, *Ragionamento-Dialogo*, 440–2.

53 "Lo mio cor è feruto – Madonna, nol so dir" (My heart is wounded,
Milady, I don't know how to say it). Jacopone da Todi, "De la beata vergine
e del peccatore (lauda 1)" (Of the Blessed Virgin and the Sinner), in *Laude*,
ed. Franco Mancini (Bari: Laterza, 1974).

54 "più di la che di qua ... i suoi occhi infocati, le sue gote molli, i suoi capegli
scompigliati, le sue labbra secche e le sue veste squarciate." Aretino,
Ragionamento-Dialogo, 441. Translation by Raymond Rosenthal, *Aretino's
Dialogues*, 267.

55 Venier, *La Zaffetta*, 57.

56 Freud, "Jokes and Their Relation to the Unconscious," 99. I am grateful
to one of the anonymous readers for the press for suggesting that Freud's
work on jokes might offer some insight into the literary dynamics I explore
here.

57 Freud, "Jokes," 100.

58 The first usage of the term as a pseudonym for gang rape that I have been
able to identify is in the manuscript version of Aretino's *La cortigiana*,
which he wrote in Rome around 1525 and never published. He would later
add Angela del Moro's name to the 1534 print edition, as discussed above.

59 Aretino referred to Titian, Angela, and himself as "un pittore da senno, un
poeta da tanto e ... una cortigiana da vero" (a wise painter, a great poet, and
a true courtesan) in a letter to Marcantonio Morosini, the podestà (magistrate)
of Treviso. Aretino to Morosini, October 1549, AEN vol. 5, pt. 5, 481

60 "E fassi figlia del Procuratore / da cà Grimani" (And she claims to be the
daughter of the procurator from the House of Grimani).Venier, *La Zaffetta*, 11.

61 "E nel venir zoso di Conseio a la scala era il cardinal di Medici vestito
   incognito con monsignor Valier e do altri che stava a veder venir zoso
   conseio. E la sera fo a dormir da una cortesana chiamata la Zaffetta, sta ...
   [left blank]" (The Cardinal de' Medici, incognito, was on the stairs with
   Monsignor Valier and two others to see the Council come down. And that
   evening, he slept at the house of a courtesan called "La Zaffetta," who
   lives ...). Sanudo, *I diarii*, vol. 57.

62 Aretino to Angela Zaffetta, December 1548:

> Quanto sia estremo il desiderio, che tiene il padre di veder la figlia,
> non accade dimostrarlo con parole a chi di figliuoli è madre. Sì che
> non mettete più legne al fuoco di quella volontà ch'io ho di godere al
> presente voi, che tale mi sète in l'amore quali mi è Adria in la carne.
> Caso che la invidia volesse mo tassare questo mio vanto di benivolen-
> zia inverso la mia signora Angela, lascio risponderle a la vostra bontà
> graziosa; ché, se bene fino da fanciulla tenera ne sono stato e ministro
> e rettore e padrone, mai altra sorte di carità non conosceste in me che
> si conosca Austria del mio sangue nasciutaci. Ma, se l'osservanza de
> l'affezione che vi porto servò sempre i termini del suo dovuto proce-
> dere nel tempo de la mia gioventù lasciva, credasi pure che il rispetto
> che tengo al vostro onore sia due volte maggiore, or ch'io mi sento ne
> la vecchiezza onestissima. Venite adunque doman da sera a cena con
> la eternità dei vostri antichi avvocati: con Tiziano, col Sansovino e con
> meco; cioè perché in loro è raddoppiata l'amorevolezza in tanto, in
> quanto voi avete mutata la vita licenziosa in continente. AEN, vol. 5,
> pt. 5, 119.

63 Aretino, *Ragionamento-Dialogo*, 383.

64 Aretino, *Ragionamento-Dialogo*, 385.

65 Aretino, *Ragionamento-Dialogo*, 384.

66 Aretino, *Ragionamento-Dialogo*, 384.

67 "Zaffetta, io 'l vo' pure dire, / s'io vi fottesse ch'io possa morire; / che ne
   la potta vostra/ sovente Amor con le piatole giostra; poi sì culo havete,/
   che v'intre." MS It. XI 66 (=6730), c. 326v, BNM. For a modern edition of
   this manuscript, see *Scritti di Pietro Aretino nel codice Marciano It. XI 66
   (=6730)*, edited by Danilo Romei (Florence: Franco Cesati, 1987).

68 LaGuardia, *Intertextual Masculinity*, 4.

69 Apostolo Zeno argued that the first edition should be dated to 1531. See
   his *Lettere di Apostolo Zeno*, 3:296 and passim.

70 Alessandro Zanco to Aretino, 27 March 1536, in AEN, vol. 9, pt. 1, 280.

71 Aretino, *Ragionamento-Dialogo*, 440.
72 Aretino, *Ragionamento-Dialogo*, Translation by Raymond Rosenthal, taken from Aretino, *Aretino's Dialogues*, 266.
73 In Venier's poem, the text of the song is slightly different: "La vedovella, quando dorme sola, / lamentarsi di me, non ha raggione" (The young widow, when she sleeps alone, has no right to complain about me). Venier, *La Zaffetta*, 33.
74 For a discussion of Gentile Sermini's tale of Scopone, a non-sexual literary *mattinata* with a male victim, see Ruggiero, *Macchiavelli in Love*, 206–7.
75 The same song was mentioned in Ruzante's dialect comedy *La Piovana* (1532) and again in Agostino Ricchi's *Tre Tiranni*, performed in Bologna in 1533. For more information on this song and some possible variations of the text, see d'Ancona, *La poesia popolare italiana*, 95–6.
76 Cited in d'Ancona, *La poesia popolare italiana*, 95.
77 For a discussion of gang rape as a rite of passage, a demonstration of sexual maturity for young men, and an initiation into prostitution for the women it dishonoured, see Jacques Rossiaud, *Medieval Prostitution*, trans. Lydia Cochrane (Oxford: Basil Blackwell, 1988), esp. ch. 2.
78 For this scene and for the argument that Giannicco is "growing up and leaving behind his youthful relationship with the Marescalco," see Aretino, "The Master of the Horse," in *Five Comedies from the Italian Renaissance*, ed. and trans. Laura Giannetti and Guido Ruggiero (Baltimore: Johns Hopkins University Press), 152 and n.
79 Venier, *La Zaffetta*, 47.
80 Venier, *La Zaffetta*, 47.
81 Venier, *La Zaffetta*, 49.
82 I am indebted to one of the anonymous readers for this insight.
83 "Intanto il porcaccio la stiracchia fino al ceppo di un mandorlo tagliato; e appoggiatole ivi la testa, le rovescia i panni in capo; e cacciatognele dove gli parve, la ringraziò del servigio con due sculacciate de le più crudele che si potesson sentire. E questo fu il cenno che si fece al secondo, il quale la travoltò sul ceppo; e facendolo a buon modo, aveva piacer grande de le punte del legno mal polito le quali le pungevano il sedere, onde ella, a suo dispetto, spingeva inverso colui che, nel compire, le fece fare il capotombolo scimiesco; e il gridar che ella face chiamò il terzo giostrante." Aretino, *Ragionamento-Dialogo*, 441. Translation by Raymond Rosenthal, in *Aretino's Dialogues*, 258.
84 Aretino, *Ragionamento-Dialogo*, 441.
85 Venier, *La Zaffetta*, 62.

86 Venier, *La Zaffetta*, 47.

87 Venier, *La Zaffetta*, 59.

88 If the Zaffetta was printed after 1532, as some scholars have argued, it may have been been written in the wake of Angela's fame due to her night with the Cardinal Ippolito de' Medici – just as Veronica Franco's night with Henri III in 1574 was probably part of the motivation behind the satiric attacks levelled at her by Maffio Venier beginning in 1575.

89 The first edition is probably Pietro Aretino, *Li dui primi canti di Orlandino del diuino messer Pietro Aretino* (Venice: [Bindoni?], [1540?]). For a modern edition of the Orlandino, see AEN, vol. 2, 215–36.

90 AEN, vol. 2, 230.

91 See the entry for "Trentuno" in Florio, *A Worlde of Wordes*. On Florio and his dictionary, see Wyatt, *The Italian Encounter with Tudor England*.

92 These include "le quattro comedie" (four of Aretino's comedies, unnamed), Aretino's courtesan dialogues, and a book Florio describes as "La p. errante del Aretino" (*The Puttana errante*, by Aretino). Wyatt, *A Worlde of Words*, Preface, n.p.

93 Shakespeare, *The Taming of the Shrew* (c. 1590–2), act 4, scene 2.

2. Fictional Ladies and Literary Fraternity

1 "Venne detto al conte Alessandro: – Sia lodato Iddio che quivvi siamo redutti senza compagnia di donne, le quali sogliano essere l'assenzio, anzi il tosco che rende amara e avvelena ogni dolce e viva compagnia. – Per che, fattosi avanti messer Benedetto Cornaro, disse: Conte, che è quello che voi dite? Anzi se cosa nessuna manca a dare perfezzione, dolcezza e vita a questo nostro solazzo, ci manca una bella compagnia di donne. A cui rispose il conte: – Cornaro, tenete pur sempre la loro ragione, che vi leveranno al ballo del capello più volte che li altri, queste ingrate." Parabosco, *Diporti: Girolamo Parabosco-Gherardo Borgogni*, 64–5. All citations are from this edition, published in 2005. The first edition is Parabosco, *I diporti di M. Girolamo Parabosco*, but the 2005 text is based on the second edition, *I diporti di m. Girolamo Parabosco, novamente ristampati, & diligentissimamente revisti* (Venice: Giovanni Griffio, 1552).

2 For a complete list of Parabosco's interlocutors and essential biographical information on all of these men, see Parabosco, *Diporti*, 60–4.

3 Parabosco's detailed description of these fishing huts suggests that perhaps he saw them up close: "cappannucci in mezo l'acque fabricati, qual di asse, qual di pietre e qual di cannucce d'alga e di luto fatti per

commodo e albergo de'pescatori" (little huts constructed on the water, some made of wooden planks, some of stone, and some of reeds and mud, created as refuges for the convenience of fishermen) (*Diporti*, 19). A painted wooden panel by Vittore Carpaccio, now known as *Hunting on the Lagoon* (1490–5, The Getty Center, Los Angeles), depicts a Venetian fishing party with a group of huts in the background that seem to fit Parabosco's description. The hunting panel was identified as the top half of another panel at the Museo Correr in Venice titled *Two Venetian Ladies* (formerly known as *Two Venetian Courtesans*).

4 "Sia laudato Iddio che quivi siamo ridutti senza compagnia di donne, le quali sogliono sempre essere l'assenzio, anzi il tosco che rende amara ed avvelena ogni dolce e viva compagnia." Parabosco, *Diporti*, 64–5.

5 "anzi se cosa nessuna manca a dare perfezzione, dolcezza e vita a questo nostro solazzo, ci manca una bella compagnia di donne." Parabosco, *Diporti*, 65.

6 For a clear and thorough introduction to the *querelle des femmes*, see King and Rabil, "The Other Voice in Early Modern Europe." A fundamental source is Kelly, "Early Feminist Theory." See also Bock, *Women in European History*, 1–31.

7 On connections between these two books and *I diporti*, see Padoan, "Fra *Decameron* e *Cortegiano*."

8 On the role of women in Castiglione's dialogue, see Kelly, "Did Women Have a Renaissance?"

9 "In quanto poi al dar lor lode, io faccio come fate voi tutti, che componete in lode loro per meglio essercitare il vostro ingegno; il quale tanto maggiore mostrate, quanto più illustrate e fate nobile soggetto per se stesso vile e tenebroso." Parabosco, *Diporti*, 67–8.

10 "pare che egli … abbia ora mai poco manco che fatto credere universalmente che le donne sieno di gran lunga più perfette e più degne che noi non siamo." Parabosco, *Diporti*, 68–9.

11 Girolamo Ruscelli, *Lettura di Girolamo Ruscelli, sopra un sonetto dell'illustriss. signor marchese della Terza alla divina signora marchesa del Vasto* (Venice: Giovanni Griffio, 1552). See Robin, *Publishing Women*, for a discussion of the book's publishing context (46–8) and Girolamo Ruscelli's literary career (110–11).

12 "Mentre vive il Ruscelli, che ha tutti i literati per amici, ognuno averà rispetto, se non a lui a gli amici suoi, né si metteranno a scrivergli contra." Parabosco, *Diporti*, 71.

13 "Anzi pure- soggiunse l'Aretino – dite che il Ruscelli sarà cagione che qualcuno si metta a scrivere contra le donne, non tanto per offender loro

quanto per farsi nome col mostrar d'avere ardito di scrivere contra un grand'uomo." Parabosco, *Diporti*, 71.

14 Parabosco, *Diporti*, 312.

15 For the term "virtual salon" and a discussion of Laura Battiferra's *Il primo libro dell'opere toscane* (Florence: Giunti, 1560) as such, see Kirkham, "Laura Battiferra degli Ammanati's First Book of Poetry," 353. See also Battiferri degli Ammannati, *Laura Battiferra and Her Literary Circle*, 36 and 52.

16 For a discussion of these clusters of poems as a "réseau" (web), see Piejus, "La première anthologie."

17 Robin, *Publishing Women*, 63.

18 Aretino to Girolamo Capello, Venice, May 1548, in AEN, vol. 4, pt. 5, 390-391. In line with my argument regarding the significance of the term, Parabosco also used the word *accademia* to describe the salon. See his letter to Pandolpho Salerno, published in 1551: "Io sto qui in Vinegia continuando la prattica del Magnifico M. Domenico Veniero, & del Magnifico Molino, & del resto della Accademia" (I remain here in Venice and continue to frequent the magnificent Messer Domenico Venier, and the magnificent Molino, and the rest of the Academy). Parabosco, *Il primo libro delle lettere famigliari*, fol. 14v.

19 The few exceptions to this rule – the prestigious Accademia della Fama founded by Venier's longtime friend Federico Badoer, the Accademia degli Uniti, and the Aldine Academy – will be discussed below.

20 On the academic *impresa* in the sixteenth century, see Roberto Ciardi, "'A Knot of Words and Things.'"

21 As James Hankins has argued, the term had at least seven distinct meanings from the beginning of the fifteenth century. See his "The Myth of the Platonic Academy of Florence."

22 "M. Sperone Speroni, che stando di stanza a Padova, onde è cittadino; quando per alcun suo affare gli occorre di venire a Venetia; tutto il tempo, che dalle facende gli avanza libero, tutto lo dispensa nella piacevole, & honorata conversatione del Magnifico M. Domenico, & di questi altri Signori, che da lui (come detto ho) sono usi a ridursi." Marcellino, *Il diamerone*, n.p.

23 On Zantani's patronage of musicians, see Feldman, *City Culture*, 67–73 and 342.

24 Parabosco and Cambio are mentioned as participants in gatherings at Zantini's house in a passage from a dedication by Toscanella to Zantani in his geographical handbook *I nomi antichi*, fols. [2]–[3]. For a transcription of the entire dedication, see Feldman, *City Culture*, 433–4.

25 See Venier's sonnet "Ben perì suon, qual suona il nome stesso" and Fenaruolo's response "Sì mi sento ne l'alma il suono impresso," first published in Fenaruolo, *Rime di Mons, Girolamo Fenaruolo*, fol. [38]. This edition was published in two variations, each with a different dedicatory letter, one from Roberto Figolino to Federico Corner and the other from Marcantonio Silvio to Domenico Venier.

26 Martin Lowry, "The 'New Academy' of Aldus Manutius." Three years later, Lowry softened his stance, noting that the earlier piece "contains a number of errors and in general suffers from the faults of having been written in an over-polemical frame of mind." Lowry, *The World of Aldus Manutius*, 213n76.

27 Chambers, "The Earlier 'Academies' in Italy," 12.

28 Chambers, "The Earlier 'Academies' in Italy," 12.

29 For his services, Bernardo Tasso received housing and a salary of 200 ducats per year. See Bolzoni, "L'Accademia Veneziana," 134n26. Bernardo's illustrious son Torquato Tasso was probably not a regular visitor to the salon, but he too turned to Venier for literary counsel.

30 For Celio Magno's involvement in the Academy, see the *Instrumento*, transcribed in Rose, "The Accademia Venetiana," 217–19.

31 See Rose, "The Accademia Venetiana," 224.

32 The original letter is lost, but there is a nineteenth-century manuscript copy in the Biblioteca Trivulziana in Milan (MS. E. 37), which also contains a copy of the academy's *Instrumento*.

33 Pagan, "Sulla Accademia 'Venetiana' o della 'Fama,'" 363. The Marcantonio Vallaresso in the *Instrumento* is probably the son of Lucieta Vallaresso, Domenico Venier's sister, mentioned in the will of their mother Foscarina Foscarini Venier (Atti notarili, Testamenti, Atti Marcon, b. 1203, no. 79, ASV).

34 The complete passage reads as follows: "io ne sono stato pregato da questi Signori miei amici, & da diversi loro Protettori; tra quali è 'l Clarissimo M. Federigo Badoaro, & M. Domenico Veniero." See Molino's letter to Tasso dated 22 January 1558, in Tasso, *Delle lettere*, vol. 2, 455.

35 Pagan, "Sulla Accademia 'Venetiana' o della 'Fama,'" 363.

36 Pagan, "Sulla Accademia 'Venetiana' o della 'Fama,'" 363.

37 Feldman, *City Culture*, 119.

38 The fundamental source on the *Compagnie della Calza* remains Lionello Venturi, "Le Compagnie della Calza (sec. XV-XVII)," *Nuovo Archivio Veneto* 16 (1908): 161–221; 17 (1909): 140–233. See also Junkerman, "Bellissima Donna," 234–54.

39 Marin Sanudo, *I diarii*, 58: 184–5.

40 A curious exception seems to have been made for twins – the *Ortolani* and
the *Floridi*, for example, each had a set of twins among their members.

41 L. Zorzi, *Il teatro e la città*, 305.

42 My account of the practices of the *Compagnie della Calza* below is based on
Venturi's "Le Compagnie della Calza" unless otherwise noted.

43 See Venturi, "Le Compagnie della Calza," 217.

44 Another member of the group, Anton Giacomo Corso, addressed a *capitolo*
to Vitturi, "Hora è da stare in villa signor mio" (Now's the time to stay in
the country, my lord), in Corso, *Le rime*, 51v–54v.

45 On Vasari's involvement in the project, see Schulz, "Vasari at Venice."

46 "Considerando, che in la nostra tenera età, havemo dado principio ad
amarsi da fradelli, e fra questa giovenil età se havemo conservadi in
unidae, e benevolentia, non ni [*sic*] par de preterir el dimostrar ad ogn'uno
per segno manifesto, e indisolubil vinculo della sempiterna amicitia nostra,
senza la qual li Stati, li Imperij, e Republiche durar non possono." Cited in
Venturi, "Le Compagnie della Calza," 200.

47 For these rules see the "Statuto dei Sempiterni," cited in Venturi, "Le
Compagnie della Calza," 200–5.

48 Cited in Venturi, "Le Compagnie della Calza," 186.

49 See Venturi, "Le Compagnie della Calza," 183, for an account of the
obscene and injurious graffiti found near the Rialto targeting an earlier
group, the *Cortesi*, just after their official constitution ceremony in 1533.

50 On Renaissance *virtù*, a complex notion that at its core defined those
qualities that set one person above another, see Laura Giannetti and Guido
Ruggiero, "Introduction: Playing the Renaissance," in *Five Comedies from
the Italian Renaissance* (Baltimore: Johns Hopkins University Press, 2003),
xi–xl.

51 On the location of Venier's palazzo, see Feldman, *City Culture*, 85n6.
Feldman points out that Venier's tax report from 1566 confirms that the
Venier family palace was located in the parish of Santa Maria Formosa
but without specifying its exact location: "A Santa Maria Formosa nella
nostra contrada ca Venier … una casa da statio dove io habito" (In Santa
Maria Formosa, in our district, Ca' Venier, the family house where I
live). Dieci Savi alle Decime (166–7), b. 130, fol. 653, ASV. Transcription
mine.

52 See Feldman, *City Culture*, 84n5, for a summary of the critical debate
regarding the exact year in which Venier fell ill.

53 "Domenico Venier … la casa del quale è un continuo ridutto di persone
virtuose così di nobili della città, come di qual si voglia altra sorte
d'huomini per professione di lettere, & d'altro rari, & eccellenti." Molino,
Rime, 7. Cited and translated in Feldman, *City Culture*, 85n7.

54 Feldman, *City Culture*, 28.

55 Official documents have not been found that confirm Parabosco's precise date of birth, but modern scholars have accepted the date of 1524 proposed by Giuseppe Bianchini. For Parabosco's biography, see Bianchini, "Girolamo Parabosco"; Bussi, *Umanità e arte di Gerolamo Parabosco;* Fiori, "Novità biografiche su tre letterati"; and, most recently, Donato Pirovano, "Nota biografica," in Parabosco, *Diporti*, 34–40.

56 "Vi promettano tanto di fama e di onore le cose che sì giovane avete concesso a le stampe, che più non ne desiderano quegli che si ritrovano atempati iscrivendo. Ma per che io vi amo, al paro di qualunque potesse invidiarvi, aciò non si atribuisca il mio lodarvi a la benivolenzia, lascio cotal negozio al Veniero. Esso Domenico Magnifico, il quale tanto sa e intende, per avermi insegnato a conoscervi, nel testimoniare la dote che vi recaste in le fasce, farane fede credendosegli. Imperoché chi è dottamente avertito, ciò che parla si nota e quel che accenna si gusta." Aretino to Parabosco, October 1549, in AEN vol. 4, pt. 5, 281.

57 Parabosco, *Il primo libro delle lettere famigliari.*

58 "Io mando a V.S. i due libri delle mie lettere amorose ... con qualche vergona, essendo certo di scemarle in gran parte quella speranza, ch'ella tuttodì dice haver di me: la quale speranza non può esser poca, se nasce in V.S. da gli amorevoli, et saggi ricordi et avvertimenti, ch'ella si degna darmi ogni hora." Parabosco, *Il primo libro delle lettere famigliari*, 3v–3r, cited in Bianchini, "Girolamo Parabosco," 421n3.

59 Parabosco, *La seconda parte delle rime*, 60–1v, cited in Bianchini, "Girolamo Parabosco," 450. The first twelve lines are cited and translated in Feldman, *City Culture*, 86. The figures mentioned above are Federico Badoer, Girolamo Molino, Domenico Venier ("the lord of the house"), Giovanni Battista Amalteo, Anton Giacomo Corso, Sperone Speroni, and Pietro Aretino.

60 Giovanni Battista (Giambattista) Amalteo (1525–1573) was the younger brother of Girolamo (1507–1574), also an author of Latin poems. Giovanni Battista was sent to London as ambassador of the Venetian Republic in 1554 and later served as secretary to Pope Pius IV at the Council of Trent.

61 "Vedete quanta grazia ha questo ... il quale fu fatto da un giovane forse di qualche speranza, se qualche altra cosa non lo traviasse spesso fuora de' suoi studii e de' suoi pensieri. Questo madrigale è fatto nello allontanarsi che egli fece da una sua donna." Parabosco, *Diporti*, 283.

62 "Se io non avessi paura di trapassare il segno della modestia, per essermi troppo a cuore l'autore di queste composizioni, io direi certamente molto più di quello ch'io dico in favor suo. E direi ad alcuni a i quali parrebbe

poco che quattro boschi d'allori circondassero loro le tempie, così par loro
essere eccellenti bevitori de l'acqua di Parnaso, e che stanno su 'l giudicare
questa e quell'altra cosa, senza mai dire bene di persona vivente, direi,
dico, che essi facessero di tali composizioni!" Parabosco, *Diporti*, 296.

63 Biographical information on Marcellino is scarce. Further evidence of his
connection with the Venier group is a little book containing his *Commento*
on a religious poem by Celio Magno titled *Deus canzone spirituale di Celio
Magno*.

64 Almost nothing is known of Marcellino's life, but his contacts included
many figures who can be tied to Venier. Marcellino may have been friends
with the humanist scholar Alessandro Citolini, who could have met Venier
through Sperone Speroni. Indeed, Citolini, like Speroni and Aretino,
was a member of the *Accademia degli Infiammati* in Padova. Marcellino's
connections to Domenico Venier are further confirmed by Alessandro
Citolini's *Tipocosmia*, an encyclopedia of sorts published in 1561, in which
both Marcellino and Venier are featured as interlocutors.

65 "per esser stato fatto il ragionamento, che è il soggetto di questa mia fatica,
in casa del Magnifico M. Domenico Veniero (come voi leggendo vedrete)
in due giorni – che Diamerone in greco suona appunto due giornate nella
nostra lingua." Marcellino, *Il diamerone.*"

66 Contributors with connections to Venier included Celio Magno, Giacomo
Zane, Giovanni Battista Amalteo, Girolamo Fenaruolo Lodovico Dolce,
and Orsatto Giustinian. For a facsimile of the volume's index, see Schutte,
"Commemorators of Irene di Spilimbergo."

67 Aretino died in 1556, and Parabosco just one year later. Other figures
associated with the salon who died in the 1550s were the Venetian
patrician Lorenzo Contarini (1515–1552) and the poet Anton Giacomo
Corso (his death date is unknown, but Parabosco published a *canzone*
lamenting his death in 1555).

68 "Orsù, di grazia, lasciamo andar queste parole, rispose il Veniero, ch'a
me non si conviene parlar di corso, poichè io non posso, colpa della mia
infermità, reggermi appena sopra le gambe" (Now, come on, let's drop this
subject, responded Venier, since it doesn't behoove me to speak of running
as I can barely stand up due to my illness). Parabosco, *Diporti*, 95.

69 "Il Magnifico M. Domenico Veniero, gentil'huomo di quel raro valore, che
a ciascuno è noto, si come hebbe da' cieli un fortissimo e molto elevato
spirito; così dalla Natura hebbe un corpo languido, & per crudele accidente
d'infermità poco sano; benche forse ciò fece la Natura con quel giudicio,
col quale molte altre cose degne di maraviglia spesso suol fare; percioche
havendo voluto dargli un intelletto così sublime, fu per avventura ben fatto,

che a quell'animo più angelico, che humano, desse un corpo sottile, magro, & oltre all'esser magro, fosse etiandio dall'infermità a maggior magrezza ridotto; accioche con la grossezza, o morbidezza sua non potesse impedire allo spirito l'espedito volo verso il cielo, là dove spesso, con gli alti suoi concetti spiegando l'ali, poggiare felicemente si vede." Marcellino, *Il diamerone*, n.p.

70 On manuscript and print sources for Domenico Venier's Tuscan poetry, see Bianco, "Sulla tradizione delle 'Rime'"; "Le *Rime* di Domenico Venier (edizione critica)," PhD diss., Università di Padova, 2001. On the tendency of Venetian aristocratic poets to circulate their poems primarily in manuscript form, see Feldman, *City Culture*, 92. Feldman points out that Venetian patrician poets closely tied to Venier's circle, such as Giacomo Zane and Girolamo Molino, did not publish full-length *canzonieri* during their lifetimes. Feldman speculates that perhaps Venetian patricians, like aristocratic Florentines, avoided "a wholesale participation in the culture of printed words as being beneath their station" (92n28).

71 *Rime diverse di molti eccellentiss. auttori nuovamente raccolte. Libro primo* [ed. Lodovico Domenichi] (Venice: Gabriele Giolito de' Ferrari, 1545).

72 Robin, *Publishing Women*, 238. For a description of the *Rime di diversi* series, see *Publishing Women*, 219–42. On the complex history of the series, see Clubb and G. Clubb, "Building a Lyric Canon"; *Biblioteca del libro italiano antico*, vol. 1, *Libri di poesia*, 243–4.

73 Aretino first sent the sonnet to Venier in 1548 with a short note attached that read as follows: "La vaghezza che avete nel dire, e la eccellenza che mostrate in averlo detto, ha causato in me la composizione de i prefati versi in vostra laude" (The beauty of what you say and the excellence that you demonstrate in saying it are what caused me to compose the above verses in praise of you). Aretino to Venier, Venice, November 1548, in AEN, vol. 4, pt.5, 95–6.

74 Corso, *Le rime*, 47r–49r.

75 Parabosco, *La seconda parte delle rime*, 6v–9r.

76 "Noi come siam usi di fare, troviamoci pur spesso per beneficio nostro in casa di quel divino spirito del chiarissimo M. Domenico Venier." This passage comes from a 1551 edition of Corso's *Le rime* that I have been unable to locate. Quoted in D. Venier, *Rime di Domenico Veniero*, ed. Serassi, xiii.

77 The date of composition can be gleaned from the poem's closing lines, which mention Phillip II's stop in Italy on his way to Brussels in 1548: "vi scrive del mese / d'Ottobre, l'anno che vienne di Spagna / Filippo nel Divin nostro Paese" (I am writing you in the month of October, the year that Philip of Spain came to our divine country). Corso, *Le rime*, 49r.

78 Corso, *Le rime*, 47r–49r.

79 "Quanto può l'arte il mostra a chi non crede," in D. Venier, *Rime di Domenico Veniero*, 74.

80 Celio Magno, "Dentro al tuo cuor più viva e bella siede," in D. Venier, *Rime di Domenico Veniero*, 74.

81 For an innovative discussion of the homoerotic elements in a shared book of *Rime* published in 1600 by Magno and Orsatto Giustinian, another Venetian patrician connected to Domenico Venier's circle, see Shannon McHugh, "The Gender of Desire: Feminine and Masculine Voices in Early Modern Italian Lyric Poetry" (PhD diss., New York University, 2015).

3. The Erotics of Venetian Dialect

1 For Venier's poems, see Ruscelli, ed., *Il sesto libro delle rime*, 108v, 127v, 129r–136v.

2 Frapolli, "Un micro-canzoniere."

3 See Venier's sonnet "Non ha tante, quant'io pene e tormenti" (the first in the series) in Ruscelli, ed., *Il sesto libro delle rime*, 129r.

4 These and many other Petrarchan commonplaces are scattered throughout Venier's poetry, but see, especially, Venier's "Veggio pur quant'io bramo, hor le due stelle," in Ruscelli, ed., *Il sesto libro delle rime*, 130r.

5 Ruscelli, ed., *Il sesto libro delle rime*, 136r.

6 Suzuki, *Metamorphoses of Helen*, 17.

7 Marlowe, *Faustus*, V.xviii, 99–100.

8 Another sonnet by Venier, "Non è men del più bello angelo in cielo" (She is no less than the most beautiful angel in heaven), offers further proof that Venier's Helen is Elena Artusi. The sonnet was written in praise of a portrait of a dead lady whose eyes like "due vaghe stelle" (two lovely stars) and "chiome d'or fin" (tresses of spun gold) enchanted the poet while she lived. While the poem itself doesn't mention the lady's name, the index at the back of the volume explains that it was written "[s]opra un ritratto di Madonna Elena Artusa, bellissima e vaghissima giovane" (on a portrait of Elena Artusa, a very beautiful and lovely young lady). See Atanagi, ed., *De le rime di diuersi nobili poeti toscani*, 11.

9 Maylender, *Storia delle accademie d'Italia*, 5: 442. On Zane's biography, see Giovanna Rabitti's "Introduzione" to her edited edition of his collected poems, *Giacomo Zane: Rime*, 11n5.

10 On Zane's connections to the Venier group, see Rabitti, "Introduzione," 23–33.

11 Zane, *Giacomo Zane: Rime*, 100.

12 Ovid, *Metamorphoses*, Book V: 572–641.

13 "Dolcemente cantò Giacomo Zane, gentiluomo patrizio veneziano, gli amori suoi e quelli in particolare che lungo esercitò con Madonna Elena

Artusi, gentildonna di famosa bellezza fra le donne di Venezia; ma con isfortunata riuscita, percioché mordendosene elle nel fiore della sua giovinezza, il poeta prese tanto dolore, che poco tempo dopo, consumato dall'infermità, se n'andò a ritrovarla nell'altra vita, essendo ancora di fresca età." Zilioli, *Vite di Gentiluomini Veneziani*, 16.

14 This *canzone* was first published in 1573 but probably composed much earlier. See Molino, *Rime*, 83v–85r.

15 Venier, "Come scese dal ciel quest'Angioletta," in Ruscelli, ed., *Il sesto libro delle rime*, 136v.

16 "Lasso chi fia, che piu d'amar n'invoglie," in Molino, *Rime*, 83v–85r.

17 For a discussion of death as orgasm in Renaissance madrigal texts, see Macy, "Speaking of Sex."

18 As Martha Feldman has noted, the composer Giovanni Nasco set a sonnet on Artusi's death, "Hor che la frale, e mortal gonna è chiusa," in his Second Book for five voices in 1551 (101n52). See Feldman, *City Culture*. The sonnet was first printed, along with Venier's own laments for Artusi, in Ruscelli, ed., *Il sesto libro delle rime* in 1553, where it is attributed to Zaccaria Pensabene (c. 217v). Biographical information on Pensabene is non-existent, but he contributed, along with Domenico Venier, to a collection in honour of another dead lady. See Atanagi, ed., *Rime di diuersi nobilissimi*.

19 Corner and Venier may have met through Aretino, who addressed at least three letters to Corner between 1545 and 1549, roughly the same period in which Corner and Venier were working on their dialect poems. Tiziana Agostini has argued that the man in question was the son of the Venetian patrician Zuanne Corner, born on 6 August 1516; see her "Benetto Corner," 152. But in a letter of 1546, Aretino addressed Corner as "figliuolo degno d'avere in padre il buon Polo Clarissimo" (son worthy of having the good and Most Illustrious Polo as a father), so our Corner was not the son of Zuanne; see AEN, vol. 4, pt. 3, 430. Instead, I believe he was the son of Polo Corner and that he was born on 27 April 1521 and died in January 1568; see Marco Antonio Barbaro, "Genealogie delle famiglie patrizie venete," vol. 3, pt. 2, 111 (references here are to the copy in the ASV). This Benetto Corner held several important political offices: one as a *Savio agli Ordini* (also called the *Savi da Mar*, an organ of the *Collegio* that was responsible for the administration of Venice's maritime territories and its fleet of warships); another as one of the *Dieci Savi alle Decime* (who can be loosely defined as the tax officers of the republic); yet another as a *Provveditore sopra Dazi* (another municipal tax office, responsible for indirect taxes); and, finally, a seat on the *Consiglio dei Pregadi (Rogati)*, later known as the

Senato (Senate). On this, see Barbaro, *Genealogie*, vol. 3, pt. 11, 111. Further proof is in notarial documents drawn up for the Venier family. A "Benetto Corner de M[esser] Polo" was witness to a codicil added to the 1553 will of Domenico's mother, Foscarina Foscarini Venier (Archivio notarile, Testamenti, Atti Marcon, busta 1203, no. 79, ASV); Domenico Venier's tax report from 1566 was signed by a "Benetto Corner alli X savi" (Benetto Corner, at the office of the Dieci savi alle decime, [Dieci savi alle Decime, busta 130, fol. 653, ASV]).

20 "Sonetti e poema in italiano di Benedetto Corner e di Domenico Venier di Venezia – Corretti da altra mano più tardi," MS Add. 12.197, BL. The codex was not discussed in any secondary sources until Feldman rediscovered it in 1981 and subsequently shared it with Tiziana Agostini. See Feldman, *City Culture*, 101, and also her "The Academy of Domenico Venier." For a description of the manuscript and a transcription of its index, see Agostini Nordio (now Agostini), "Poesie dialettali di Domenico Venier." See also Frapolli, "Un micro-canzoniere"; and Rossi, "The Illicit Poetry of Domenico Venier."

21 For an overview of poetry in Venetian dialect in the Renaissance, see Brevini, "Petrarchismo e antipetrarchismo in dialetto." Brevini's discussion focuses on Leonardo Giustinian, Andrea Calmo, Giambattista Maganza (who wrote not in Venetian but in pavano), and Maffio Venier. For a description and index of the largest manuscript collection of sixteenth-century Venetian dialect poetry, along with a list of the authors represented, see Ferrari, "Il *Lamento dei pescatori veneziani*."

22 See Love, *The Culture and Commerce of Texts*, 177.

23 On the history of the use of Venetian dialect, see Ferguson, *A Linguistic History of Venice*.

24 "[S]i veggono le toscane voci miglior suono avere, che non hanno le viniziane, piú dolce, piú vago, piú ispedito, piú vivo; né elle tronche si vede che sieno e mancanti, come si può di buona parte delle nostre vedere, le quali niuna lettera raddoppiano giamai." Pietro Bembo, *Prose della volgar lingua; Gli Asolani; Rime*, edited by Carlo Dionisotti (Turin: TEA, 1989), 111 (I.15).

25 "[N]on solamente i viniziani compositori di rime con la fiorentina lingua scrivono, se letti vogliono essere dalle genti, ma tutti gli altri italiani ancora." Bembo, *Prose della volgar lingua*, 111 (I.15).

26 The phrase comes from a *sonetto caudato* that begins with equal xenophobia: "Non vogio, e questa è la mia intention,/ che chi no intende bene la proprietà/ del parlar familiar che se usa qua/ leza del mio sonetto né canzon" (I don't wish – and this is my intention – for anyone who

doesn't understand the properties of the common way of speaking that we use here to read any of my sonnets or *canzoni*). This sonnet is found in a sixteenth-century manuscript that contains poems attributed to Venier and other members of his circle (MS It IX 173 (6282), 175r, BNM).

27 See Ferguson, *A Linguistic History of Venice*, 212.

28 "Sì come bene ispesso la grossezza de i villani cibi, o Magnifico S. Domenico, incitano l'appetito a una avidità di gola, che altra delicatura di signorili vivande non mai la mossero al piacere del mangiare in tal modo, così a le volte il triviale de i suggetti infimi aguzzano lo ingegno con certa ansia di prontitudine che in sorte alcuna d'eroiche materie non dimostrossi mai tali. Sì che nel comporre per recrear lo intelletto in lingua, in stile, e in foggia veneziana, laudo sommamente i sonetti, i capitoli, e gli strammotti, che ho visti, letti, e intesi da voi, da altri, e da me. Imperoché ci sono drento alcuni spirti che destano le orecchie a chi gli sente, con certe iscosse di risa, che non si può dir meglio. Girolamo fratel vostro, e il Cornaro padron mio, vagliano assai (oltre la eccellenza che aparisce in le altissime carte loro) in la galantaria de gli andari in facezie sì dolci; e come parmi avervi detto in iscrittis, l'altro dì andai in estasi sì fu nuovo il piacere che mi penetrò per tutto i sentimenti non so che bulesco in canzone, recitatami da uno de i sopra detti gentiluomini in barca." Aretino to Domenico Venier, Venice, November 1548, AEN, vol. 4, pt. 5, 392. As Feldman has noted in *City Culture*, Aretino's triads here (*lingua/stile/foggia; sonetti/ capitoli/strammotti; visti/letti/intesi*) pay homage to the correlative sonnet type for which Venier was famous (100n50).

29 Corso's birth and death dates are unknown. For a quick biographical sketch, see Parabosco, *Diporti*, 64n1.

30 Corso, *Le rime*, 48r.

31 "Rime in lingua veneziana di diversi … ," fol. 155v, MS It. Cl. IX, 173 (6282), BNM.

32 Parabosco, *Il primo libro delle lettere famigliari.*

33 See Pilot, "Poesie vernacole."

34 This sonnet is the best-known example of what Dámaso Alonso and Carlos Bousoño have dubbed the "correlative sonnet," a type that seems to have been invented by Venier. See their *Seis calas en la expresión literaria española*, 56, for a discussion of this technique. For a discussion of the correlative sonnet in the context of Petrarchism throughout Europe, see Forster, *The Icy Fire*.

35 Thiene was an intimate of Venier's friend Giovanni Battista Maganza ("il Magagnò") and was known as Begotto in pavano. His versions of Venier's poem are "La caecchia, el sogatto e 'l fogaron," in Maganza, ed., *La prima*

parte de le rime di Magagnò, 54v–55r; and "Tuogia la soga, el fuogo e el vereton," in Maganza, ed., *La terza parte de le rime di Magagnò*, n.p. On these "translations" of Venier's sonnet, see Milani, "Di un omaggio pavano a Domenico Venier."

36 Calmo, *Le bizarre, faconde et ingegnose rime pescatorie*, 92.

37 "Rime di Dom.[eni]co Veniero, e d'altri," MS It. Cl. IX 248 (7071), fol. 50, BNM. I have translated "zueca" ("civetta" in Italian), literally "owl" – as admirer, since "fare la civetta" means "to flirt."

38 "Proposte e risposte del Veniero a varj illustri poeti," in D. Venier, *Rime*, 71–97.

39 MS It. Cl. IX 248 (7071), fol. 39r–40v, BNM.

40 See Brevini, "Petrarchismo e antipetrarchismo in dialetto," in *La poesia in dialetto*, 1: 563–604.

41 For more on Dolce, see Terpening, *Lodovico Dolce*.

42 For a transcription of the text, as well as a discussion of the three manuscript copies, see Tiziana Agostini, "Benetto Corner, poeta dialettale e bulesco." Agostini was evidently unaware of the print edition, which is held by the Biblioteca Apostolica Vaticana, Rome: [Corner?], *Cinquanta stanze de Arcibrauo venetiano*.

43 Cited in Agostini, "Benetto Corner," 159.

44 Bull-baiting during Carnival was a Venetian tradition going back at least to the fourteenth century. See Boccaccio's tale of the wily Frate Alberto and the gullible Lisetta, set in Venice, for a fourteenth-century description of this custom: *Decameron*, IV.2. See also Giacomo Franco's *Habiti delle donne veneziane intagliate*, which contains an engraving of courtesans bull-baiting.

45 Agostini, "Benetto Corner," 170.

46 MS Add. 12.197 fol. 1r, BL. Note the Venetian forms of the Italian names Benedetto (which in Venetian usually becomes "Benetto," as above) and Domenico (in Venetian, "Domenego").

47 *Provveditori alla Sanità*, Necrologi, 1550, ASV.

48 MS Add. 12.197, 36r–37r, BL.

49 "Capitolo del Ven[ier] a mad[onna] Helena," in MS Add. 12.197, fol. 41v–42r, BL. For a modern transcription of the poem, see Agostini, "Poesie dialettali di Domenico Venier," 52–6. The poem had been previously transcribed and published by Antonio Pilot, who suspected that it was by Venier due to its allusions to the poet's illness. His uncertainty suggests, however, that the version of the poem that he saw was not the British Library codex, since there it is clearly attributed to Venier. See Antonio Pilot, "Un peccataccio di Domenico Venier."

50 Dante Alighieri, *La vita nuova e le rime*, ed. Andrea Battistini (Rome: Salerno editrice, 1995), 10.

51 MS Add. 12.197, fol. 42v, BL.

52 Ibid., fol. 43r.

53 "Quelle veramente se intendino esser meretrice quale non essendo maridate haveranno comercio et pratica con uno over più homeni. Se intendano etiam meretrice quelle che avendo marito non abitano con sui mariti, ma stanno separate et habbino commercio con uno over più homeni" (Prostitutes are to be considered those women who, while unmarried, have commerce and intercourse with one or more men. Furthermore, prostitutes are to be considered those women who while married do not live under one roof with their husbands but live apart from them and have intercourse with one or more men). Senato terra, reg. 32, fol. 126, 21 February 1542 m.v. (i.e. 1543), ASV. Cited and translated in Rosenthal, *The Honest Courtesan*, 67.

54 *Il catalogo di tutte le principali et più honorate cortigiane di Venetia* (n.p. [c. 1565?]), a catalogue purporting to list the names, addresses, and go-betweens of the most famous courtesans of Venice, identifies four of the women as married. For a modern edition, see Dittico, *Il catalogo*.

55 MS Add. 12.197, fol. 87r and 89r.

56 MS Add. 12.197, fol. 18r–18v.

57 MS Add. 12.197, fol. 50r.

58 Ruggiero, *Binding Passions*, 5–7, 10–11. See also Brown, *Venetian Narrative Painting*, 173–81, 185, 187, for a discussion of Elisabetta Condulmer, a married courtesan who did not reside with her husband.

59 MS Add. 12.197, fol. 69r.

60 MS Add. 12.197, fol. 72r.

61 MS Add. 12.197, fol. 72v.

62 MS Add. 12.197, fol. 25r.

63 MS Add. 12.197, fols. 48v–49r.

64 MS Add. 12.197, fol. 59v.

65 MS Add. 12.197, fol. 48r.

4. Dialect and Homosociality from Manuscript to Print

1 "Lascierò i desideri delle cose caduche; fuggirò le passioni; ingegnerommi d'imitare, s'io potrò, V.M. la quale, come dotata di alto sapere, avvedutasi di non potere ottener l'intera salvezza del corpo, a conservar l'animo con ogni studio si è rivolta; e ritrahendolo fuori della tenebrosa caligine delle cure mondane, hallo condotto nella luce de' celesti pensieri." Manuzio

to Venier, Venice, 11 February 1555, in Manuzio, *Lettere volgari di M. Paolo Manutio*, 93r–v.

2 Domenico Venier, *Rime*. This is the unique edition of Venier's collected works, and includes a biography as well as a collection of poems and letters addressed to Venier.

3 "Egli nell'età sua giovinetta poco curando la immaginaria dottrina, e la rea conversazione di Pietro Aretino, dietro a cui andava follemente perduto Lorenzo il fratello. E per questo Domenico e nel parlare e nello scrivere si tenne sempre entro i limiti della più castigate modestia, laddove l'altro dalla rea scuola di quel pessimo uomo guasto e corrotto, e pubblicò scritture laide." Serassi, "La vita del Veniero," in Domenico Venier, *Rime*, v.

4 Clusters of the poems appear in the following manuscripts: "Rime in lingua veneziana di diversi ... ," MS It. Cl. IX 173 (6282), BNM, Venice; "Rime, canzoni, et sonetti di Maffio Veniero," MS It. Cl. IX 217 (7061), BNM, Venice; "Rime di Dom.[eni]co Veniero, e d'altri," MS It. Cl. IX 248 (7071), BNM, Venice; "Rime di diversi autori del secolò XVI," MS It. Cl. IX 492 (6297), BNM, Venice.

5 "Sonetti e poema in italiano di Benedetto Corner e di Domenico Venier di Venezia – Corretti da altra mano più tardi," MS Add. 12.197, fol. 207r, BL, London.

6 MS Add. 12.197, fol. 203v.

7 MS Add. 12.197, fol. 203v. I have translated "in sti canei" – literally, "in these reeds" – as "in public," since the term was widely used by Venetian poets of the time to refer to the city in the middle of the reed-filled lagoon.

8 MS Add 12.197, fol. 204r.

9 MS Add 12.197, fol. 204r. Italics mine.

10 MS Add 12.197, fol. 206v.

11 On the continuities between manuscript and print, see Richardson, *Printing, Writers, and Readers*, 5–9. On manuscript culture in Venice, see Balduino, "Petrarchismo veneto."

12 MS It. Cl. IX 173 (6282), BNM. For a description of the manuscript and a list of incipits of poems in it that have been attributed to Maffio Venier, see Agostini Nordio (now Agostini), "La Strazzosa, canzone di Maffio Venier," 41–5. For an index of the manuscript and more descriptive information, see Ferrari, "Il *Lamento dei pescatori veneziani*."

13 My attribution of the codex to Giovanni Querini is based on the assertions of Agostini Nordio, "La Strazzosa," 41. On Querini, see Dazzi, *Il fiore della lirica venezia*, 1: 421–6. While Agostini is convinced that the entire codex is in a single hand (with the exception of two brief notes on fols. 71 and

221, added, she says, by a later hand), Dazzi argues that a second copyist added to the collection after Querini's death.

14 Querini's attributions are often off-target and should be taken with a grain of salt. The question of the authorship in this large codex is especially complex given that it is a collection of poems copied from myriad sources, and it cannot be fully addressed here.

15 The earliest attestation of a sonnet with a "tail" is found in Guido Cavalcanti's "Di vil matera mi conven parlare," which had a coda of only two rhymed lines, both *endecassillabi* (ABBA ABBA CDE DCE FF). The form was widely used by Domenico Venier and his circle for their satiric and often erotic poems in Venetian dialect. A well-known example is Maffio Venier's "Veronica, ver unica puttana," a modern edition of which can be found in M. Venier and V. Franco, *Il libro chiuso di Maffio Venier*, 37–40. In sixteenth-century Venetian dialect poetry, the *sonetto caudato* usually consists of a classic fourteen-line sonnet followed by a coda of one or more tercets, each composed of a *settenario* and two *endecassillabi*.

16 MS It Cl. IX 173 (6282), fol. 163r, BNM. The copyist has transcribed the name "Corso" in capital letters, a practice that was standard in printed poetry anthologies.

17 See MS It. Cl. IX 173 (6282), fols. 163v–165r, BNM; and MS Add. 12.197, fols. 19v, 177r–180r, BL.

18 The sonnet appears in MS Add. 12.197, fol. 19v, BL; and MS It. Cl. IX 173 (6282), fol. 163v, BNM.

19 Ruscelli, ed., *Il sesto libro delle rime*, 129r.

20 Following is a list of the sixteenth-century editions of *La caravana* of which I am aware: *Delle rime piaseuoli di diuersi auttori: nuouamente raccolte da m. Modesto Pino, et intitolate La carauana. Parte prima* (Venice: Sigismondo Bordogna, 1565); *Delle rime piaseuoli di diuersi auttori nuouamente raccolte da m. Modesto Pino, & intitolate la Carauana.* Parte prima (Venice: Sigismondo Bordogna, 1573); *Delle rime piaseuoli di diuersi auttori. Nuouamente raccolte da m. Modesto Pino, & intitolate la Carauana. Parte prima* (Venice: Domenico Farri, 1576); *Delle rime piaceuoli di diuersi auttori. Raccolte da Modesto Pino, & intitolate La carauana. Parte prima* (Venice: Domenico Farri, 1578); *Delle rime piacevoli di diversi avtori. Raccolte da m. Modesto Pino, & initolate La Carauana. Parte prima* (Venice: Presso Altobello Salicato, 1580); *Delle rime piaceuoli di diuersi auttori raccolte da m. Modesto Pino, & intitolate La carauana. Parte prima* (Venice: Fabbio & Agostin Zoppini fratelli, 1584).

21 Dazzi, *Il fiore della lirica veneziana*, 1: 325–6. Caravia dedicated *La morte de Giurco e Gnagni* (undated, but first edition probably printed in 1550) to Aretino.

22 "Onde havendomi già alcuni anni faticato di raccoglier da diversi auttori diverse forme di rime scritte ne la natia lingua Veneziana, ho deliberato essendo così persuaso da gli amici, di ragunarle insieme, & a diletto, & utile vostro pubblicarle." *Delle rime piaseuoli di diuersi auttori. Nuouamente raccolte da m. Modesto Pino, & intitolate la Carauana. Parte prima*, [2v]. All subsequent citations are taken from this 1576 edition, hereafter *La caravana*.

23 "Leggete adunque con lieto animo o benigni lettori questa prima parte, nella quale con modi piacevolissimi scorgerete molti sensi allegorici" (Read, then, with a happy spirit, o benevolent readers, this first part, in which, with many pleasurable expressions you will discern many allegorical meanings). *La caravana*, [2v].

24 Benedetto Clario, *Il primo canto de Orlando furioso*.

25 Ludovico Ariosto, *Orlando furioso e Cinque Canti*, 2 vols., edited by Sergio Zatti (Turin: UTET, 1997), vol. 1, 84.

26 *La caravana*, 3v.

27 *La caravana*, 20v.

28 On "lettere parlanti," see Nardelli, *La lettera e l'immagine*. The story of Aristotle's downfall at the hands of Phyllis, a popular medieval legend, was recorded by the thirteenth-century Norman poet Henry d'Andeli in his "Lai d'Aristote." On the image of the mounted Aristotle in manuscript marginalia, see Smith, *The Power of Women*, esp. chap. 4, "Body It Forth."

29 See *La caravana*, 42r–46r. For the entire sequence, see MS Add. 12.197, fols. 156v–174v, BL. Venier experimented with Petrarch's conceit in his Italian poetry, as well, as in his sonnet "No ch'io nol dissi mai, donna gradita," first published in Ruscelli, ed., *Il sesto libro*, 133r.

30 Giovanni Mario Crescimbeni (1663–1728) mentioned *La caravana* and these two dialect poems as part of a discussion of parodies of Petrarch in his *L'istoria della volgar poesia*, 319.

31 The rhyme scheme is as follows: ABBA AcccA/ ABBA AcccA/ BCCB BaaaB/ BCCB BaaaB/ CAAC CbbC/ CAAC CbbC/ Cbba. The six stanzas are arranged in pairs, and the three rhyme sounds are arranged according to the principle of *retrogradatio*, that is, the first two stanzas begin with A, the second two with C, and the final two with C.

32 *La caravana*, 42r.

33 Corner's two poems are "Sel dissi mai che in to la mia scuella" (MS Add. 12.197, fols. 161r–162v, BL) and "Sel dissi mai, ch'a son de campanella" (MS Add. 12.197, fols. 163v–165r. BL).

34 For "Cagozzo fantolin, frasca cornua" see *La caravana*, 48v; MS Add. 12.197, fols. 74v–75r, BL; and MS It. Cl. IX 248 (7071), fol. 35r, BNM. For "Maliazo la mare che t'ha fatto," see *La caravana*, 51r, and MS Add. 12.197,

fol. 6r, BL. For "Chi dirave che 'l mosto imbriagasse," see *La caravana*, 50r, and MS Add. 12.197, 6v–7r, BL.

35 *La caravana*, 48v. While Modesto Pino's version of the poem reads "le varole" (the Venetian term for chickenpox), this is likely a printing error; MS Add. 12.197, BL, has "la verola" (the witch), which makes more sense in this context.

36 A *capitolo* by Corner to Venier implies that Artusi lived with Novello in the parish of San Marcuola before her move to San Pantalon. Corner laments that "chi se stà puttana a San Marcuola, / sconvien anch'esser a San Pantalon; / che l'esser bona no s'impara a scuola" (she who was a whore when she lived in San Marcuola might as well be one in San Pantalon, since being good is not something one learns at school). MS Add. 12.197, fol. 139r, BL.

37 On invectives against Cupid in sixteenth-century music and poetry, see Paolo Fabbri, "Andrea Gabrieli," 249–72. Fabbri attributes Corner's "Cagozzo fantolin, frasca cornua" to Alessandro Caravia, after Dazzi, *Il fiore della lirica veneziana*, 1: 344.

38 MS Add. 12.197, fol. 10r, BL. In the version printed in *La caravana*, two lines are missing from the third stanza of Venier's poem. This is probably an unintentional printing error given that this omission alters the regular rhyme scheme to which all of the other stanzas adhere (AbAccddeeF). The omitted lines are "Morir da dogia? / Cappe, mo togia" (stanza 3, vv. 8–9).

39 *La caravana*, 52r.

40 "Quella notte, co zonsia alle palae, / brusì la barba a un Zaffo co un sospiro, / e arsì do stuore, che iera bagnae" (That night, when I arrived at the dock, I burned the beard off a policeman with just one sigh, and I also burned up two tarps that were wet). *La caravana*, 52v.

41 Ms. It. Cl. IX 248 (7071), fols. 46r–47r, BNM ("Morosetta mia cara quel affanno") and fols. 47r–46r ("Se te soio Corner, se mi t'inganno").

42 Ms. It. Cl. IX 248 (7071), fol. 47v, BNM.

43 *La caravana*, 53v.

44 *Versi alla venitiana* (1613).

45 In the context of Venetian dialect poetry, Ingegneri is often referred to by the Venetianized variant of his name, "Anzolo Ingegner," as in the title of the *Versi*. For Ingegneri's life and a bibliography of his works, see Doglio's modern edition of his treatise *Della poesia rappresentativa e del modo di rappresentare le favole sceniche*.

46 *Versi alla venitiana* (1613), 6.

47 "quei versi che cantava qualche volta in fisolera, quando andavamo a balotar, che ve piaceva tanto; cussì tratte da una banda le rè, e le fossine,

e i burchiei, e el pesce, me ho conzà sora un costrao, e sì ho scritte ste puoche cossette, parte composte da i primi Cittadini de sta nostra citate, e parte dal vostro povero servidor, e cussì, co le è ve le mando perché podè cantarle con la vostra bella novizia, che da niovo havè trovao." *Versi alla venitiana* (1613), 6. The fisherman-turned-poet in this passage recalls the many similar figures in Andrea Calmo's fanciful letters, published in four books beginning in 1548.

48 All but the last four poems attributed to Ingegneri in the *Versi* had been published earlier as an addendum to Ingegneri's translation of Ovid's *Remedia Amoris* (The cure for love). See his *De' rimedi contra l'amore*, 39r–56v, where the poems are labelled "Versi a la Venitiana del Medemo" (Poetry in the Venetian style, by the same [author]).

49 *Versi alla venitiana* (1613), 60, and MS Add. 12.197, fol. 128r, BL.

50 MS Add. 12.197, fol. 128r, BL.

51 *Versi alla venitiana* (1613), 76. For some other examples of the colloquial phrase "un do da drio" (in the sense of "a kick in the behind"), see Cortelazzo, *Dizionario*, 476.

52 *Versi alla venetiana* (1617).

53 Romano, *Aggionta*. The copy of the *Aggionta* held at the Biblioteca Bertoliana (Vicenza) is bound in with the *Versi*. The *Biblioteca delle Facoltà di Giurisprudenza e Lettere e Filosofia* at the University of Milan has an edition with an identical title printed by Francesco Grossi.

54 On these volumes, see Miller, "New Information."

55 Romano, *Aggionta*, n.p. See also MS Add. 12.197, fol. 7v, BL (here there are slight variations in the orthography).

56 See Romano, *Aggionta*, n.p., and "Tocca pi la camisa, che 'l zippon," MS Add. 12.197, fol. 75v–76r, BL.

57 The Malipiero family was one of the powerful patrician families of Venice. This admirer of Artusi is mentioned three times in MS Add.12.197, fols. 39v, 68r, and 76r, BL, though never identified by first name.

5. Women Writers between Men: Gaspara Stampa and Veronica Franco

1 "Poi che di seguir' io vostre pedate, / Per me l'ardente mio desir non empio; / Voi, d'ogni cortesia ricetto, e tempio, / A' venir dopo voi la man mi date." Stampa, *The Complete Poems*, ed. Tower and Tylus, 261. Unless indicated, all citations and translations of Stampa are from this edition.

2 "E con tanto mio diletto converso con coloro che sanno, per aver occasione ancora d'imparare, che, se la mia fortuna il comportasse, io farei tutta la mia vita e spenderei tutto 'l mio tempo dolcemente nell'accademie degli

uomini virtuosi." Letter 17, in Franco, *Lettere*, 60. English translation in Franco, *Poems and Selected Letters*, 34.

3 On Stampa, see *The Complete Poems*. For Stampa's life and works, see Bassanese, *Gaspara Stampa*; and "Gaspara Stampa," in *Italian Women Writers*, 404–13. On Stampa's involvement with the Venier group, see Salza, "Madonna Gasparina Stampa." See also Erspamer, "Petrarchismo e manierismo," 189–222.

4 On Stampa as a musician, see De Rycke, "On Hearing the Courtesan"; Feldman, "The Courtesan's Voice"; and Smarr, "Gaspara Stampa's Poetry for Performance."

5 According to Bassanese, Stampa met Collaltino di Collalto in 1548 or 1549, and in 1549 she sent him a group of her poems: *Gaspara Stampa*, 17. Salza points out that the Duke of Ferrandina, whose death Stampa commemorated in one of her sonnets, died in February 1549. See Salza, "Madonna Gasparina Stampa," 250n3.

6 Gaspara Stampa, *Rime di Madonna* (1554). The press was headed at the time by the Venetian typographer Plinio Pietrasanta, but owned in part by Girolamo Ruscelli, which suggests that he may have had a hand in publishing Stampa's book. On Ruscelli and Pietrasanta, see Paolo Trovato, *Con ogni diligenza corretto: La stampa e le revisioni editoriali dei testi letterari italiani (1470–1570)* (Bologna: Il Mulino, 1991), 253–4.

7 On Franco (1546–1591), see Rosenthal, *The Honest Courtesan*, as well as her "Veronica Franco's *Terze Rime*." For an analysis of Franco's strategies of negotiating and displaying her relationships with her male interlocutors, see Jones, "City Women and Their Audiences"; and *The Currency of Eros*, ch. 5.

8 For a reprint from 1565, see Fulvio Dittico, *Il catalogo*. See the same, pp. 72–3, for the entries on Paola Fracassa (here Paola Franca) and Veronica Franco. On the *Catalogo*, its purpose, and its print history, see Rosenthal, *The Honest Courtesan*, 274n89 and 288n19.

9 Franco, *Terze rime*. This book was printed without the name of a publisher or the date of publication, but the dedication is dated 1575.

10 Franco, *Lettere familiari a diversi*. This volume was printed without the name of a publisher or date of publication, but Franco's dedication is dated 1580.

11 For a discussion of Giacomina da Seravallo, a possible prostitute who was kept in a *casinò* run by a group of Venetian nobles, see Ruggiero, *Binding Passions*, 43–4.

12 See Domenico Venier, "Ne 'l bianco augel, che 'n grembo a Leda giacque," in *Rime*, ed. Serassi, 37. For a discussion of this sonnet and female singers

associated with the Venier group, including Gaspara Stampa, see Feldman, *City Culture*, 103–9.

13 On the question of Stampa's presence at Ca Venier, see Feldman, who argues that "although she was probably not a regular at their meetings, her close ties with intimates of the academy – especially Parabosco and Molino – and the sonnet she addressed to Venier make her presence there very likely." *City Culture*, 106.

14 "Rime di Dom.[eni]co Veniero, e d'altri," MS It. Cl. IX, 248 (7071), fol. 37r. This excerpt comes from Venier's *capitolo* "Quando ve digo che nessun ve passa" (When I tell you that no one surpasses you). Tantalizingly, the last page (two folios) of the poem has been cut out of the manuscript, perhaps because it contained either obscene content or sensitive information.

15 Corner's response is "Po far Domenedio et non me passa," in MS It. Cl. IX 492 (6297), fol. 176v–178r, Biblioteca Nazionale Marciana, Venice.

16 "Quel che vù fè, Madonna, el feu da vù?" in MS Add 12.197, fols. 50r–50v, BL.

17 On female impersonation in Ortensio Lando's anthology of "women's" letters, *Lettere di molte valorose donne* (1548), see Ray, *Writing Gender*, 45–80.

18 MS Add 12.197, fol. 23r, BL.

19 These are "Si ch'i v'ha ditto 'l vero o ch'i s'insunia" (Whether they are telling you the truth or making it up), MS Add 12.197, fols. 28r–30v, BL; and "Missier mio caro, e' m'ha tanto piasesto" (My dear sir, it pleased me so much), MS Add 12.197, fols. 31–33v.

20 MS Add 12.197, fol. 33v.

21 Ortensio Lando, *Sette libri de' cathaloghi* (Venice: Giolito, 1552), 475.

22 Lodovico Domenichi, ed., *Rime diverse d'alcune nobilissime, et virtuosissime donne, raccolte per M. Lodovico Domenichi* (Lucca: Vicenzo Busdragho, 1559. The poems included here are the three that had appeared in Ruscelli, ed., *Il sesto libro delle rime* (1553), along with "Questo felice e glorioso tempio" (which had appeared in Ruscelli's *Tempio alla divina signora donna Giovanna d'Aragona* in 1554), and the previously unpublished "Dotto, saggio, gentil, chiaro Bonetto," a sonnet to the poet Giovan Iacopo Bonetti.

23 I have been unable to further identify Giovanni Scrittore. As Julia Hairston suggested to me in a private communication, it is possible that the surname "Scrittore" (which means, literally, "Writer") is a pseudonym invented to disguise the writer's identity. The sonnet praising Franco appeared in a volume she edited to commemorate the death of Estore Martinengo: *Rime di diversi eccellentissimi auttori nella morte dell'illustre sign. Estor Martinengo Conte di Malpaga Estor Martinengo conte di Malpaga. Raccolte, et mandate all'illustre, et valoroso colonnello il s. Francesco Martinengo*

suo fratello, conte di Malpaga. Dalla signora Veronica Franco ([Venice]: n.p., [1575?]).

24 Manfredi's letter to Franco appeared in his *Lettere brevissime di Mutio Manfredi* (Venice: Francesco Rondinelli, 1596), 249. See Rosenthal, *The Honest Courtesan*, for a discussion of the letter (151–2) and a reproduction of the 1596 print version (n.p., between page 152 and 153).

25 D'Aragona, *Rime*. For a modern edition of d'Aragona's poetry and letters, see d'Aragona, *The Poems and Letters*. For a discussion of d'Aragona's *Rime* in the context of correspondence poetry, see Hairston, "'Di sangue illustre & Pellegrino,'" in *The Body in Early Modern Italy*, 158–75. For d'Aragona's biography and a discussion of her literary production, see Hairston, "Aragona, Tullia d' (1505/1510–1556)" in *Encyclopedia of Women in the Renaissance: Italy, France, and England*, ed. Anne R. Larsen, Diana Robin, and Carole Levin (Santa Barbara: ABC-CLIO, 2007), 26–9. For a discussion of the "poetics of group identity" in the work of d'Aragona and the Lyonnaise poet Pernette du Guillet, see Jones, "The Poetics of Group Identity," in Jones, *The Currency of Eros*, 37–79.

26 See Aretino's letter to Sperone Speroni, 6 June 1537, in AEN, vol. 4, pt. 1, 209–11; and Nicolò Franco, *Il vendiammiatore, poemetto in ottava rima di Luigi Tansillo; e la Priapea, sonetti lussuriosi-satirici di Niccolò Franco* (Pe-King, n.d. [Paris: J.C. Molino, 1790]), 114.

27 As Virginia Cox points out, Franco's publications were printed clandestinely, probably to avoid censorship. Cox notes that this was not due only to the erotic content of Franco's work, since even her irreproachable verse collection commemorating the death of Ettore Martinengo (1575) and her "sober and often moralizing" *Lettere* (1580) were printed without naming the publisher. See Cox, *Lyric Poetry*, 14 and n.

28 Tullia d'Aragona, *Il Meschino, altramente detto il Guerrino, fatto in ottava rima dalla signora Tullia d'Aragona* (Venice: Giovanni Battista and Melchiorre Sessa, 1560). This text is the first epic poem to have been published by a woman, although some scholars have questioned its attribution to d'Aragona. On this controversy, see Hairston, who attributes the *Meschino* definitively to d'Aragona and notes that references to it are already present in d'Aragona's *Rime* ("Introduction," in d'Aragona, *The Poems and Letters*, 47). As Hairston points out, d'Aragona's authorship of *Il Meschino* was first questioned over a hundred years ago by Enrico Celani (in d'Aragona, *Le rime di Tullia d'Aragona*, lvi–lxiii). For a more recent discussion of doubts regarding the poem's attribution to d'Aragona, see Cox, *Women's Writing*, 312n167.

29 On this see Cox, *Lyric Poetry*, 119. A ready example of changing social mores regarding courtesans is Sperone Speroni's early *Dialogo d'Amore*, first published in 1534 but composed around 1528, which features none other than a young Tullia d'Aragona as interlocutor, whom Speroni treats relatively respectfully (despite the circumscribed role he assigns her). But in 1575, Speroni published *Orazione contro le cortegiane* (Oration against courtesans), probably under pressure from censors. D'Aragona probably met Speroni, along with Bernardo Tasso and Girolamo Molino, in Venice in 1528 (she may have returned in 1535), well before all three of these men began to frequent Domenico Venier's salon in the 1540s. In his youth, Molino wrote a few encomiastic sonnets to d'Aragona, exhorting her to stay and keep him company in Venice, but these were not published until 1573, almost two decades after his death.

30 D'Aragona also had contacts outside of Florence. For a discussion of some previously unknown figures in her *Rime*, including two Romans (Latino Giovenale and Tiberio Nari) and one Milanese man who was involved in Sienese politics (Francesco Crasso), see Julia L. Hairston, "Out of the Archive: Four Newly-Identified Figures in Tullia d'Aragona's *Rime della Signora Tullia di Aragona et di diversi a lei* (1547)," *MLN* 118, no. 1 (2003): 257–63.

31 This was the second time that d'Aragona had been charged and then excused for such a violation. The first incident occurred in Siena in 1544. See Salvatore Bongi, "Il velo giallo di Tullia d'Aragona," in *Rivista critica della letteratura italiana* 3, no. 3 (1886): 85–95.

32 On Tullia's petition and the manuscript sonnets in praise of her, see Julia L. Hairston, "Di sangue illustre," 172–5.

33 For further discussion of the context of Venetian patrician women's writing, see Marina Zancan, "L'intellettualità femminile nel primo Cinquecento: Maria Savorgnan e Gaspara Stampa," *Annali d'italianistica* 7 (1989): 42–65. The only Venetian patrician woman poet to attain any prominence in the sixteenth century was Olimpia Malipiero, whose work appeared in lyric anthologies of the period. But even Malipiero is an exception, since she spent most of her life in Florence, where she apparently was less bound by Venetian cultural norms for women. For a modern edition of two of Malipiero's poems, see Cox, *Lyric Poetry*, 212 and 341 (and 395 for some biographical information).

34 "Alla virtuosa Madonna Gasparina Stampa," in Girolamo Parabosco, *Lettere amorose* di M. Girolamo Parabosco. Libro Primo (Venice: Domenico Farri, 1545), 20b–21b, cited in Salza, "Madonna Gasparina Stampa," 15–16.

35 It has been suggested more than once that Stampa met Collaltino at one of Domenico Venier's literary gatherings, but I am not aware of concrete evidence that would confirm these claims. I suspect their origins may lie in the romanticized "autobiography" of Stampa in Carrer, *Anello di sette gemme*, which consists of a set of fictitious letters in Stampa's voice addressed to Ippolita Mirtilla, with whom the real Stampa exchanged poems. In one of these letters, Correr has his Stampa recount that she first saw Collalto at the villa of the Venetian poet Trifone Gabriele on the island of Murano and was later introduced to him at Domenico Venier's house by Girolamo Molino. That said, there is some literary evidence that alludes to connections between Stampa and these figures – for example, both Stampa and Venier wrote sonnets commemorating Trifone Gabriele's death in 1549.

36 For biographical information on Francesco Sansovino (the son of the sculptor Jacopo), as well as a discussion of his role in the Venetian literary sphere, see Paul F. Grendler, "Francesco Sansovino and Italian Popular History 1560–1600," *Studies in the Renaissance* 16 (1969): 139–80. For a discussion of Girolamo Ruscelli's life and works, see Robin, *Publishing Women*, 110–111. For a collection of essays on Ruscelli, see Paolo Marini and Paolo Procaccioli, eds., *Girolamo Ruscelli dall'accademia alla corte alla tipografia: atti del convegno internazionale di studi, Viterbo, 6–8 ottobre 2011* (Manziana (Roma): Vecchiarelli, 2012).

37 Ruscelli, ed., *Il sesto libro delle rime*. The three sonnets by Stampa are "Vieni Amor' a veder la gloria mia," "Ò hora, ò stella dispietata, e cruda," and "Fà ch'io riveggia Amor, prima ch'io moia" (69).

38 Stampa's sonnet to Venier is "Se voi non foste à maggior cose volto," in Stampa, *The Complete Poems*, 261.

39 "Gaspara Stampa è costretta a discender bene in basso dal posto in cui la nostra ammirazione l'aveva collocata: essa si mette in ischiera, se non con quelle 'sciaguratelle' e 'sgualdrinette' da pochi quattrini, come le dicevano, con quelle altre disgraziate, di cui le più conosciute finora eran Tullia d'Aragona e Veronica Franco." Salza, "Madonna Gasparina Stampa," 94.

40 Franco and Stampa, *Rime*, ed. Abdelkader Salza (Bari: Laterza, 1913), 365.

41 Giovanni Alfredo Cesareo, "Gaspara Stampa, signora non cortigiana," in *Giornale d'Italia*, 12 February 1914; and Greggio, "In difesa di Gaspara Stampa." See the second part of Salza's study, "Madonna Gasparina Stampa e la società veneziana del suo tempo (nuove discussioni)," 217n2, for a lengthy list of responses to the first article.

42 "Fu donna; e di solito la donna, quando non si dà a scimmiottare l'uomo, si serve della poesia sottomettendola ai suoi affetti, amando il proprio

amante o i propri figli più della poesia." Benedetto Croce, *Conversazioni critiche, II* (Bari: Laterza, 1916), 225.

43 On Tullia d'Aragona's musical activities, see Feldman, "The Courtesan's Voice." On Franco as musician, see Rosenthal, *The Honest Courtesan,* 317n58.

44 On the duality of the siren in early modern literature and art, see Elena Laura Calogero, "'Sweet aluring harmony': Heavenly and Earthly Sirens in Sixteenth- and Seventeenth-Century Literature and Visual Culture," in *Music of the Sirens,* ed. Linda P. Austern and Inna Naroditskaya (Bloomington: Indiana University Press, 2006), 140–75.

45 Parabosco's letter, which will be discussed in detail below, is "Alla virtuosa Madonna Gaspara Stampa," in Parabosco, *Lettere amorose di m. Girolamo Parabosco* (Venice: Giolito, 1545) 24r-v.

46 "mille, & mille spirti gentili, & nobili: i quali udito havendo i dolci concenti vostri, v'hanno dato nome di divino sirena." Perissone Cambio, dedication to *Il primo libro de madrigali a 4 voci* (Venice, 1545). Cited and translated in Feldman, *City Culture,* 373.

47 For the image of Franco as siren, see the sonnet by Giovanni Scrittore, "Qual gratia, o qual destin, che da la morte," in *Raccolte, et mandate all'illustre, et valoroso colonnello il s. Francesco Martinengo suo fratello* ([Venice?]: [1575?]). Cited and translated in Rosenthal, *The Honest Courtesan,* 95–6.

48 Aretino to Gianambrogio degli Eusebi, 1 June 1537, in AEN, vol. 4 pt. 1, 204.

49 AEN, vol. 6 pt. 2, 177. In the same passage, Aretino pokes fun at the aging Marchesa of Mantua, Isabella d'Este (1474–1539): "Tutti i segni, tutti i cieli et tutti i pianetti calculate dal quadrante affermano che la mostruosa Marchesana di Mantova la quale ha i denti de hebano e le ciglia di avorio, dishonestamente brutta et arcidishonestamente imbellettata, partorirà in senettute sua senza copula maritale: et un simile miraculo farà la signora Veronica Gambara meretrice laureata" (All the signs, the heavens, and the planets, calculated with a compass, confirm that the monstrous Marchesa of Mantua, who has teeth the color of ebony and eyelashes the color of ivory, dishonestly ugly and super-dishonestly made-up, will give birth in her old age without marital copulation – and a similar miracle will be worked by the lady Veronica Gambara, prostitute laureate). For a discussion of the circulation and reception of Aretino's prognostications, see Edward Hutton, *Pietro Aretino, the Scourge of Princes* (London: Constable, 1922), 100–2. On Gambara (1485–1550), who by the middle of the sixteenth century had become after Vittoria Colonna the second most

frequently published woman poet of her time, see Diana Maury Robin, "Gambara, Veronica," in *Encyclopedia of Women in the Renaissance: Italy, France, and England*, eds. Diana Maury Robin, Anne R. Larsen, and Carole Levin (Santa Barbara: ABC-CLIO, 2007), 160–2.

50 For the argument that Stampa was a member of the Accademia dei Dubbiosi, see Greggio, "In difesa di Gaspara Stampa," 28–31.

51 Ruscelli, ed., *Il sesto libro delle rime.*

52 I have verified Salza's observation that a note on the frontispiece records that the book was "Di Girolamo Ferlito dato al Signor Fabrizio Valguarnera" (Given to Signor Fabrizio Valguarnera by Girolamo Ferlito). See Salza, "Madonna Gasparina Stampa," 71. For Salza's transcription of many, but not all, of Ferlito's glosses, see Salza, 71–2n3.

53 "Nobile Venetiano, sempre infermo in letto, secco dalla metà in giù, troppo accurato e famoso poeta nella lingua nostra." Cited in Salza, "Madonna Gasparina Stampa," 72n3.

54 Ruscelli, ed., *Il sesto libro delle rime*, 69. The copy of the book that belonged to Ferlito is now held at the Biblioteca Nazionale di Firenze, Rinasc. Op. Gen. 314 Libri VI 1553.

55 "Sonetto sopra Mad. Gaspara Stampa di autore incerto," in MS Vaticano latino 9948, f. 211r, Biblioteca Apostolica Vaticana. At the bottom of the page, a note reads "Il fine dei XXI sonetti sopra Mad. Gaspara Stampa" (The last of twenty-one sonnets on Madonna Gaspara Stampa), suggesting that "Fermati, viator" was part of a sequence. The other twenty sonnets do not appear in this codex, nor have I been able to locate them elsewhere. Previously, "Fermati viator" was thought to exist only in an early nineteenth-century copy (Milan, Biblioteca Trivulziana, Miscellanea 115), first brought to critical attention by Salza. For a transcription from this version, see Salza, "Madonna Gasparina Stampa," 73. For a description of the Trivulziana codex and list of its contents, see Porro-Lambertenghi, *Trivulziana*, 259. As Bianchi has noted, the transcriber of the sonnet notes in the Trivulziana codex that he copied it from a manuscript belonging to Alessandro Padoani, the same man who once owned the sixteenth-century codex now in the Vatican Library. See Bianchi, *La scrittura poetica femminile nel Cinquecento veneto*, 35–6n3. It seems plausible that the Trivulziana version was copied from the Vatican manuscript.

56 The famous sixteenth-century Venetian dialect poet Andrea Calmo wrote at least thirty-seven satiric epitaphs. For a modern edition of these as well as some information about this theme in Venetian poetry, see Gino Belloni's edition of Calmo's *Le bizarre, faconde et ingegnose rime pescatorie* (Venice: Marsilio, 2003), 147–67.

57 MS It. Cl. IX 173 (6282), BNM, "Rime in lingua veneziana di diversi autori."

58 The complete text is as follows: "Post mortem sia sepolta in questo fosso, / Diana ladra, spoca, sodomita, / Qual fu sì amica della merda in vita, /Che poi morta ciascuno li cagrà adosso. / Morta che sia, non si saprà di certo / Come li uscirà l'alma o per qual porta, / Perché trovata sia nel letto morta / Co la bocca la potta il cul aperto" (After her death, may she be buried in this ditch: Diana the dirty sodomite and thief, who was such a good friend to shit in life that when she is dead everyone will shit all over her. When she is dead, we won't know how her spirit will leave her body, or through which door, because she will be found dead in her bed with her mouth, her cunt, and her ass wide open). "Rime in lingua veneziana di diversi ... " MS It. Cl. IX 173 (6282), BNM, fol. 96r. The same codex contains several other satiric epitaphs in various poetic forms, including "La in quel canton ti xe, manina Ghisi" (45v), "Qui giace quel meschin del gobbo Dandolo" (octave 123r), and "Son quel Molin, che feva la mia vita" (214v).

59 For a discussion of several examples, see Tessa Storey, "Chapter 1: Themes and Issues in Literature and Image," in *Carnal Commerce in Counter-Reformation Rome* (Cambridge: Cambridge University Press, 2008), 25–56. See also Kurz, "Italian Models."

60 The earliest extant edition of this text is *Lamento d'una cortigiana ferrarese quale per hauere il mal franzese si conduxe andare in carrecta. Composto per Andrea Venitiano* (Siena: Michelangelo de' Libri, 1520). For a discussion of the 1520 edition, see Henry, "Whorish Civility." For a modern edition of the text and a discussion of its attribution, see Giovanni Aquilecchia, "Per l'attribuzione del *Lamento d'una cortigiana ferrarese*," in *Tra latino e volgare. Per Carlo Dionisotti* (Padua: Antenore, 1974), 3–25. For an incisive critical analysis of the *Lamento* and a discussion of the "indexical or deitic function" of the prostitute, who is pointed to as "both exposed body and embodied transgression," see Shemek, "Mi mostrano a ditto tutti quanti."

61 The satirist is probably alluding to the same "magnifico Andrea Gritti" who is named by Cassandra Stampa in her 1576 will as the father of Gaspara Stampa's two daughters, Elisabetta and Sulpizia. This man was probably not the Doge of the same name (1455–1538) who was almost seventy years Stampa's senior, but perhaps he was a younger relative. For a transcription of the will and some discussion of Gritti's identity, see Emilia Veronese Cesaracciu, "Il testamento di Cassandra Stampa: contributi alla biografia di Gaspara," in *Atti e memorie dell'Accademii patavina di scienze, lettere, ed arti. Memorie della Classe di scienze morali, lettere ed arti*, 89.3 (1976–1977): 89–96. Cited in Stefano Bianchi, *La scrittura poetica femminile nel Cinquecento veneto*, 35n1.

62 Salza, in "Madonna Gasparina Stampa secondo nuove indagini," 75, argues that Stampa's literary mentor was Giovanni Francesco Fortunio (1470–1517), the author of the first Italian grammar, *Regole grammaticali della volgar lingua* (1516). But since Fortunio died before Stampa was born, it seems unlikely that he is the figure addressed by Stampa in her *Rime* and then alluded to by the anonymous satirist.

63 Stampa, "Mille fiate a voi volgo la mente" (A thousand times I've turned my thoughts to you), in *The Complete Poems*, 300–1. Spira, a poet and humanist from Viterbo, exchanged poems with Domenico Venier, Sperone Speroni, and Benedetto Varchi, among others. Several of Spira's poems were set to music during his lifetime, including his sonnet, "Et a noi restarà fra sdegn' & ire," which appeared in Girolamo Parabosco's *Madrigali a cinque voci* (Venice: Gardano, 1546).

64 See Cox, *Women's Writing in Italy*, 109–10.

65 Stampa, *The Complete Poems*, 260–1.

66 Parabosco's *capitolo*, "Magnifico Venier, se ben li conto," was printed in Domenico Venier, *Rime di Domenico Veniero*, 118–19.

67 Stampa, *The Complete Poems*, 260–1.

68 Stampa, *Rime*, 129.

69 See Girolamo Molino, *Rime*, 104r.

70 Girolamo Molino, *Rime*, 104r.

71 "Credete voi, dolce Signora mia, che mai per adietro io habbia voluto credere che un huomo in un sol punto possa ardere et agghiacciare? Credete che io avessi mai pensato di poter vedere una donna al mondo perfetta in tutte le virtù? Credete voi che io avessi mai creduto che il canto delle Sirene avesse forza di trare gli ascoltanti fuora di loro stessi? Certo non, ma per innanzi potrò io più questo negare … Che dirò io di quella angelica voce, che qualhora percuota l'aria de' suoi divini accenti, fa tale sì dolce harmonia, che non pura a guisa di Sirena fa d'ognuno, che degno d'ascoltarla … ma infonde spirto e vita nelle più fredde pietre, facendole per soverchia dolcezza lacrimare? Potete adunque, bellissima e graziosissima Signora Gasparina, esser sicura che ogni huomo, che vi vede, v'habbia da rimaner perpetuo servitore. De' quali benché io sia forse il più indegno per virtù, non sarò già per amore, e da hora inanzi in ogni cosa, che io conoscerò potervi piacere, ve ne mostrarò chiarissimo segno." Parabosco, *Lettere amorose*, 24r–v.

72 For a modern edition, see Cambio, *Il primo libro di madrigali a quattro voci*.

73 "… si sa bene homai, e non pure in questa felice città, ma quasi in ogni parte, niuna donna al monda amar più la musica di quello che fate voi, né

altra più raramente possederla … ," cited in Salza, "Madonna Gasparina Stampa," 18.

74 See Fenaruolo, *Rime*, fol. [38].

75 Girolamo Parabosco, *La prima parte delle rime di M. Girolamo Parabosco* (Venice: Botietta, 1546), fol. 20v.

76 See Alonso and Bousoño, *Seis calas en la expresión literaria española*, 56.

77 For a list of print and manuscript sources for this sonnet, see Balduino, "Petrarchismo veneto e tradizione manoscritta," 258n26.

78 Parabosco, *Diporti*, 302–3.

79 Stampa, *Rime*, 97.

80 On the use of the burlesque *capitolo* in the sixteenth century, see Longhi, *Lusus*.

81 The complete passage is as follows: "Molto vagamente pur' in quest' anni stessi hanno il mio Signor Domenico Veniero, et altri nobilissimi ingegni introdotto di scrivere in versi sciolti, e di terze rime, alcuni soggetti piacevolissimi, & principalmente volendo contrafar la pedanteria … & non so se questa, nè altra lingua habbia sorte di componimento così piacevole. De' quali io ò in questo stesso volume, ò (se pur questo venisse soverchiamente grande) in qualche altro spero di farne dar fuori alcuni, che sieno per pienamente dilettare ogni bello spirito" (Even in these very years my Signor Domenico Venier and other most noble talents have very charmingly introduced writing in blank verse and *terze rime* on some very pleasurable subjects, principally wanting to make a burlesque on pedantry … and I don't know if this, or any other language may have a sort of composition so pleasing. Some of these I, either in this same volume, or [should it yet become excessively long] in some other one, hope to issue, so that they may delight utterly every beautiful spirit). Girolamo Ruscelli, *Del modo de comporre in versi, nella lingua italiana* (Venice, 1559), lxxviii, cited and translated in Martha, *City Culture*, 100n50.

82 Rosenthal, "Veronica Franco's *Terze Rime*."

83 Gugliemo Gonzaga (1538–1587), the son of Federico II (Aretino's patron in the 1520s), was an amateur composer and one of the most important musical patrons in the sixteenth century.

84 On Marco Venier, see Rosenthal, *The Honest Courtesan*, 50–1, and Zorzi, *Cortigiana veneziana*, 115–33. Both identify Veronica's interlocutor as Marco Venier (1537–1602), son of Francesco and only distantly related to Domenico. This may well be the right man, but it seems worth noting that both Domenico Venier and his mother Foscarina mention in notarial documents a Marco Antonio Venier, who was the illegitimate son of Domenico's brother Girolamo (and thus Domenico's nephew). See

Domenico Venier's tax report of 1565, ASV Dieci savi alle Decime, b. 130, fol. 653, and Foscarina Venier's will of 1553, ASV, Atti notarili, Testamenti, Atti Marcon 1203/79.

A poet named Marco Venier contributed ten sonnets to a lyric anthology compiled by Dionigi Atanagi in 1565. See Atanagi, ed., *De le rime di diversi nobili poeti toscani*, 132r–134v. The same anthology contains a good number of poems by Domenico Venier, Celio Magno, Orsatto Giustinian, and many others associated with the Venier circle.

85 The copy in the Biblioteca Nazionale Centrale di Firenze (Rinasc. F 251) labels the first poem as "Del Magnifico Messer Marco Veniero alla Signora Veronica Franca" (From the Magnificent Sir Marco Venier to the Lady Veronica Franco), while the copy in the Biblioteca Nazionale Marciana di Venezia (Rari V 494 1) does not. Antonio Cicogna mentions three copies of the book, two with Marco Venier's name (one of these is possibly the copy in Florence) and one without (the copy currently held in the Marciana) in Cicogna, *Delle iscrizioni veneziane*, 5: 421.

86 On Luigi d'Este, who was also a patron of Torquato Tasso, see Rosenthal, *The Honest Courtesan*, 303n97.

87 Fratta, *Della dedicatione de' libri*. See Richardson, *Printing, Writers, and Readers*, 56–7.

88 Fratta, *Della dedicatione de' libri*, fols. 3r–v.

89 Fratta, *Panegirico nel felice dottorato*. For a description of the volume, see Rosenthal, *The Honest Courtesan*, 101–2, and for biographical information on Fratta, *Panegirico*, 302n89.

90 On Henri III in Venice, see Pierre de Nolhac and Angelo Solerti, *Il viaggio in Italia di Enrico III Re di Francia e le feste a Venezia, Ferrara, Mantova e Torino* (Turin: L. Roux, 1890).

91 "All'altissimo favor che la Vostra Maestà s'e degnata di farmi, venendo all'umile abitazione mia, di portarne seco il mio ritratto … io non sono bastevole di corrispondere." Franco, *Lettere*, 30.

92 The sonnets for Henri III are "Come talor dal ciel sotto umil tetto" (As sometimes from heaven to a humble roof), which retells the story of the king's visit to Franco's house, and "Prendi, re per virtù sommo e perfetto" (Take, king, supreme and perfect in virtue), in which Franco offers the king an enamelled medallion of her own image (the portrait she mentions in the dedication letter). On Franco and Henri III, see Rosenthal, *The Honest Courtesan*, 102–11, 124, 247, 304n100.

93 "In quel vostro sì celebre concorso / d'uomini dotti e di giudicio eletto, / da cui vien ragionato e ben discorso, / come, senza poter formar un detto / dovev'io ne la scola circostante uom tal visitar egro infermo

in letto?" (In that assembly of yours, so famous, of learned men of distinguished judgment, who know how to argue and discourse so well, how was I, unable to say one word, amid an academy such as yours, to visit an invalid, confined to bed?). Franco, *Poems and Selected Letters*, 153.

94 *Rime di diuersi eccellentissimi auttori nella morte dell'illustre sign. Estor Martinengo conte di Malpaga* ([Venice?]: [1575?]). For a discussion of Franco's role in compiling the volume, and of its contents, see Rosenthal, *The Honest Courtesan*, 91–7.

95 For the argument that Francesco Martinengo is the "colonello" lamented by Franco in *capitolo* 15, and for biographical information on the Martinengo brothers, see Rosenthal, *The Honest Courtesan*, 91–2.

96 The letter is cited and translated in Rosenthal, *The Honest Courtesan*, 92.

97 The other contributors to the volume are Andrea Menichini, Marco Stecchin, Orazio Toscanella, Giovanni Scrittore, Valerio Sali, and Antonio Cavassico.

98 For a modern edition of Franco's sonnets, see Franco, *Rime*, 171–8. The quote comes from "Mentre d'Estor vorrei pianger la morte," *Rime*, 166.

99 See Cox, *Women's Writing in Italy*, 153.

100 On the poetic debate between Veronica Franco and Maffio Venier, see Rosenthal, *The Honest Courtesan*, 45–57 and 153–96; and "Veronica Franco's *Terze Rime*." See also Dolora Chapelle Wojciehowski, "Veronica Franco vs. Maffio Venier: Sex, Death, and Poetry in Cinquecento Venice," *Italica* 83, nos. 3–4 (2006): 367–90. On Maffio Venier, the fundamental source remains Ruggieri, *Maffio Venier*. For a discussion of Maffio's literary output, his impact on dialect poetry, and his poetic debate with Veronica Franco, see Zorzi, *Cortigiana veneziana*, 93–111. Three of the *capitoli* can be found in "Rime, canzoni, et sonetti di Maffio Veniero," MS It. Cl. IX 217 (7061), BNM, a codex copied in the early seventeenth century by a single hand. For a short description of the codex, including a list of incipits of its contents, see Agostini Nordio (now Agostini), "La Strazzosa," 45–7. As Agostini points out, several of the poems in this codex, although attributed to Maffio, are by Domenico instead. The poems addressed to Franco are "Franca credéme che per San Maffio" (MS It. Cl. IX 217 (7061), fol. 45r, BNM); "An fia, comuodo? A che muodo zioghemo?" (MS It. Cl. IX 217 (7061), fol. 59v, BNM); "Veronica, ver unica puttana" (MS It. Cl. IX 217 (7061), fol. 56r, BNM). A different codex contains Maffio's dialect sonnet, "El retratto e la impresa è bona e bella" (MS It. Cl. IX 173 [6282], fols. 253v–254r, BNM), written after an engraved portrait of Franco that was probably intended as a frontispiece for her *Terze rime*. All of these were first edited by Dazzi, in *Il fiore della*

lirica veneziana, vol. 2, *Il libro chiuso di Maffio Venier (la tenzone con Veronica Franco)* (Venice: Neri Pozza, 1956). On Franco's poetic battle with Maffio Venier, see Dazzi, *Il fiore*, 51–7.

101 Franco is mentioned along with Azzalina, Savorgnan, and many others in Maffio Venier's *capitolo* "Daspuò che son entrà in pensier sì vario," in MS It. Cl. IX 217 (7061), 83v–86r, BNM.

102 Dazzi, ed., *Il libro chiuso di Maffio Venier*, 23–7. The two manuscript copies of the poem are "Franca, credeme che per San Maffio," in MS It. Cl. IX 217 (7061), 45r–48r, BNM and the variant "Franca, credeme che al corpo de Lio," in MS It. Cl. IX 173 (6282), 409v–411r, BNM. The latter was probably an attempt to mask the author's identity.

103 Here I am indebted to Rosenthal, who argues provocatively that Marco and Maffio Venier were using Franco as a pawn in their own battle for authority (*The Honest Courtesan*, 51).

104 Dazzi, ed., *Il libro chiuso*. This volume forms part of Dazzi's four-volume anthology of Venetian dialect poetry, *Il fiore della lirica veneziana*.

105 *Versi alla venitiana*, (1613), 97–9.

106 Franco, *Rime*, ed. Bianchi, 92–4.

107 *Versi alla venitiana* (1613), 97.

108 BNM, MS It. Cl. IX 217 (7061): "Rime, canzoni, et sonetti di Maffio Veniero," 63r–65v. For a short description of the codex including a list of incipits of its contents, see Agostini Nordio (now Agostini), "La Strazzosa," 45–7. As Agostini points out, several of the poems in this codex are attributed to authors other than Venier in other sources.

109 "Adesso, che le zanze xe compìe, e che qualche un se l'ha desmentegà, / vogio da valent'huomo far le mie" (Now that the chatter has finished, and some people have forgotten, I want to make my own [chatter], as a gentleman would). BNM, MS It. Cl. IX 217 (7061), 63r.

110 BNM, MS It. Cl. IX 217 (7061), 63r.

111 MS It. Cl. IX 217 (7061), 63r–65v, BNM.

112 For a summary of the debate on Franco among Italian literary critics and commentators from the eighteenth to the twentieth century, see Zorzi, *Cortigiana veneziana*, 8–18.

113 Stampa's sonnet is "O notte, a me più chiara, e più beata" (O night, to me more luminous and blessed), *Rime* 104 (150). On Franco's eroticism and her reworking of Ovid's *Amores* and *Ars Amatoria*, see Robin, "Courtesans, Celebrity, and Print Culture," 35–59.

114 Franco, *Poems and Selected Letters*, 56–7.

115 Franco, *Poems and Selected Letters*, 58–9.

116 Franco, *Poems and Selected Letters*, 68–9.

117 For a brief analysis of *capitoli* 1 and 2 that focuses on Franco's insistence on literary collaboration as a prerequisite for erotic fulfilment, see Jones and Rosenthal, "Introduction: The Honored Courtesan," in Franco, *Poems and Selected Letters*, 14. See also Rosenthal's earlier argument that Franco is "redefining the Petrarchan muse as poetic collaborator rather than disembodied and silent addressee" in *The Honest Courtesan*, 185.

118 Franco, *Poems and Collected Letters*, 70–1. I have adapted the translation to a more literal one for clarity.

119 See their "Introduction: The Honored Courtesan," in Franco, *Poems and Collected Letters*, 14.

120 Franco, *Poems and Collected Letters*, 64–5.

121 Parabosco, *Rime*, fol. 65v.

122 Franco, *Poems and Collected Letters*, 66–7.

Bibliography

PRIMARY SOURCES

Manuscripts

London, British Library (BL)

MS Add. 12.197: "Sonetti e poema in italiano di Benedetto Corner e di
    Domenico Venier di Venezia – Corretti da altra mano più tardi."

Paris, Bibliothèque nationale de France (BNF)

MS Italien 563: "Rime oscene d'anonimo, in dialetto."

Rome, Biblioteca Apostolica Vaticana (BAV)

MS Barberiniano latino 3775.
MS Vaticano latino 9948.

Venice, Archivio di Stato di Venezia (ASV)

Avogaria di Comun.
Dieci savi alle decime.
Notarile.
Atti.
Testamenti.
Provveditori alla Sanità
Necrologi.
Sant'Uffizio.
Senato terra.

Venice, Biblioteca del Museo Correr

MS Codice Cicogna 664: Emanuele Cicogna, "*La puttana errante* e *Il trentuno della Zaffetta.*"
MS Cicogna 2039: Emanuele Cicogna, "Il catalogo de tutte le principal, et piu onorate cortigiane di Venetia."
MS 33.D.76: Giuseppe Tassini, "Cittadini veneziani."
Misc. Codici, I: Toderini, Teodoro. "Genealogie delle famiglie Venete ascritte alla cittadinanza originaria." 4 vols.

Venice, Biblioteca Nazionale Marciana (BNM)

MS It. Cl. VII 925–928 (8584–8597): Marco Barbaro, "Genealogie delle famiglie patrizie venete."
MS It. Cl. VII 15–18 (8304–8307): Girolamo Alessandro Cappellari, "Il campidoglio Veneto."
MS It. Cl. IX 171 (6092): Celio Magno, "Rime di Celio Magno, e di altri a lui dirette con altre cose in prosa. Autografo."
MS It. Cl. IX 173 (6282): "Rime in lingua veneziana di diversi."
MS It. Cl. IX 217 (7061): "Rime, canzoni, et sonetti di Maffio Veniero."
MS It. Cl. IX 248 (7071): "Rime di Dom.[eni]co Veniero, e d'altri."
MS It. Cl. IX 271 (6096): "Poesie varie di varii Autori."
MS It. Cl. IX 272 (6645): "Rime di diversi del secolo XVI."
MS It. Cl. IX 273 (6646): "Rime d'autore Veneziano Anonimo, mandate a Roma nel 1573 con lettera dedicatoria."
MS It. Cl. IX 288 (6072): "Commedie varie del secolo XVI."
MS It. Cl. IX 307 (7564): "Rime di vari autori."
MS It. Cl. IX 308 (7007): "Rime anonime, fra le quali ... Maffio Veniero."
MS It. Cl. IX 348 (7203): "Rime di diversi autori."
MS It. Cl. IX 380 (6372): "Poesie in dialetto veneziano e in italiano di vari autori."
MS It. Cl. IX 453 (6498): "Leggenda di Santa Margherita; Canzoni spirituali; Poesie varie, cioè sonetti, capitoli, e canzoni di diversi anonimi dei sec. XV e XVI, in pezzi volanti."
MS It. Cl. IX 492 (6297): "Rime di diversi autori del secolo XVI."
MS It. Cl. IX 589 (9765): Domenico Venier, "Frammento di canzoniere autografo."
MS It. Cl. IX 691 (12098): "Poesie veneziane del sec.[olo] XVI."
MS It. Cl. X 1 (6394): "Istoria delle vite de' poeti italiani, di Alessandro Zilioli veneziano."

Print (including modern editions)

Aragona, Tullia d'. *Il Meschino, altramente detto il Guerrino, fatto in ottava rima dalla signora Tullia d'Aragona*. Venice: Giovanni Battista and Melchiorre Sessa, 1560.

– *The Poems and Letters of Tullia d'Aragona and Others: A Bilingual Edition*. Edited and translated by Julia L. Hairston. Toronto: Iter Inc., 2014.

– *Rime della Signora Tullia di Aragona; et di diversi a lei*. Venice: Gabriele Giolito de' Ferrari, 1547.

– *Le rime: cortigiana del secolo XVI*, edited by Enrico Celani. Bologna: Commissione per i testi di lingua, 1969.

Arcadelt, Jacob. *Opera omnia*. 10 vols. Edited by Albert Seay. [Rome]: American Institute of Musicology, 1965.

Aretino, Pietro. *Al gran marchese del Vasto dui primi canti di Marphisa del divino Pietro Aretino*. Venice: n.p., [1532?].

– *Aretino's Dialogues*. Translated by Raymond Rosenthal. Toronto: University of Toronto Press, 2005.

– *La Cortigiana*. Venice: Francesco Marcolini, 1534.

– *Dialogo, nel quale la Nanna il primo giorno insegna a la Pippa sua figliuola a esser puttana*. Turin [Venice?]: P.M.L. [Francesco Marcolini?], 1536.

– *Edizione nazionale delle opere di Pietro Aretino*. Edited by Giovanni Aquilecchia and Angelo Romano. Rome: Salerno editrice, 1992.

– *Lettere*. Edited by Paolo Procaccioli. 6 vols. Rome: Salerno editrice, 1997–2002.

– *Li dui primi canti di Orlandino del diuino messer Pietro Aretino*. Venice: [Bindoni?], [1540?].

– *Opera nova del fecundissimo giovene Pietro pictore Arretino, zoè strambotti sonetti capitoli epistole barzellette & una desperata*. Venice: Nicolo Zopino, 1512.

– *Poemi cavallereschi*. Edited by Danilo Romei. Rome: Salerno editrice, 1995.

– *Poesie varie*. Edited by Giovanni Aquilecchia and Angelo Romano. Rome: Salerno editrice, 2002.

– *La prima parte de Ragionamenti di M. Pietro Aretino cognominato il Flagello de prencipi, il Veritiero, el Divino, divisa in tre giornate, la contenenza de le quali si porra ne la facciata seguente*. Bentigodi [London]: [John Wolfe], 1584.

– *Ragionamento della Nanna, et della Antonia, fatto in Roma sotto una ficaia, composto dal diuino Aretino per suo capricio, a corretione de i tre stati delle donne*. Paris [Venice?]: Ubertinus Mazzola [Francesco Marcolini?], 1534.

– *Les Ragionamenti ou Dialogues du divin Pietro Aretino. Texte italien et traduction complete par le traducteur des Dialogues de Luisa Sigea*. Edited by Alcide Bonneau. Paris: Isadore Lisieux, 1882.

– *Ragionamento: Dialogo.* Introduction by Giorgio Barberi Squarotti. Edited by Carla Forno. Milan: Biblioteca Universale Rizzoli, 1998.

– *Scritti di Pietro Aretino nel codice Marciano It. XI 66 (=6730).* Edited by Danilo Romei. Florence: Franco Cesati, 1987.

– *Teatro.* Edited by Giorgio Petrocchi. Milan: Mondadori, 1971.

Ariosto, Ludovico. *Orlando furioso e Cinque Canti.* 2 vols. Edited by Sergio Zatti. Turin: UTET, 1997.

Atanagi, Dionigi, ed. *Rime di diversi nobilissimi, et eccellentissimi autori, in morte della Signora Irene delle Signore di Spilimbergo. Alle quali si sono aggiunti versi latini di diversi egregij poeti, in morte della medesima Signora.* Venice: 1561.

–, ed. *De le rime di diversi nobili poeti toscani, raccolte da M. Dionigi Atanigi. Libro primo-[secondo].* 2 vols. Venice: Lodovico Avanzo, 1565.

Baschet, Armand. "Documents concernant la personne de messer Pietro Aretino," *Archivio storico italiano,* 3rd ser., 3 (1866): 107–130.

Battiferri degli Ammannati, Laura. *Laura Battiferra and Her Literary Circle: An Anthology.* Edited and translated by Victoria Kirkham. Chicago: University of Chicago Press, 2006.

Bembo, Pietro. *Prose di m. Pietro Bembo nelle quali si ragiona della volgar lingua.* Venice: Giovanni Tacuino, 1525.

– *Prose della volgar lingua; Gli Asolani; Rime.* Edited by Carlo Dionisotti. Turin: TEA, 1989.

Boccaccio, Giovanni. *Decameron.* Edited by Vittore Branca. Torino: Einaudi, 1991.

Bruno, Giordano. *Il candelaio.* Biblioteca rara 18. Milan: G. Daelli, 1863.

Cairns, Christopher S. "Domenico Bollani, a Distinguished Correspondent of Pietro Aretino – Some Identifications." *Renaissance News* 19, no. 3 (Autumn 1966): 193–205.

Calmo, Andrea. *Le bizarre, faconde et ingegnose rime pescatorie.* Edited by Gino Belloni. Venice: Marsilio, 2003.

– *Le bizzarre, faconde, et ingeniose rime pescatorie ... Et il commento di due sonetti del Petrarcha, in antiqua materna lingua per Andrea Calmo.* Venice: Giovanni Battista Bertacagno, 1553.

Cambio, Perissone. *Il primo libro di madrigali a quatro voci.* Venice, 1547. Mod. ed. Martha Feldman. Sixteenth-Century Madrigal, vol. 3. New York: Garland, 1989.

Catullus, Gaius Valerius. *The Poems of Catullus.* Translated by Charles Martin. Baltimore: Johns Hopkins University Press, 1990.

Citolini, Alessandro. *La tipocosmia di Alessandro Citolini da Serravalle.* Venice: Vincenzo Valgrisi, 1561.

Clario, Benedetto. *Il primo canto de Orlando furioso in lingua venetiana. Composto per Benedetto Clario per dar piacer a gli suoi amici.* Venice: Bindoni, 1554.

Componimenti poetici delle più illustri rimatrici d'ogni secolo, edited by Luisa Bergalli. Venice: Antonio Mora, 1726.

[Corner, Benetto]. *Cinquanta stanze de Arcibravo venetiano. Ne le quali egli narra cose oltra modo terribili et grandi, non mai più intese, della sua destrezza, gagliardia, et fatti. Con un sonetto amoroso.* Venice: n.p., n.d.

Corso, Anton Giacomo. *Le rime di M. Anton' Giacomo Corso.* Venice: a San Luca a segno della Cognitione, 1550.

Crescimbeni, Giovan Mario. *L'istoria della volgar poesia.* 2 vols. Venice: L. Basegio, 1730.

Dante Alighieri. *La vita nuova e le rime.* Edited by Andrea Battistini. Rome: Salerno editrice, 1995.

Dazzi, Manlio, ed. *Il fiore della lirica veneziana.* 4 vols. Venice: Neri Pozza Editore, 1956.

Della nuova scielta di lettere di diversi nobilissimi huomini, et eccell. ingegni, scritte in diverse materie, fatta da tutti i libri sin'hora stampati, libro primo [-e secondo]. Venice, 1574.

Delle rime di diversi nobili huomini eccellenti poeti nel la lingua thoscana. Nuovamente ristampate. Libro secondo, 2nd ed. Venice: Gabriele Giolito de' Ferrari, 1548.

[Libro terzo] delle rime di diversi nobilissimi et eccellentisimi autori nuovamente raccolte. Edited Andrea Arrivabene. Venice: Bartolomeo Cesano, 1550.

Delle rime piaseuoli di diversi auttori: nuovamente raccolte da m. Modesto Pino, et intitolate la carauana. Parte prima. Venice: Sigismondo Bordogna, 1565.

Delle rime piaseuoli di diuersi auttori nuouamente raccolte da m. Modesto Pino, & intitolate la Carauana. Parte prima. Venice: Sigismondo Bordogna, 1573.

Delle rime piaseuoli di diuersi auttori. Nuouamente raccolte da m. Modesto Pino, & intitolate la Carauana. Parte prima. Venice: Domenico Farri, 1576.

Delle rime piaceuoli di diuersi auttori. Raccolte da Modesto Pino, & intitolate La carauana. Parte prima. Venice: Domenico Farri, 1578.

Delle rime piacevoli di diversi avtori. Raccolte da m. Modesto Pino, & initolate La Carauana. Parte prima. Venice: Presso Altobello Salicato, 1580.

Delle rime piaceuoli di diuersi auttori raccolte da m. Modesto Pino, & intitolate La carauana. Parte prima (Venice: Fabbio & Agostin Zoppini fratelli, 1584.

Dialogo dello Zoppino: de la vita e genealogia di tutte le cortigiane di Roma. Edited by Gino Lanfranchi. Milan: L'Editrice del libro raro, 1922. See also *Ragionamento del Zoppino.*

Dittico, Fulvio. *Il catalogo delle principali e piu onorate cortigiane di Venezia nel Cinquecento: con uno studio su il libertinaggio sotto la dominante di Fulvio Dittico.* Venice: Edizioni della Fortuna, 1956.

Domenichi, Lodovico, ed. *Rime diverse d'alcune nobilissime, et virtuosissime donne, raccolte per M. Lodovico Domenichi.* Lucca: Vicenzo Busdragho, 1559.

Fenaruolo, Girolamo. *Rime di Mons. Girolamo Fenaruolo.* Venice: Giorgio
Angelieri, 1574.

Florio, John. *A Worlde of Wordes, or Most Copious, and Exact Dictionarie in Italian
and English, Collected by Iohn Florio.* London: By Arnold Hatfield for Edw.
Blount, 1598.

Franco, Giacomo. *Habiti delle donne veneziane intagliate in rame nuovamente da
Giacomo Franco.* Venice: n.p., 1614.

Franco, Niccolò. *Le pistole vulgari.* Venice: Gardane, 1542.

– *Il vendiammiatore, poemetto in ottava rima di Luigi Tansillo; e la Priapea, sonetti
lussuriosi-satirici di Niccolò Franco.* Pe-King [Paris]: n.p. [J.C. Molino], n.d.
[1790].

Franco, Veronica. *Terze rime di Veronica Franco al serenissimo signor duca di
Mantova et di Monferrato.* [Venice]: n.p., [1575?].

– *Lettere familiari a diversi.* [Venice]: n.p., [1580].

– *Poems and Selected Letters.* Edited by Ann Rosalind Jones and Margaret F.
Rosenthal. Chicago: University of Chicago Press, 1998.

– *Rime.* Edited by Stefano Bianchi. Milan: Gruppo Ugo Mursia, 1995.

– *Lettere.* Edited by Stefano Bianchi. Rome: Salerno, 1998.

Franco, Veronica, ed. *Rime di diuersi eccellentissimi auttori nella morte dell'illustre
sign. Estor Martinengo conte di Malpaga. Raccolte, et mandate all'illustre, et
valoroso colonnello il s. Francesco Martinengo suo fratello, conte di Malpaga. Dalla
signora Veronica Franco.* [Venice]: n.p., [1575?].

Franco, Veronica, and Gaspara Stampa. *Rime.* Edited by Abdelkader Salza.
Bari: Laterza, 1913.

Fratta, Giovanni. *Panegirico nel felice dottorato dell'illustre, et eccell.mo sig.
Gioseppe Spinelli digniss. rettor de legisti, et caualier splendidissimo. Raccolto da
Giovanni Fratta gentil'huomo veronese, et Academico Animoso.* Padua: Lorenzo
Pasquati, 1575.

– *Della dedicatione de' libri, con la corretion dell'abuso, in questa materia introdotto,
dialoghi del sig. Giouanni Fratta, nobile veronese.* Venice: Giorgio Angelieri,
1590.

Ingegneri, Angelo. *De' rimedi contra l'amore fatto volgare ... da A. Ingegneri, con
aggiunta di vari novi componimenti.* Bergamo: Comin Ventura, 1604.

Lando, Ortensio. *Sette libri de cathaloghi a' varie cose appartenenti, non solo
antiche, ma anche moderne: opera utile molto alla historia, et da cui prender si po
materia di fauellare d'ogni proposito che ci occorra.* Venice: Giolito, 1552.

Maganza, Giovanni Battista (Magagnò), ed. *La prima parte de le rime di
Magagnò, Menon, e Begotto in lingua rustica padovana, con una tradottione del
primo canto de M. Ludovico Ariosto.* Padua: Grazioso Perchacino, 1558.

– *La terza parte de le rime di Magagnò, Menon e Begotto. Nuovamente poste in luce.* Venice: Bolognino Zaltiero, 1569.

Magno, Celio. *Deus canzone spirituale di Celio Magno. Con vn discorso sopra di quella dell'eccellentissimo signor Ottauio Menini. Un commento dell'eccellentissimo signor Valerio Marcellini, & due lettioni dell'eccellentissimo signor Theodoro Angelucci.* Venice: Domenico Farri, 1597.

Manfredi, Muzio. *Lettere brevissime di Mutio Manfredi.* Venice: Francesco Rondinelli, 1596.

Manuzio, Paolo. *Lettere volgari di M. Paolo Manutio, divise in quattro libri.* Venice: Aldo Manuzio, 1560.

Marcellino, Valerio. *Il diamerone … ove con vive ragioni si mostra, la morte non esser quel male, che'l senso si persuade. Con una dotta, e giudiciosa lettera over discorso intorno alla lingua volgare.* Venice: Gabriele Giolito de' Ferrari, 1564.

Milani, Marisa. "Di un omaggio pavano a Domenico Venier." *Quaderni veneti* 18 (1993): 179–86.

– *Contro le puttane: rime venete del XVI secolo.* Bassano del Grappa: Ghedina & Tassotti, 1994.

– *Streghe e diavoli nei processi del S. Uffizio: Venezia, 1554–1587.* Bassano del Grappa: Ghedina and Bassottim, 1994.

Molino, Girolamo. *Rime di M. Girolamo Molino: nouamente venute in luce.* Venice: n.p., 1573.

Parabosco, Girolamo. *Lettere amorose di m. Girolamo Parabosco.* Venice: Giolito, 1545.

– *La prima parte delle rime di M. Girolamo Parabosco.* Venice: Tomaso Botietta (Giovanni Farri e fratelli), 1546.

– *Rime di M. Girolamo Parabosco.* Venice: Giolito, 1547.

– *I diporti di m. Girolamo Parabosco.* Venice: Giovanni Griffio, [1551?].

– *Il primo libro delle lettere famigliari di M. Girolamo Parabosco. Et il primo libro de' suoi madrigali nuovamente posti in luce.* Venice: Giovanni Griffio, 1551.

– *La seconda parte delle rime di m. Girolamo Parabosco.* Venice: Francesco e Pietro Rocca, 1555.

– *I quattro libri delle lettere amorose.* Edited by Thomaso Porcacchi. Venice, 1561. Rev. ed. 1607.

– *Diporti: Girolamo Parabosco-Gherardo Borgogni.* Edited by Donato Pirovano. Rome: Salerno, 2005.

Pasquino, *Consigli vtilissimi dello eccellente dottore mastro Pasquino a tutti li gentilhuomini, officiali procuratori, notari, artisti, brauazzi, & altri che vengono di nouo a Roma, tradutti de greco in latino, & de latino in vulgar.* Rome: n.p., [1530?].

Petrarca, Francesco. *Trionfi, rime estravaganti, codice degli abbozzi.* Edited by
    Vinicio Pacca and Laura Paolino. Milan: Mondadori, 1996.
– *Canzoniere.* Edited by Marco Santagata. Milan: Mondadori, 1996.
Procaccioli, Paolo. *"Ragionamento* e *Dialogo* di Pietro Aretino." In *Letteratura
    Italiana Einaudi,* vol. 2, edited by Alberto Asor Rosa. Turin: Einaudi, 1993.
*Ragionamento del Zoppino fatto frate, e Lodovico puttaniere, dove contiensi la vita
    e genealogia di tutte le cortigiane di Roma.* Venice: Francesco Marcolino, 1539.
    See also *Dialogo dello Zoppino.*
*Rime di diversi signori napoletani e d'altri. Nuovamente raccolte et impresse. Libro
    settimo.* Edited by Lodovico Dolce. Venice: Gabriele Giolito de' Ferrari, 1556.
Rime diverse di molti eccellentiss. auttori nuovamente raccolte. Libro primo. Edited
    by Lodovico Domenichi. Venice: Gabriele Giolito de' Ferrari, 1545.
Rime di diversi autori eccellentiss. Libro nono. Cremona: Vincenzo Conti, 1560.
*Rime diverse di molti eccellentiss. auttori nuovamente raccolte. Libro primo, con
    nuova additione ristampato,* 2nd ed. Edited by Lodovico Domenichi. Venice:
    Gabriele Giolito de' Ferrari, 1546.
Rime di diversi nobili huomini et eccellenti poeti nella lingua thoscana. Libro secondo.
    Venice: Gabriele Giolito de' Ferrari, 1547.
*Rime diverse in lingua genovese le quali per la novità de' soggetti sono molto
    dilettevoli da leggere.* Pavia: Gieronimo Bartoli, 1588.
Romano, Remigio, ed. *Aggionta ai versi alla venetiana di bellissime poesie, raccolti
    per il signor Remigio Romano.* Vicenza: Angelo Salvadori, 1619.
Ruscelli, Girolamo. *Lettura di Girolamo Ruscelli, sopra un sonetto dell'illustriss.
    signor marchese della Terza alla divina signora marchesa del Vasto.* Venice:
    Giovanni Griffio, 1552.
Ruscelli, Girolamo, ed. *Il sesto libro delle rime di diversi eccellenti autori,
    nuovamente raccolte, et mandate in luce. Con un discorso di Girolamo Ruscelli.*
    Venice: al segno del Pozzo [Giovanni Maria Bonelli], 1553.
Sanudo, Marin. *I diarii di Marino Sanuto.* 58 vols. Edited by Rinaldo Fulin et al.
    Venice: F. Visentini, 1879–1903.
Sansovino, Francesco. *Delle cose notabili della città di Venetia.* Venice: Altobello
    Salicato, 1587.
Speroni, Sperone. *Opere di M. Sperone Speroni degli Alvarotti: tratte de' Mss.
    originali.* 5 vols. Venice: Domenico Occhi, 1740.
Stampa, Gaspara. *The Complete Poems: The 1554 Edition of the "Rime," a Bilingual
    Edition.* Edited by Troy Tower and Jane Tylus. Chicago: University of
    Chicago Press, 2010.
– *Rime di madonna Gaspara Stampa.* Venice: Plinio Pietrasanta, 1554.
– *Rime di Madonna Gaspara Stampa, con alcune altre di Collaltino, e di Vinciguerra,
    conti di Collato, e di Baldassare Stampa.* Edited by Luisa Bergalli. Venice:
    Francesco Piacentini, 1738.

La tariffa delle puttane di Venegia, accompagné d'un catalogue des principales courtisanes de Venise, tiré des archives vénitiennes (XVIe siècle) et traduit pour la première fois en français. Edited by Guillaume Apollinaire. Paris: Bibliothèque des curieux, 1911.

Tasso, Bernardo. *Rime di messer Bernardo Tasso. Divise in cinque libri nuovamente stampate.* Venice: Gabriele Giolito de' Ferrari, 1560.

– *Delle lettere di M. Bernardo Tasso.* Venice: Gabriele Giolito de' Ferrari, 1560.

Il terzo libro dell'opere burlesche di M. Francesco Berni ... e di altri autori. Florence [=Naples]: n.p., 1723.

Todi, Jacopone da. *Laude.* Edited by Franco Mancini. Bari: Laterza, 1974.

Toscanella, Orazio. *I nomi antichi, e moderni delle provincie, regioni, città, castella, monti, laghi, fiumi, mari, golfi, porti, & isole dell'Europa, dell'Africa, & dell'Asia; con le graduationi loro in lunghezza, e larghezza & una breve descrittione delle suddette parti del mondo ...* Venice, 1567.

Vasari, Giorgio. *Le vite de' più eccellenti pittori, scultori, ed architetti.* Florence, 1550.

Vecellio, Cesare. *Habiti antichi, et moderni di tutto il mondo.* Venice: Sessa, 1598.

Venier, Domenico. *Rime di Domenico Veniero, raccolte ora la prima volta.* Edited by Pierantonio Serassi. Bergamo: Pietro Lancellotto, 1751.

Venier, Lorenzo. *La puttana errante: Poème en quatre chantes de Lorenzo Veniero.* Paris: Isidore Liseux, 1883.

– *La puttana errante.* Edited by Nicola Catelli. Milan: Unicopli, 2005.

– *La Zaffetta.* Edited by Gino Raya. Catania: Tirelli, 1929.

Venier, Maffio. *Poeti antichi del dialetto veneziano divisi in due volumi,* vol. 2: *Poesie di Maffeo Veniero arcivescovo di Corfù e di altri.* Venice: Al negozio di libri all'Apollo, dalla Tipografia di Alvisopopoli, 1817.

– *Canzoni e sonetti.* Edited by Attilio Carminati. Venice: Corbo e Fiore, 1993.

– *Poesie diverse.* Edited by Attilio Carminati. Venice: Corbo e Fiore, 2001.

Venier, Maffio, and Veronica Franco. *Il libro chiuso.* Edited by Manlio Torquato Dazzi. Venice: Neri Pozza, 1956.

Versi alla venitiana, zoè, canzon, satire, lettere amorose, matinae, canzonete in aieri moderne et altre cose belle. Opera del signor Anzolo Inzegner, et d'altri bellissimi spiriti. Vicenza: per il Brescia, 1613.

Versi alla venitiana, zoè canzon, satire, lettere amorose, matinae, canzonete in aieri moderni, & altre cose belle. Vicenza: Angelo Salvadori, 1617.

Zane, Giacomo. *Rime di M. Giacomo Zane.* Venice: Domenico, e Gio. Battista Guerra, fratelli, 1562.

– *Giacomo Zane: Rime.* Edited by Giovanna Rabitti. Padua: Antenore, 1997.

Zeno, Apostolo. *Lettere di Apostolo Zeno cittadino veneziano istorico e poeta cesareo nelle quali si contengono molte notizie attenenti all'istoria letteraria de' suoi tempi.* 6 vols. Venice: F. Sansoni, 1785.

SECONDARY SOURCES

Agostini Nordio (now Agostini), Tiziana. "Benetto Corner poeta dialettale e bulesco." In *Tra commediografi e letterati: Rinascimento e Settecento veneziano*, edited by Tiziana Agostini and Emilio Lippi, 151–70. Ravenna: Longo editore, 1997.

– "Poesie dialettali di Domenico Venier." *Quaderni veneti* 14 (1991): 33–56.

– "Rime dialettali attribuite a Maffio Venier. Primo regesto." *Quaderni veneti*, no. 2 (1985): 7–23.

– "La Strazzosa, canzone di Maffio Venier. Edizione critica." In *Contributi rinascimentali*, edited by Tiziana Agostini Nordio and Valerio Vianello, 9–131. Abano Terme (Padova): Francisci, 1982.

Alonso, Dámaso. *Pluralità e correlazione in poesia*. Bari: Adriatica, 1971.

Alonso, Dámaso, and Carlos Bousoño. *Seis calas en la expresión literaria española (prosa, poesía, teatro)*. Madrid: Editorial Gredos, 1970.

Althusser, Louis. "Idéologie et appreils idéologiques d'état." In *Positions, 1964–1975*, 67–125. Paris: Éditions Sociales, 1976.

Ancona, Alessandro d'. *La poesia popolare italiana*. Livorno: Francesco Vigo, 1878.

Aquilecchia, Giovanni. "Aretino's *Sei giornate*: Literary Parody and Social Reality." In *Women in Italian Renaissance Culture and Society*, edited by Letizia Panizza, 453–62. Oxford: European Humanities Research Centre, University of Oxford, 2000.

– "Per l'attribuzione del lamento d'una cortigiana ferrarese." In *Tra latino e volgare. Per Carlo Dionisotti*, 3–25. Padua: Antenore, 1974.

Armellini, Mariano. "Un censimento della città di Roma sotto il pontificato di Leone X tratto da un codice inedito dell'archivio Vaticano." Offprint from *Gli studi in Italia* IV–V. Rome: A. Befani, 1882.

Bakhtin, Mikhail. *Rabelais and His World*. Bloomington: Indiana University Press, 1984.

Balduino, Armando. "Petrarchismo veneto e tradizione manoscritta." In *Petrarca, Venezia e il Veneto*, edited by Giorgio Padoan, 243–70. Florence: Leo S. Olschki, 1976.

– "Restauri e ricuperi per Maffio Venier." *Medioevo e Umanesimo* 35 (1979): 231–63.

Barzaghi, Antonio. *Donne o cortigiane? La prostituzione a Venezia: documenti di costume dal XVI al XVIII secolo*. Verona: Bertani, 1980.

Barzman, Karen-Edis. *The Florentine Academy and the Early Modern State: The Discipline of Disegno*. Cambridge: Cambridge University Press, 2000.

Bassanese, Fiora A. *Gaspara Stampa*. Boston: Twayne, 1982.

– "Gaspara Stampa." In *Italian Women Writers: A Bio-Bibliographical Sourcebook,* edited by Rinaldina Russell, 404–13. Westport: Greenwood Press, 1994.

Benjamin, Walter. *The Arcades Project.* Boston: Harvard University Press, 1999.

Benzoni, Gino. "Aspetti della cultura urbana nella società veneta del '500-'600: le accademie." *Archivio Veneto* 108 (1977): 87–159.

– "L'accademia: appunti e spunti per un profilo." *Ateneo veneto* 26 (1988): 37–58.

Bernstein, Jane A. *Music Printing in Renaissance Venice: The Scotto Press, 1539–1572.* New York: Oxford University Press, 1998.

Bertolo, Fabio Massimo. *Aretino e la stampa: strategie di autopromozione a Venezia nel Cinquecento.* Rome: Salerno, 2003.

Bianchi, Stefano. *La scrittura poetica femminile nel Cinquecento veneto: Gaspara Stampa e Veronica Franco.* Manziana (Roma): Vecchiarelli, 2013.

Bianchini, Giuseppe. "Girolamo Parabosco: scrittore e organista del secolo XVI." *Miscellanea di Storia Veneta* 2, no. 6 (1899): 207–486.

Bianco, Monica. "Domenico Venier e l'epitaffio di Pietro Aretino." *Quaderni veneti* 41 (2005): 129–36.

– "Le rime di Domenico Venier (edizione critica)." PhD diss., Università degli studi di Padova, 2000.

– "Sulla tradizione delle 'Rime' di Domenico Venier." In *Petrarca in barocco: cantieri petrarcheschi: due seminari romani,* edited by Amedeo Quondam, 331–6. Rome: Bulzoni, 2004.

Bock, Gisela. *Women in European History.* Translated by Allison Brown. Oxford: Blackwell Publishing, 2002.

Boerio, Giuseppe. *Dizionario del dialetto veneziano.* Venice: A. Santini, 1829.

Bolzoni, Lina. "L'Accademia Veneziana: splendore e decadenza di una utopia enciclopedica." In *Università accademie e società scientifiche in Italia e in Germania dal cinquecento al settecento,* edited by Laetitia Boehm and Ezio Raimondi, 117–67. Bologna: Il Mulino, 1981.

Bongi, Salvatore. *Annali di Gabriel Giolito de' Ferrari da Trino di Monferrato, stampatore in Venezia.* 2 vols. Rome: Ministero della Pubblica Istruzione, 1890.

– "Il velo giallo di Tullia d'Aragona." *Rivista critica della letteratura italiana* 3, no. 3 (1886): 85–95.

Boucher, Bruce. *The Sculpture of Jacopo Sansovino.* 2 vols. New Haven: Yale University Press, 1991.

Breitenberg, Mark. *Anxious Masculinity in Early Modern England.* Cambridge: Cambridge University Press, 1996.

Brevini, Francesco. "Petrarchismo e antipetrarchismo in dialetto." In *La poesia in dialetto: Storia e testi dalle origini al Novecento*, vol. 1, 563–604. Milan: Mondadori, 1999.

Brown, Patricia Fortini. *Art and Life in Renaissance Venice*. New York: Harry N. Abrams, 1997.

– *Private Lives in Renaissance Venice: Art, Architecture, and the Family*. New Haven: Yale University Press, 2004.

– *Venetian Narrative Painting in the Age of Carpaccio*. New Haven: Yale University Press, 1988.

Burchard, Jean. *Diarium sive rerum urbanarum commentarii 1483–1506*, vol. 3. Edited by Louis Thuasne. Paris: E. Leroux, 1883.

Bussi, Francesco. *Umanità e arte di Gerolamo Parabosco, madrigalista, organista e poligrafo (Placenza, 1524 c.-Venezia, 1557)*. Piacenza: Liceo Musicale G. Niccolini, 1961.

Butler, Judith. *Bodies That Matter: On the Discursive Limits of "Sex."* New York: Routledge, 1993.

– *Gender Trouble: Feminism and the Subversion of Identity*. New York: Routledge, 1990.

Cairns, Christopher. *Pietro Aretino and the Republic of Venice: Researches on Aretino and His Circle in Venice, 1527–1556*. Florence: Leo S.Olschki, 1985.

Calogero, Elena Laura. "'Sweet aluring harmony': Heavenly and Earthly Sirens in Sixteenth- and Seventeenth-Century Literature and Visual Culture." In *Music of the Sirens*, edited by Linda P. Austern and Inna Naroditskaya, 140–75. Bloomington: Indiana University Press, 2006.

Campbell, Julie D. *Literary Circles and Gender in Early Modern Europe: A Cross-Cultural Approach*. Aldershot: Ashgate, 2006.

Carroll, Linda L. "Carnival Rites as Vehicles of Protest in Renaissance Venice." *Sixteenth Century Journal* 16 (1985): 487–502.

Carrer, Luigi. *Anello di sette gemme*. Venice: Co' tipi del Gondoliere, 1838.

Cesareo, Giovanni Alfredo. "Gaspara Stampa, signora non cortigiana." *Giornale d'Italia*, 12 February 1914.

Chambers, David. "The Earlier 'Academies' in Italy." In *Italian Academies of the Sixteenth Century*, edited by David Chambers and François Quiviger, 1–14. London: Warburg Institute, 1995.

Chemello, Adriana. "Donna di palazzo, moglie, cortigiana: ruoli e funzioni sociali della donna in alcuni trattati del Cinquecento." In *La corte e il 'Cortigiano,'* edited by Amedeo Quondam, 113–32. Rome: Bulzoni, 1980.

Chojnacka, Monica. *Working Women of Early Modern Venice*. Baltimore: Johns Hopkins University Press, 2001.

Chojnacki, Stanley. *Women and Men in Renaissance Venice: Twelve Essays on Patrician Society*. Baltimore: Johns Hopkins University Press, 2000.

Cian, Vittorio. *Galanterie italiane del secolo XVI*. Torino: n.p., 1887.

Ciardi, Roberto. "'A Knot of Words and Things': Some Clues for Interpreting the *Imprese* of Academies and Academicians." In *Italian Academies of the Sixteenth Century*, edited by David Chambers and François Quiviger, 37–60. London: Warburg Institute, 1995.

Cicogna, Emmanuele Antonio. *Delle inscrizioni veneziane*. 6 vols. Venice: Giuseppe Orlandelli, 1824.

Clubb, Louise George, and William G. Clubb. "Building a Lyric Canon: Gabriel Giolito and the Rival Anthologists, 1545–1590: Part I." *Italica* 68, no. 3 (1991): 332–44.

Cohen, Elizabeth S. "Back Talk: Two Prostitutes' Voices from Rome c. 1600." *Early Modern Women: An Interdisciplinary Journal* 2, no. 95 (2007): 95–126.

– "'Courtesans' and 'Whores': Words and Behavior in Roman Streets." *Women's Studies* 19, no. 2 (1991): 201–8.

Cohn, Samuel K. *Women in the Streets: Essays on Sex and Power in Renaissance Italy*. Baltimore: Johns Hopkins University Press, 1996.

Cortelazzo, Manlio. *Dizionario veneziano della lingua e della cultura popolare nel XVI secolo*. Padua: La Linea Editrice, 2007.

Cox, Virginia. *Lyric Poetry by Women of the Italian Renaissance*. Baltimore: Johns Hopkins University Press, 2013.

– *The Prodigious Muse: Women's Writing in Counter-Reformation Italy*. Baltimore: Johns Hopkins University Press, 2011.

– *Women's Writing in Italy, 1400–1650*. Baltimore: Johns Hopkins University Press, 2008.

Croce, Benedetto. *Conversazioni critiche, II*. Bari: Laterza, 1916.

Da Mosto, Andrea. *L'Archivio di Stato di Venezia, indice generale, storico, descrittivo ed analitico*. Rome: Biblioteca d'Arte, 1937.

Da Rif, Bianca Maria. *La letteratura "alla bulesca": Testi rinascimentali veneti*. Padua: Editrice Antenore, 1984.

Dalla Man, Leone. *Un discepolo di Pietro Aretino: Lorenzo Venier e i suoi poemetti osceni*. Ravenna: Tipografia Nazionale, E. Lavagna e figli, 1913.

Davis, Natalie Zemon. "The Reasons of Misrule: Youth Groups and Charivaris in Sixteenth-Century France." *Past and Present* 50 (1971): 41–75.

– *Society and Culture in Early Modern France*. Stanford: Stanford University Press, 1975.

Dean, Trevor, and K.J.P. Lowe. *Marriage in Italy, 1300–1650*. Cambridge: Cambridge University Press, 1998.

De Rycke, Dawn. "On Hearing the Courtesan in a Gift of Song: The Venetian Case of Gaspara Stampa." In *The Courtesan's Arts: Cross-Cultural Perspectives*, edited by Martha Feldman and Bonnie Gordon, 124–32. Oxford: Oxford University Press, 2006.

Diberti-Leigh, Marcella. *Veronica Franco, donna, poetessa e cortigiana del Rinascimento*. Ivrea, Italy: Priuli & Verlucca, 1988.

Dionisotti, Carlo. "La letteratura italiana nell'età del concilio di Trento." In *Geografia e storia della letteratura italiana*, 183–204. Turin: Einaudi, 1967.

Doglio, Maria Luisa. *Della poesia rappresentativa e del modo di rappresentare le favole sceniche*. Modena: Panini, 1989.

Eisenbichler, Konrad. *The Sword and the Pen: Women, Politics, and Poetry in Sixteenth-Century Siena*. Notre Dame: University of Notre Dame Press, 2012.

Erspamer, Francesco. "Petrarchismo e manierismo nella lirica del secondo cinquecento." In *Storia della cultura veneta: il seicento*, vol. 4, pt. 1, edited by Girolamo Arnaldi and Manlio Pastore Stocchi, 189–222. Vicenza: Neri Pozza, 1983.

Fabbri, Paolo. "Andrea Gabrieli e le composizioni su diversi linguaggi: La giustiniana." In *Andrea Gabrieli e il suo tempo: Atti del convegno internazionale (Venezia 16–18 Settembre 1985)*, edited by Francesco Degrada, 249–72. Florence: Leo S. Olschki Editore, 1987.

Fahy, Conor. "Three Early Renaissance Treatises on Women." *Italian Studies* 11 (1956): 30–55.

– "Women and Italian Cinquecento Literary Academies." In *Women in Italian Renaissance Culture and Society*, edited by Letizia Panizza, 438–52. Oxford: Oxford University Press, 2000.

Faraone, Christopher A., and Laura McClure. *Prostitutes and Courtesans in the Ancient World*. Madison: University of Wisconsin Press, 2006.

Feldman, Martha. "The Academy of Domenico Venier, Music's Literary Muse in Mid-Cinquecento Venice." *Renaissance Quarterly* 44, no. 3 (1991): 476–512.

– *City Culture and the Madrigal at Venice*. Berkeley: University of California Press, 1995.

– "The Courtesan's Voice: Petrarchan Lovers, Pop Philosophy, and Oral Traditions." In *The Courtesan's Arts: Cross-Cultural Perspectives*, edited by Martha Feldman and Bonnie Gordon, 105–23. Oxford: Oxford University Press, 2006.

Ferguson, Ronnie. *A Linguistic History of Venice*. Florence: Leo S. Olschki, 2007.

Ferrari, Mattia. "Il *Lamento dei pescatori veneziani* e il MS. Marc. It. IX 173 (=6282)." Tesi di laurea. Università Ca' Foscari di Venezia, 2012.

Ferraro, Joanne Marie. *Marriage Wars in Late Renaissance Venice*. Oxford: Oxford University Press, 2001.

Fido, Franco, ed. *Il paradiso dei buoni compagni: Capitoli di storia letteraria veneta.* Padua: Editrice Antenore, 1988.

Findlen, Paula. "Humanism, Politics and Pornography in Renaissance Italy." In *The Invention of Pornography: Obscenity and the Origins of Modernity, 1500–1800,* edited by Lynn Hunt, 49–108. New York: Zone Books, 1996.

Finucci, Valeria. *The Lady Vanishes: Subjectivity and Representation in Castiglione and Ariosto.* Stanford: Stanford University Press, 1992.

– *The Manly Masquerade: Masculinity, Paternity, and Castration in the Italian Renaissance.* Durham: Duke University Press, 2003.

Finucci, Valeria, and Regina M. Schwartz, eds. *Desire in the Renaissance: Psychoanalysis and Literature.* Princeton: Princeton University Press, 1994.

Fiori, Giorgio. "Novità biografiche su tre letterati piacentini del Cinquecento: Lodovico Domenichi, Luigi Cassoli, Girolamo Paraboschi." *Bollettino storico piacentino* 97 (2002): 73–111.

Forster, Leonard. *The Icy Fire: Five Studies in European Petrarchism.* London: Cambridge University Press, 1969.

Foucault, Michel. "The Discourse on Language." In *The Archaeology of Knowledge and the Discourse on Languages,* 215–37. New York: Harper and Row, 1972.

– *The History of Sexuality.* 3 vols. Translated by Robert Hurley. New York: Vintage Books, 1990.

Frantz, David O. *Festum Voluptatis: A Study of Renaissance Erotica.* Columbus: Ohio State University Press, 1989.

Frapolli, Massimo. "Un micro-canzoniere di Domenico Venier in antologia." *Quaderni veneti* 33 (2001): 29–68.

Freccero, John. "The Fig Tree and the Laurel: Petrarch's Poetics." *Diacritics* 5 (1975): 34–40.

Freedman, Luba. *Titian's Portraits through Aretino's Lens.* University Park: Pennsylvania State University Press, 2005.

Freud, Sigmund. "Jokes and Their Relation to the Unconscious." In *The Standard Edition of the Complete Works of Sigmund Freud,* vol. 8, translated by James Strachey. London: Hogarth Press and the Institute of Psychoanalysis, 1966.

Gardiner, Judith Kegan, ed. *Masculinity Studies and Feminist Theory: New Directions.* New York: Columbia University Press, 2002.

Gaylard, Susan. *Hollow Men: Writing, Objects, and Public Image in Renaissance Italy.* New York: Fordham University Press, 2013.

Giannetti, Laura. *Lelia's Kiss: Imagining Gender, Sex, and Marriage in Italian Renaissance Comedy.* Toronto: University of Toronto Press, 2009.

Giannetti, Laura, and Guido Ruggerio, eds. and trans. *Five Comedies from the Italian Renaissance.* Baltimore: Johns Hopkins University Press.

Il gioco dell'amore: le cortigiane di Venezia dal Trecento al Settecento. Milan: Berenice, 1990.

Girard, René. *Mensonge romantique et vérité Romanesque.* Paris: Grasset, 1961. Translated by Yvonne Freccero as *Deceit, Desire, and the Novel: Self and Other in Literary Structure.* Baltimore: Johns Hopkins University Press, 1965.

Graf, Arturo. *Attraverso il Cinquecento.* Turin: Loescher, 1888.

Greenblatt, Stephen. *Renaissance Self-Fashioning from More to Shakespeare.* Chicago: University of Chicago Press, 1980.

Greggio, Elisa. "In difesa di Gaspara Stampa." *Ateneo Veneto* 1 (1915): 5–149.

Grendler, Paul F. *Critics of the Italian Words (1530–1560): Anton Francesco Doni, Nicolò Franco & Ortensio Lando.* Madison: University of Wisconsin Press, 1969.

– "Form and Function in Italian Renaissance Popular Books." *Renaissance Quarterly* 46, no. 3 (1993): 451–85.

– "Francesco Sansovino and Italian Popular History 1560–1600." *Studies in the Renaissance* 16 (1969): 139–80.

– "The Roman Inquisition and the Venetian Press, 1540–1605." *Journal of Modern History* 47, no. 1 (1975): 48–65.

Hairston, Julia L. "Out of the Archive: Four Newly-Identified Figures in Tullia d'Aragona's Rime della Signora Tullia di Aragona et di diversi a lei (1547)." *MLN* 118, no. 1 (2003): 257–63.

Hairston, Julia L., and Walter Stephens, eds. *The Body in Early Modern Italy.* Baltimore: Johns Hopkins University Press, 2010.

Hankins, James. "The Myth of the Platonic Academy of Florence." *Renaissance Quarterly* 44, no. 3 (1991): 429–75.

Henry, Chriscinda. "'Whorish Civility' and Other Tricks of Seduction in Venetian Courtesan Representation." In *Sex Acts in Early Modern Italy: Practice, Perversion, Performance,* edited by Allison M. Levy, 109–24. Burlington: Ashgate, 2010.

Hickson, Sally. "More than Meets the Eye: Giulio Romano, Federico II Gonzaga, and the Triumph of Trompe-l'oeil at the Palazzo del Te in Mantua." In *Disguise, Deception, Trompe-l'oeil: Interdisciplinary Perspectives,* edited by Leslie Boldt-Irons, Corrado Federici, and Ernesto Virgulti, 41–60. New York: Lang Publishing, 2009.

Horodowich, Elizabeth. *Language and Statecraft in Early Modern Venice.* New York: Cambridge University Press, 2008.

Hunt, Lynn Avery, ed. *The Invention of Pornography: Obscenity and the Origins of Modernity, 1500–1800.* New York: Zone Books, 1993.

Hutton, Edward. *Pietro Aretino, the Scourge of Princes*. London: Constable, 1922.

Jones, Ann Rosalind. "City Women and Their Audiences: Louise Labé and Veronica Franco." In *Rewriting the Renaissance: The Discourses of Sexual Difference in Early Modern Europe*, edited by Margaret W. Ferguson, Maureen Quilligan, and Nancy J. Vickers, 299–316. Chicago: Chicago University Press, 1986.

– *The Currency of Eros: Women's Love Lyric in Europe, 1540–1620*. Bloomington: Indiana University Press, 1990.

– "Surprising Fame: Renaissance Gender Ideologies and Women's Lyric." In *The Poetics of Gender*, edited by Nancy K. Miller, 74–95. New York: Columbia University Press, 1986.

Junkerman, Anne Christine. "Bellissima Donna: An Interdisciplinary Study of Venetian Sensuous Half-length Images of the Early Sixteenth Century." PhD diss., University of California, Berkeley, 1988.

Keener, Shawn Marie. "Virtue, Illusion, *Venezianità*: Vocal Bravura and the Early *Cortigiana Onesta*." In *Musical Voices of Early Modern Women: Many-Headed Melodies*. Aldershot: Ashgate, 2005.

Kelly, Joan. "Did Women Have a Renaissance?" In *Women, History, and Theory*, 19–50. Chicago: University of Chicago Press, 1984.

– "Early Feminist Theory and the *Querelle des Femmes*, 1400–1789." *Women, History, and Theory*, 65–109. Chicago: University of Chicago Press, 1984.

King, Margaret L., and Albert Rabil, Jr., eds. "The Other Voice in Early Modern Europe: Introduction to the Series." In *The Other Voice in Early Modern Literature*. Chicago: University of Chicago Press, 1998.

Kirkham, Victoria. "Laura Battiferra degli Ammanati's 'First Book' of Poetry: A Renaissance Holograph Comes Out of Hiding." *Rinascimento* 36 (1996): 351–91.

Klapisch-Zuber, Christiane. *Women, Family, and Ritual in Renaissance Italy*. Translated by Lydia G. Cochrane, 261–82. Chicago: University of Chicago Press, 1985.

Kurz, Hilde. "Italian Models of Hogarth's Picture Stories." *Journal of the Warburg and Courtald Institutes* 15, nos. 3/4 (1952): 136–58.

Labalme, Patricia H., Laura Sanguineti White, and Linda Carroll. "How to (and How Not to) Get Married in Sixteenth-Century Venice (Selections from the Diaries of Marin Sanudo)." *Renaissance Quarterly* 52, no. 1 (1999): 43–72.

LaGuardia, David. *Intertextual Masculinity in French Renaissance Literature: Rabelais, Brantôme and the Cent Nouvelles Nouvelles*. Aldershot: Ashgate, 2008.

Lanza, Alfonso. *La lirica amorosa veneziana del secolo XVI*. Verona: R. Cabianca, 1933.

Larivaille, Paul. *Pietro Aretino fra Rinascimento e manierismo*. Rome: Bulzoni, 1980.

– *La vita quotidiana delle cortigiane nell'Italia del Rinascimento: Roma e Venezia nei secoli XV e XVI*. Milan: Rizzoli, 1983.

Lawner, Lynne. *Lives of the Courtesans: Portraits of the Renaissance*. New York: Rizzoli, 1987.

– *I modi: The Sixteen Pleasures: An Erotic Album of the Italian Renaissance: Giulio Romano, Marcantonio Raimondi, Pietro Aretino, and Count Jean-Frederic-Maximilien de Waldeck*. Evanston: Northwestern University Press, 1988.

Lévi-Strauss, Claude. *The Elementary Structures of Kinship*. Boston: Beacon Press, 1969.

Lippi, Emilio. "Un inedito intermezzo cinquecentesco 'alla bulesca.'" In *Tra commediografi e letterati: Rinascimento e Settecento veneziano*, edited by Tiziana and Emilio Lippi Agostini, 129–50. Ravenna: Longo editore, 1997.

Longhi, Silvia. *Lusus, il capitolo burlesco nel Cinquecento*. Padua: Antenore, 1983.

Lorenzi, Giovanni Battista, ed. *Leggi e memorie venete sulla prostituzione fino alla caduta della Repubblica*. Venice: a spese del conte di Oxford, 1870–72.

Love, Harold. *The Culture and Commerce of Texts: Scribal Publication in Seventeenth-Century England*. Amherst: University of Massachusetts Press, 1998.

Lowry, Martin. "The 'New Academy' of Aldus Manutius: A Renaissance Dream." *Bulletin of the John Rylands Library* 58 (1976): 378–420.

– *The World of Aldus Manutius: Business and Scholarship in Renaissance Venice*. Ithaca: Cornell University Press, 1979.

Luzio, Alessandro. *Pietro Aretino nei primi suoi anni a Venezia e la corte dei Gonzaga*. Turin: Ermanno Loescher, 1888.

– *Un pronostico satirico di Pietro Aretino*. Bergamo: Instituto italiano delle arti grafiche, 1900.

Macy, Laura. "Speaking of Sex: Metaphor and Performance in the Italian Madrigal." *Journal of Musicology* 14, no. 1 (1996): 1–34.

Marini, Paolo, and Paolo Procaccioli, eds. *Girolamo Ruscelli dall'accademia alla corte alla tipografia: atti del convegno internazionale di studi, Viterbo, 6–8 ottobre 2011*. Manziana (Rome): Vecchiarelli, 2012.

Marlowe, Christopher. *The Tragicall History of D. Faustus*. London: Printed by V. S[immes] for Thomas Bushell, 1604.

Marsand, Antonio. *I manoscritti italiani della Regia Biblioteca Parigina*. Parigi: Stamperia reale, 1835.

Martin, John Jeffries, and Dennis Romano, eds. *Venice Reconsidered: The History and Civilization of an Italian City-State, 1297–1797*. Baltimore: Johns Hopkins University Press, 2000.

Masson, Georgina. *Courtesans of the Italian Renaissance*. London: Secker & Warburg, 1975.

Maylender, Michele. *Storia delle accademie d'Italia*. 5 vols. Bologna: L. Cappelli, 1926–1930.

Mazzuchelli, Giovanni Maria. *La vita di Pietro Aretino, scritta dal conte Giammaria Mazucchelli*. Brescia: Pietro Pianta, 1763.

McClure, Laura K. *Courtesans at Table: Gender and Greek Literary Culture in Athenaeus*. New York: Routledge, 2003.

McHugh, Shannon. "The Gender of Desire: Feminine and Masculine Voices in Early Modern Italian Lyric Poetry." PhD diss., New York University, 2015.

Milani, Marisa. "'L'incanto' di Veronica Franco." *Giornale storico della letteratura italiana* 262, no. 518 (1985): 250–63.

– "Un omaggio pavano a Domenico Venier." *Quaderni veneti* 18 (1993): 179–86.

– *Streghe e diavoli nei processi del S. Uffizio: Venezia, 1554–1587*. Bassano del Grappa: Ghedina & Tassotti, 1994.

– "Da accusati a delatori: Veronica Franco e Francesco Barozzi." *Quaderni veneti* 23 (1996): 9–34.

Miller, Roark. "New Information on the Chronology of Venetian Monody: The 'Raccolte' of Remigio Romano." *Music & Letters* 77, no. 1 (1996): 22–33.

Milligan, Gerry. "Masculinity and Machiavelli: How to Avoid Effeminacy, Perform Manliness and Be Wary of the Author." In *Seeking Real Truths: Multidisciplinary Perspectives on Machiavelli*, edited by Patricia Vilches and Gerald Seaman, 149–72. Boston: Brill Academic Press, 2007.

– "The Politics of Effeminacy in 'Il cortegiano.'" *Italica* 83, nos. 3/4 (2006): 345–66.

Milligan, Gerry, and Jane Tylus, eds. *The Poetics of Masculinity in Early Modern Italy and Spain*. Essays and Studies, vol. 22. Toronto: Centre for Reformation and Renaissance Studies, Victoria University in the University of Toronto, 2010.

Molmenti, Pompeo. *La storia di Venezia nella vita privata*. 3 vols. Trieste: Edizioni LINT, 1973.

Moulton, Ian Frederick. *Before Pornography: Erotic Writing in Early Modern England*. New York: Oxford University Press, 2000.

Muir, Edward. *Civic Ritual in Renaissance Venice*. Princeton: Princeton University Press, 1981.

– *Ritual in Early Modern Europe*. Cambridge: Cambridge University Press, 2005.

Nardelli, Franca Petrucci. *La lettera e l'immagine: Le iniziali parlanti nella tipografia italiana (secc. 16–18)*. Florence: Leo S. Olschki, 1991.

Nolhac, Pierre de and Angelo Solerti, *Il viaggio in Italia di Enrico III Re di Francia e le feste a Venezia, Ferrara, Mantova e Torino*. Turin: L. Roux, 1890.

Nuovo vocabolario illustrato della lingua italiana. Edited by Giacomo Devoto and Gian Carlo Oli. Milan: Le Monnier, 1987.

Padoan, Giorgio. "Fra *Decameron* e *Cortegiano*: l'autunno della novella nei *diporti* del Parabosco." In *Il paradiso dei buoni compagni: Capitoli di storia letteraria veneta*, edited by Franco Fido, 74–85. Padua: Editrice Antenore, 1988.

– *Momenti del Rinascimento veneto*. Padua: Antenore, 1978.

– *Rinascimento in controluce: poeti, pittori, cortigiane e teatranti sul palcoscenico rinascimentale*. Ravenna: A. Longo, 1994.

Pagan, Pietro. "Sulla Accademia 'Venetiana' o della 'Fama.'" *Atti dell'Istituto Veneto di Scienze, Lettere ed Arti* 132 (1973–4): 359–92.

Panizza, Letizia, ed. *Women in Italian Renaissance Culture and Society*. Oxford: Legenda European Humanities Research Centre, University of Oxford, 2000.

Pavan, Elisabeth. "Police des moeurs, société et politique à Venise à la fin du Moyen Age." *Revue Historique* 264 (1981): 241–88.

Petrella, Giancarlo. "'Ad instantia d'Hippolito Ferrarese': Un cantimbanco editore nell'Italia del Cinquecento." In *Paratesto*, 8 (2011), 23–79.

Phillippy, Patricia. "'Altera Dido': The Model of Ovid's Heroides in the Poems of Gaspara Stampa and Veronica Franco." *Italica* 69, no. 1 (1992): 1–18.

Piejus, Marie Francoise. "La première anthologie de poèmes féminins." In *Le pouvoir et la plume: Incitation, contrôle, e répression dans l'Italie du XVIe siècle*, 193–213. Paris: Université de la Sorbonne Nouvelle, 1982.

Pilot, Antonio. "Un peccataccio di Domenico Venier." *Fanfulla della domenica* 28, no. 30 (1906). Reprint, Rome: F. Centenari.

– "Poesie vernacole inedite di Celio Magno, di Giovanni Querini, del Parabosco, e di Giacomo Mocenigo." *Fanfulla della domenica* 31, no. 16 (1909). Reprint, Rome: n.p.

Porro-Lambertenghi, Giulio. *Trivulziana; catalogo dei codici manoscritti*. Turin: Stamperia di G.B. Paravia, 1884.

Pucci, Paolo. "Decostruzione disgustoza e definizione di classe nella *Tariffa delle puttane di Venegia*." *Rivista di letteratura italiana* 28, no. 1 (2010): 29–49.

Quaintance, Courtney. "Defaming the Courtesan: Satire and Invective in Sixteenth-Century Italy." In *The Courtesan's Arts: Cross-Cultural Perspectives*, edited by Martha Feldman and Bonnie Gordon, 199–208. Oxford: Oxford University Press, 2006.

Ray, Meredith Kennedy. *Writing Gender in Women's Letter Collections of the Italian Renaissance*. Toronto: University of Toronto Press, 2009.

Richardson, Brian. *Manuscript Culture in Renaissance Italy*. Cambridge: Cambridge University Press, 2009.

– *Printing, Writers, and Readers in Renaissance Italy.* Cambridge: Cambridge University Press, 1999.

Richter, Bodo. "Petrarchism and Anti-Petrarchism among the Veniers." *Forum Italicum* 3 (1969): 20–39.

Robin, Diana Maury. "Courtesans, Celebrity, and Print Culture." In *Italian Women and the City,* edited by Janet Levarie Smarr and Daria Valentini, 35–59. Madison: Farleigh Dickinson University Press, 2003.

– *Publishing Women: Salons, the Presses, and the Counter-Reformation in Sixteenth-Century Italy.* Chicago: University of Chicago Press, 2007.

Robin, Diana, Carole Levin, and Anne Larsen. *Encyclopedia of Women in the Renaissance: Italy, France, and England.* Santa Barbara: ABC-CLIO, 2007.

Rosand, David. *Myths of Venice: The Figuration of a State.* Chapel Hill: University of North Carolina Press, 2001.

– "*Venetia figurata*: The Iconography of a Myth." In *Interpretazioni veneziane: Studi distoria dell'art in onore di Michelangelo Muraro,* edited by David Rosand, 177–96. Venice: Aresenale Editrice, 1984.

Rosand, Ellen. "Music in the Myth of Venice." *Renaissance Quarterly* 30, no. 4 (1977): 511–37.

Rose, Paul Lawrence. "The Accademia Venetiana: Science and Culture in Renaissance Venice." *Studi veneziani* 11 (1969): 191–242.

Rosenthal, Margaret F. *The Honest Courtesan: Veronica Franco, Citizen and Writer in Sixteenth-Century Venice.* Chicago: University of Chicago Press, 1992.

– "Venetian Women Writers and Their Discontents." In *Sexuality and Gender in Early Modern Europe,* edited by James Grantham Turner. Cambridge: Cambridge University Press, 1993.

– "Veronica Franco's *Terze Rime*: The Venetian Courtesan's Defense." *Renaissance Quarterly* 42 (1989): 227–57.

– "A whore's vices are really virtues": The Erotics of Satire in Pietro Aretino's *Ragionamenti.*" In *Aretino's Dialogues,* translated and edited by Raymond Rosenthal, xi–xxiv. Toronto: University of Toronto Press, 2005.

Ross, Sarah Gwyneth. *The Birth of Feminism: Woman as Intellect in Renaissance Italy and England.* Cambridge, MA: Harvard University Press, 2009.

Rossi, Daniella. "The Illicit Poetry of Domenico Venier: A British Library Codex." *The Italianist* 30, no. 1 (2010): 38–62.

Rossiaud, Jacques. "Fraternités de jeunesse et niveau de culture dans les villes du Sud-est à la fin du moyen âge." *Cahiers d'Histoir* 1–2 (1976): 67–102.

– *Medieval Prostitution.* Translated by Lydia Cochrane. Oxford: Basil Blackwell, 1988.

Rubin, Gayle. "The Traffic in Women: Notes Towards the Political Economy of Sex." In *Toward an Anthropology of Women,* edited by Rayna R. Reiter, 157–210. New York: Monthly Review Press, 1975.

Ruggieri, Nicola. *Maffio Venier arcivescovo e letterato veneziano del Cinquecento.* Udine: Tip. Arturo Bosetti, 1909.

Ruggiero, Guido. *Binding Passions: Tales of Magic, Marriage, and Power at the End of the Renaissance.* New York: Oxford University Press, 1993.

– *The Boundaries of Eros: Sex Crime and Sexuality in Renaissance Venice.* New York: Oxford University Press, 1985.

–, ed. *A Companion to the Worlds of the Renaissance.* Malden: Blackwell Publishers, 2002.

– *Machiavelli in Love: Sex, Self, and Society in the Italian Renaissance.* Baltimore: Johns Hopkins University Press, 2007.

– "Marriage, Love, Sex and Renaissance Civic Morality." In *Sexuality and Gender in Early Modern Europe: Institutions, Texts, Images,* edited by James Grantham Turner, 10–30. Cambridge: Cambridge University Press, 1993.

– "Prostitution: Looking for Love." In *A Cultural History of Sexuality in the Renaissance,* vol. 3, edited by Bette Talvacchia, 157–74. Oxford: Berg, 2011.

– *Violence in Early Renaissance Venice.* New Brunswick: Rutgers University Press, 1980.

– "Who's Afraid of Giuliana Napolitana? Pleasure, Fear, and Imagining the Arts of the Renaissance Courtesan." In *The Courtesan's Arts: Cross-Cultural Perspectives,* edited by Martha Feldman and Bonnie Gordon, 280–92. Oxford: Oxford University Press, 2006.

Salked, Duncan. "History, Genre and Sexuality in the Sixteenth Century: The Zoppino Dialogue Attributed to Pietro Aretino." *Mediterranean Studies* 10 (2001): 49–116.

Salza, Abdelkader. "Madonna Gasparina Stampa, secondo nuove indagini." *Giornale storico della letteratura italiana* 62 (1913): 1–101.

– "Madonna Gasparina Stampa e la società veneziana del suo tempo (nuove discussioni)." *Giornale storico della letteratura italiana* 66 (1917): 217–306.

Salzberg, Rosa. *Ephemeral City: Cheap Print and Urban Culture in Renaissance Venice.* Manchester: Manchester University Press, 2014.

– "In the Mouths of Charlatans: Street Performers and the Dissemination of Pamphlets in Renaissance Italy." *Renaissance Studies* 24, no. 5 (2010): 638–53.

Samuels, Richard S. "Benedetto Varchi, the Accademia degli Infiammati, and the Origins of the Italian Academic Movement." *Renaissance Quarterly* 29, no. 4 (1976): 599–634.

Santore, Cathy. "Danaë: The Renaissance Courtesan's Alter Ego." *Zeitschrift für Kunstgeschichte* 54 (1991): 412–27.

– "Julia Lombardo, 'Somtuosa Meretrize': A Portrait by Property." *Renaissance Quarterly* 41, no. 1 (1998): 44–83.

Scarabello, Giovanni. "Le 'signore' della Repubblica." In *Il gioco dell'amore: le cortigiane di Venezia dal Trecento al Settecento. Catalogo della mostra*, 11–35. Milan: Berenice Art Books, 1990.

Schiavon, Alessandra. "Per la biografia di Veronica Franco: nuovi documenti." *Atti dell'Istituto Veneto di Scienze, Lettere ed Arti* 137 (1978–79): 243–56.

Schulz, Juergen. "Vasari at Venice." *The Burlington Magazine* 103, no. 705 (1961): 500–11.

Schutte, Anne Jacobson. "Commemorators of Irene di Spilimbergo." *Renaissance Quarterly* 45, no. 3 (1992): 524–36.

– "Irene di Spilimbergo: The Image of a Creative Woman in Late Renaissance Italy." *Renaissance Quarterly* 44, no. 1 (1991): 42–61.

Sedgwick, Eve Kosofsky. *Between Men: English Literature and Male Homosocial Desire*. New York: Columbia University Press, 1985.

– *Epistemology of the Closet*. Berkeley: University of California Press, 1990.

Shemek, Deanna. *Ladies Errant: Wayward Women and Social Order in Early Modern Italy*. Durham: Duke University Press, 1998.

– "'Mi mostrano a ditto tutti quanti': Disease, Deixis, and Disfiguration in the *Lamento di una cortigiana ferrarese*." In *Medusa's Gaze: Essays on Gender, Literature, and Aesthetics in the Italian Renaissance, in Honor of Robert J. Rodini*, edited by Paul A. Ferrara, Eugenio Giusti, and Jane Tylus, 49–64. Lafayette: Bordighera Press, 2004.

Shephard, Alexandra. *Meanings of Manhood in Early Modern England*. Oxford: Oxford University Press, 2003.

Simons, Patricia. "Homosociality and Erotics in Italian Renaissance Portraiture." In *Portraiture: Facing the Subject*, edited by Joanna Woodall, 29–51. Manchester: Manchester University Press, 1997.

Smarr, Janet L. "Gaspara Stampa's Poetry for Performance." *Journal of the Rocky Mountain Medieval and Renaissance Association* 12 (1991): 61–84.

Smith, Susan L. *The Power of Women: A Topos in Medieval Art and Literature*. Philadelphia: University of Pennsylvania Press, 1995.

Sperling, Jutta Gisela. *Convents and the Body Politic in Late Renaissance Venice*. Chicago: University of Chicago Press, 1999.

Storey, Tessa. *Carnal Commerce in Counter-Reformation Rome*. Cambridge: Cambridge University Press, 2008.

Storia della cultura veneta. 6 vols. Vicenza: N. Pozza, 1976.

Suzuki, Mihoko. *Metamorphoses of Helen: Authority, Difference, and the Epic*. Ithaca: Cornell University Press, 1989.

Talvacchia, Bette. *Taking Positions: On the Erotic in Renaissance Culture*. Princeton: Princeton University Press, 1999.

Tassini, Giuseppe. *Veronica Franco, celebre poetessa e cortigiana del secolo XVI.* Venice: Alfieri, 1969.

Terpening, Ronnie H. *Lodovico Dolce, Renaissance Man of Letters.* Toronto: University of Toronto Press, 1997.

Tiraboschi, Girolamo. *Storia della letteratura italiana.* 4 vols. Milan: Niccolò Bettoni, 1833.

Turner, James Grantham. "*I modi* and Aretino: I, The 'Toscanini Volume' in Context." *The Book Collector* 60 (2011), 559–70.

– *Libertines and Radicals in Early Modern London: Sexuality, Politics, and Literary Culture, 1630–1685.* Cambridge: Cambridge University Press, 2002.

– *Schooling Sex: Libertine Literature and Erotic Education in Italy, France, and England, 1534–1685.* Oxford: Oxford University Press, 2003.

–, ed. *Sexuality and Gender in Early Modern Europe: Institutions, Texts, Images.* New York: Cambridge University Press, 1993.

Trovato, Paolo. *Con ogni diligenza corretto: La stampa e le revisioni editoriali dei testi letterari italiani (1470–1570).* Bologna: Il Mulino, 1991.

Ulivioni, Paolo. *Accademie e cultura in Italia dalla Controriforma all'Arcadia, Il caso veneziano.* Milan: Archivio Storico Civico e Biblioteca Trivulziana, 1979.

Venturi, Lionello. "Le Compagnie della Calza (sec. XV–XVII)." *Nuovo Archivio Veneto* 16 (1908): 161–221; 17 (1909): 140–233.

Verheyen, Egon. *Palazzo del Te in Mantua: Images of Love and Politics.* Baltimore: Johns Hopkins University Press, 1977.

Veronese Cesaracciu, Emilia. "Il testamento di Cassandra Stampa: contributi alla biografia di Gaspara." In *Atti e memorie dell'Accademia patavina di scienze, lettere, ed arti. Memorie della classe di scienze morali, lettere ed arti* 89, no. 3 (1976–7): 89–96.

Vianello, Valerio. *Il letterato, l'accademia, il libro: contributi sulla cultura veneta del cinquecento.* Biblioteca Veneta, no. 6. Padua, 1988.

Vickers, Nancy J. "Diana Described: Scattered Woman and Scattered Rhyme." *Critical Inquiry* 8, no. 2 (1981): 265–79.

Walker, Jonathan. "*Bravi* and Venetian Nobles, c. 1550–1650." *Studi veneziani* 36 (1998): 85–114.

Waddington, Raymond B. *Aretino's Satyr: Sexuality, Satire and Self-Projection in Sixteenth-Century Literature and Art.* Toronto: University of Toronto Press, 2004.

Wiegman, Robyn. "Unmaking: Men and Masculinity in Feminist Theory." In *Masculinity Studies and Feminist Theory: New Directions,* edited by Judith Kegan Gardiner, 31–59. New York: Columbia University Press, 2002.

Wilson, Bronwen. *The World in Venice: Print, the City and Early Modern Identity.* Toronto: University of Toronto Press, 2005.

Wojciehowski, Dolora Chapelle. "Veronica Franco vs. Maffio Venier: Sex, Death, and Poetry in Cinquecento Venice." *Italica* 83, nos. 3–4 (2006): 367–90.

Wyatt, Michael. *The Italian Encounter with Tudor England: A Cultural Politics of Translation*. Cambridge: Cambridge University Press, 2005.

Zancan, Marina. "L'intellettualità femminile nel primo Cinquecento: Maria Savorgnan e Gaspara Stampa." *Annali d'italianistica* 7 (1989): 42–65.

Zilioli, Alessandro. *Vite di Gentiluomini Veneziani del secolo DVI tratte dalle Vite dei poeti italiani di Alessandro Zilioli ed ora per la prima volta pubblicate*. Venice: Antonelli, 1848.

Zorzi, Alvise. *Cortigiana veneziana: Veronica Franco e i suoi poeti, 1546–1591*. Milan: Camunia, 1986.

Zorzi, Lodovico. *Il teatro e la città: saggi sulla scena italiana*. Turin: G. Einaudi, 1977.

Index